W9-BUE-479

Cultural Change
and Your Church

Cultural Change and Your Church

*Helping Your Church Thrive
in a Diverse Society*

Michael Pocock
and
Joseph Henriques

Baker Books

A Division of Baker Book House Co
Grand Rapids, Michigan 49516

Published by Baker Books
a division of Baker Book House Company
P.O. Box 6287, Grand Rapids, MI 49516-6287

Printed in the United States of America

ISBN 0-8010-9135-7

Library of Congress Cataloging-in-Publication Data is on file at the Library of Congress, Washington, D.C.

For current information about all releases from Baker Book House, visit our web site:
http://www.bakerbooks.com

To our wives,
Penny Pocock and Bonnie Henriques,
lifelong partners and educators

And to our parents,
George and Millie Pocock and Bento and Mariana Henriques,
who dared to dream of America,
realized that dream,
and passed it on to their children

Contents

Preface

Whether you live in Seattle or Selma, Washington D.C. or Washington-on-the-Brazos, Texas, Miami or Minneapolis, Alabama, Los Angeles, Latrobe, Pennsylvania, or anywhere in between, you know that your community is in the middle of cultural change. Some areas of our country are already incredibly diverse, other places less so, but most communities are in the middle of rapid cultural changes.

Looking around you in church on Sundays, you may discover that everyone looks pretty much like you. Although there may be churches for several different cultures in your town, individual churches still don't look anything like a cross section of their community. Single-ethnicity churches can be wonderful places, places where newcomers to America feel at home with familiar language, culture, fellowship, and worship. But is there something wrong with this picture?

As America grows more culturally diverse, people who work together all week, go to school together, serve in the armed forces together, and play the same sports together ought to feel comfortable together in church. Many churches dream of being "a New Testament–type church," but the churches of that era were incredibly diverse. They had people in them from every corner of the Roman Empire and beyond. Fourteen different nationalities are mentioned by Luke as being present on the day of Pentecost—a sure sign of what the Holy Spirit intended to do in drawing people from every people, tongue, and nation into the body of Christ worldwide.

As people from diverse backgrounds multiply in America, many want to experience a church that feels more like the community at large rather than an almost "foreign" enclave within the neighborhood. Second-generation Chinese, Koreans, Japanese, and Filipinos, all now speaking English, are forming "Pan Asian" churches as their next step toward assimilation into the American church scene. Multicultural churches are flourishing in most major metropolitan areas. We are going to introduce you to some of them in this book.

The arrival of unprecedented numbers of more culturally diverse people also makes America itself a mission field. Both Joe Henriques and I have served with our wives overseas—Joe in his father's native Portugal, I in Venezuela. Joe and I are both children of immigrants. I am an immigrant from Great Britain. After ministry overseas and teaching others to do ministry around the world, we both have a deep sense of urgency to help this country rise to the challenge of international ministry in our own adopted land. We long to see people of every national, ethnic, and cultural background fellowshiping together in churches nationwide.

Some years ago, Joe sensed God leading him to establish People of the World, a ministry to help American churches respond to newcomers from abroad. To this end he has led workshops across the country on international outreach in American communities. As a chaplain (Lt. Col) in the Air National Guard, he frequently leads training sessions on handling diversity in the armed forces. He has taught courses in multicultural ministry at Capitol Bible Seminary in Maryland. In 2001 Joe became vice president and dean of the Moody Graduate School in Chicago, where he continues to lead students and faculty toward a global awareness in ministry.

Following our service in Venezuela, my wife and I continued to mobilize others for international ministry through The Evangelical Alliance Mission. Some fourteen years ago I joined the faculty of Dallas Theological Seminary where I serve as chairman and professor in the department of world missions and intercultural studies. For five years I served as advisor to international students. I have continued to travel internationally in the cause of missions, but like Joe, I have become increasingly aware that our own adopted country is a mission field of international dimensions. My wife's ministry as principal of Casa View Baptist School in Dallas has made her sensitive to the differing ethnic backgrounds of children and their parents. Since 1980, Bonnie Henriques has been actively involved with diverse peoples. She was immersed in the founding and developing of the International Christian Church and School in Portugal as well as People of the World in the United States.

Joe and I have an immigrant's sense of gratitude for the opportunities afforded us in this country. Our parents searched for and discovered the reality that most of us know—that America is a land of incredible possibilities for those with a willing spirit and a heart to work. Now we want to give back to America something in return for all we have received. That "something" is the insight we have gained from ministry to those of other cultures around the world, in the hope that these insights and experiences will help American churches thrive in their increasingly diverse communities.

How can you make the most of this book? If your aim is to understand how and why America is changing and how to respond in a biblically effective manner, you have the right book in your hand! The best use of it comes when several of you get together—a church's leadership team, concerned individuals, or a class in ministry preparation aimed at effectiveness in the new, more diverse America. Read the book a chapter at a time, then get together to discuss the implications for you and your church. There are discussion questions at the close of each chapter. When it's time to take some concrete steps, you'll find organizations and resources listed in the resources section that will help you. All the members of a leadership team could read the book in preparation for a retreat or workshop where various possibilities for response to your community can be discussed.

In this book Joe and I have repeatedly emphasized the positive contributions newcomers have made to America. We all know this is a nation of immigrants, a kaleidoscope which, as it turns, reveals a constantly changing yet wonderful pattern of people in a single society. As we moved toward publication, the unprecedented events of September 11, 2001, occurred. The attacks on the World Trade Center in New York and on the Pentagon and the crash of the United Airlines plane in Pennsylvania were absolutely horrific. We worried that our book might fall on deaf ears in a nation angered by what foreign enemies could do on our own soil. At a distance of two months since those attacks, we are actually heartened by the response of the American people. Most of us have been able to separate in our minds the awful acts of a few and the peaceful goodwill of the majority of newcomers to our country, whatever their religion, culture, or national background.

Americans are showing a remarkable ability to rise above pettiness and ethnic mistrust in the face of attacks by people of a foreign origin. Citizens and newcomers alike have shown acts of kindness for each other. People of many national backgrounds in New York, a place renowned for gruff and distant relationships in public, have shown tenderness and love in the aftermath of these awful events.

We are convinced that the principles we deal with in this book are as applicable after September 11, if not more so, than they were before that sunniest yet darkest of days. American churches have the opportunity to demonstrate both the spirit of America and the Spirit of Christ in the context that surrounds them. God bless you as you learn to help your church thrive in a culturally diverse society.

Michael Pocock
November 2001

Acknowledgments

Mike Pocock wishes to thank the following for their assistance:

Jim Kinney, Wendy Wetzel, and Mary Suggs of Baker Books for their encouragement, editorial expertise, and patience in the production of this book

Lynn Maynard of Campus Crusade for Christ for researching parallel publications in multicultural ministry

Toni Martin, my administrative assistant at Dallas Seminary, for her valuable research ideas and her efforts to protect my time

Dianne Whittle, TESOL Coordinator at Dallas Seminary, for reading parts of the manuscript and delivering cogent critiques

The students of my Fall 2000 class "Ministry in Multicultural America" for reading and commenting on the manuscript as it progressed

Dallas Theological Seminary for the sabbatical year 1999–2000 during which much of this manuscript was researched and produced

Brannon Claxton and Sylvia Green of Grandview Baptist Church for their historical insights about East Grand Avenue Baptist, Dallas, and its engagement with a culturally changing community

Lanny Elmore of First Baptist Dallas for help in understanding their many separate language chapels, and Patti Lane of the Intercultural Office of the Texas General Conference of the Southern Baptist Convention

Jim Thames, associate academic dean, Dallas Seminary, who helped me understand the issues facing Reinhardt Bible Church in dealing with its multicultural community

Jack Matlick of CAM International for insights into Cristo Viene Hispanic Church in Dallas

Derrah Jackson of International Students Incorporated, Dallas-Fort Worth, for details on international student enrollment in U.S. colleges and universities and ministry to them; Derrah facilitates matchups between Dallas Seminary students and international students on area campuses, an invaluable ministry

Mark and Dee Jobe, pastor and shepherdess of New Life Community Church, Chicago, my guides to a dynamic multicultural urban ministry in Chicago

Harold and Thelma Reynolds of Tulsa who helped me feel the excitement and value of hosting international exchange students

Martin Hironaga, Allison White, and Mike Maden for showing me the beauty of multicultural ministry among Southeast Asians at New Life Fellowship and Common Grace Ministry and their coworkers Vibol and Bouye in East Dallas

Shigeko Hironaga who gives constantly of her TESOL expertise to the community of East Dallas and the TESOL program of Dallas Seminary

Charles Kemp, senior lecturer in nursing and public health at Baylor College of Medicine, a man who after serving in Vietnam during the war has given the people of Southeast Asia twenty-five years of public health service in East Dallas

Huang Soo Kim of Faith Lutheran Church, Surrey, British Columbia

Arnold Wong of the Asian American Baptist Church in Richardson, Texas, and Philip Gee of Arlington Chinese Church, Arlington, Texas

Librarians at Southern Methodist University and Dallas Theological Seminary for valuable research assistance and the generous use they allowed of both their facilities

Eliseo Mejia and Edward Retta for their understanding of the Hispanic community and agenda

Willie Peterson, Eddie Lane of Dallas Seminary and the Urban Evangelical Mission, and Wayne Mitchell for their interpretation of the African American community

Pivotal in the production of this book, David Largent and Samira Khaled, "electronic messiahs" of Dallas Seminary Information Services, who "exorcised" the electronic demons from my computer and helped me stay sane!

Matt DeMoss of Bibliotheca who arranged the text and standardized the chapters and helped this book emerge as an integrated work before sending it off to the publishers

My wife, Penny, whose loving encouragement and patience carried me through this project.

Lastly my thanks to our brothers and sisters in Christ of our Home Team at Lake Ridge Bible Church, who, led by Joe and Loan Reigel, prayerfully supported me through this entire project

From Joe Henriques:

The fingerprints of many people are found throughout my chapters. Bonnie, my wife and gifted coworker, researched many books and articles on the subject of immigration and assimilation. This research enabled us to toss around, analyze, synthesize, and evaluate ideas that eventually settled into my writings.

Readers made invaluable suggestions, using years of respective professional experience as their unique grid. This special group included a foreign missionary, Greek professor, engineer, veteran intercultural ministry workers, and leaders in government, education, and business. They included Bob and Jean Davis, Ned Donaldson, Tom and Lorenda Dyson, Dr. Tom Edgar, and Jack and Barbara Tapping.

Al Butkovich, Ned Donaldson, and I spent hours planning and doing training workshops for multicultural ministry. Lessons learned from those experiences are woven throughout these pages. Of course my real teachers and heroes are the many men and women in local churches who have poured hours of creative and sacrificial effort into developing specially designed ministries to their ethnically diverse communities. What they have taught me seeps into virtually every paragraph.

The home and cultural setting provided by my Portuguese father and Puerto Rican mother—Bento and Mariana—taught me two important values: love for America and loyalty to my ethnic heritage. My daughter, Tori Busenitz, contributed long hours to proofreading rough drafts. And I am deeply grateful to my sons—Ben, Jonathan, Justin, and Matthew—for their patience and prayers as I worked.

Finally, I was blessed with very special editors. It was Dianne Hurst who first—literally—cut each of the original chapters into sections, in order to visually show me how to properly align arguments. Then Baker Books assigned Mary Suggs to edit our book. Mary's keen eye for detail and a sense for consistent, flowing thought kept my conversation steady on the straight and narrow path. As with Mike, I thank Jim Kinney and Wendy Wetzel for being our guides from start to finish.

Ultimately, it is because of Jesus Christ that I had the compulsion to write. Because of his great love, I want the people of the world to know him too.

Kaleidoscope America
Michael Pocock

Here from all nations, all tongues and all peoples
Countless the crowd but their voices are one;
Vast is the sight and majestic their singing—
"God has the victory: He reigns from the throne."

Christopher M. Idle

I held the end of a cardboard tube up to the sunlight and, holding the other end to my eye, stared through an opaque glass lens. To my delight a marvelous pattern of brightly colored pieces came into focus. A slight twist of my hand made all the angular points of color form another pattern, just as beautiful as the one before. Another turn of the cardboard barrel and yet another pattern formed. What an enchanted moment for a ten-year-old boy who had never seen television or a single movie!

Fifty years later, in the year 2002, Toys R Us doesn't even carry kaleidoscopes, but that does not matter to me now. I am more interested in the kaleidoscopic movement all around me. It was true at the turn of the millennium and during each century and even each decade in the progress of the American adventure that the face of our country had been changing; the people who live here form an increasingly diverse pattern.

More than forty years ago, John F. Kennedy called the United States "a nation of immigrants."[1] Even Native Americans came here thousands of years ago as immigrants from Asia.[2] Today we are more diverse than ever.[3] Global events such as wars in Southeast Asia, unrest and famine in Africa, and civil strife in Latin America have pushed people to more stable areas in the United States, Canada, and western Europe. The promise of freedom, security, and prosperity all serve as magnets to draw people to America and the West.

The result of changing immigration laws and the migration of people to the United States in recent years is that we now look different as a nation.[4] Whereas immigrants once came mainly from Europe (apart from African Americans and Native Americans), they are now coming from other areas of the world. The first Europeans to come were from many different nations, and for years after they arrived, they spoke their own languages at home and at church, but they learned English, looked similar to one another, and formed what we call the Anglo peoples. This gave America a relatively homogeneous look until the 1960s, when changes in socio-political theories and immigration policy had an impact on the makeup of our immigrant population. Immigrants began to *look* more distinct and compose large, distinct blocks of people, making the process of assimilation, widely assumed to be the goal of immigrants, more difficult.[5] Michael Novak chronicled this phenomenon in his book *The Rise of the Unmeltable Ethnics.*[6] These are issues we will deal with in later chapters.

In spite of changes in the look and feel of America, there remain an essential continuity, unity, and beauty that we can identify as America. There are changes in communities and changes in the churches that serve them. Wonderful examples exist of churches that intentionally orient their people to the changes going on in their community and help them respond in positive ways. For example, Scofield Memorial Church in Dallas teamed up with a traditional overseas mission board, SIM International, to form the International Friendship Ministry. They sponsor special workshops to raise the awareness of the congregation about growing ethnic diversity and help initiate interaction between church members and the newer ethnic arrivals in their community.[7]

But many Christians and local churches have failed to "do the right thing" in response to ethnic change. They have faithfully responded to Christ's Great Commission in Matthew 28:19–20, sending missionaries around the globe, but they have not always been so diligent or even

friendly when the peoples of the world have come to their neighborhood! Resistance to newcomers is the subject of our next chapter, but
here we want to emphasize that, historically, immigrants are a desirable addition to the American scene. Obviously, America is built on
immigration. Both communities and entire church movements have
benefited. We can illustrate this by the case of the Hispanic peoples.

Hispanic Immigrants

Hispanics have always been a part of the American landscape and
currently represent an immigration boom from Latin America. *The Economist*, says:

> It is almost 400 years [now just over that] . . . April 30, 1598—since Don
> Juan de Oñate's expedition waded across the Rio Grande, gave thanks,
> and claimed the lands to the north for Spain. It is also 150 years since the
> annexation of the south-west after the Mexican-American war, and the
> centenary of Puerto Rico's entry into the Union after the Spanish Ameri-
> can war. History, it seems, is asking the United States to reflect on its
> Spanish speakers. It is high time.[8]

Hispanics form an integral part of the United States. Although they
were not called Hispanics until the mid-twentieth century, Spanish-
speaking peoples inhabited Florida and the entire region of what we call
the southwestern United States from the arrival of the conquistadors in
the 1500s. Hispanics have a historical place in America, and their numbers are increasing rapidly through birth and voluntary migration. The
1990 census counted thirty million Hispanics and that number had
grown to thirty-four million by the year 2000.

Having ministered in Latin America, I am familiar with this wonderful *gente*, or people. Through my experiences with them, both in Latin
America and the United States, I have come to appreciate them deeply.
They are participating in a wide spectrum of American life, from the
president's cabinet, the armed forces, and educational leadership to the
food and restaurant industry, construction, and social services. I recently
listened as expert Hispanic masons laid brick for nearby houses. They
sang and chatted as they worked, and I admired the finished job.

Like other immigrant groups, Hispanics are overwhelmingly industrious, but because there has been a rapid increase in their numbers,
we hear opposition to Hispanic immigration from certain quarters
throughout our country. People complain they will be a drain on our
economy, that they will be on welfare, and that they won't learn to speak

English. The truth is, however, that many Hispanics quickly rise to middle-class status.

> Even poor Latinos have middle-class aspirations. According to David Hayes Bautista, the head of the Centre for the Study of Latino Health at the University of California at Los Angeles, Latinos have the highest rate of male participation in the labour force, the lowest use of public assistance and the highest rate of family formation. Latinos spend nearly twice as much as blacks on mortgages, and, although most arrive with no capital and take rockbottom jobs, they are reaching the middle class in increasingly large numbers. In Los Angeles there are now around 450,000 middle-class Latino households, three times as many as in 1980.[9]

The buying power of Latinos is 452.4 billion dollars annually.[10] Imagine the income for states from sales taxes on that amount of money, let alone the impact for federal tax income! These people are contributing to the national wealth.

Some worry about America becoming a Third World country, especially if we permit newcomers to keep using their own language.[11] But Roger Hernandez says it is absurd to imagine that Spanish is a threat to the predominantly spoken English language:

> No one of any standing in any serious Hispanic organization is suggesting that the United States become an officially bilingual nation, and everyone recognizes that the dominant language of this country is and always will be English. . . . Most polls say that over 90 percent of new immigrant Latinos want to learn English, and Latino parents want their children taught in English at school.[12]

Although the rate of Hispanic immigration is alarming to some Americans, they should be aware that most Hispanics share the same basic values as the majority of Americans, and often their values are even stronger in areas of family and faith. And most Hispanic immigrants are industrious. Peter Salins, author of *Assimilation, American Style*, says immigrants have been "indispensable to America's economic growth."[13]

Hispanics are predominantly Roman Catholic, and they are deeply spiritual people. But as in Latin America, so in the States, large numbers are becoming evangelical. Edward Retta notes that Hispanics in the United States were 95 percent Roman Catholic in 1971 but were 26 percent evangelical by 1988, and that figure had risen to some 44 percent in the mid-1990s. Although only 10 percent of all students in graduate schools in Texas were Hispanic in 1992, nationally, there are more Hispanics in Protestant than in Roman Catholic seminaries.[14]

As we think of the American kaleidoscope, we should remember that so-called ethnic groups like Hispanics are themselves a kaleidoscope. They represent many nationalities and ethnicities from indigenous Indian peoples to those of African and European descent. In a process similar to the formation of the United States, millions from other countries have made their way to Latin America and settled there. People from other parts of the world have become such an integral part of the Southern Hemisphere that a country like Peru has had a president named Alberto Fujimori, a descendant of Japanese immigrants.

Like all other peoples in America, Hispanics have their share of challenges, but they desire to succeed in the land they have chosen, while not forgetting their roots in Latin America. The United States bears the indelible and delightful mark of Hispanic presence from San Diego to San Luis Obispo, from the Sierra Nevada to San Antonio. The music of Latin America throbs throughout the country, its food is enjoyed in every city, and its architecture displayed throughout the Southwest. The spiritual impact of evangelists like Luis Palau has touched the lives of thousands across the country, and new directions in completing the Great Commission have been pioneered by Luis Bush of the A.D. 2000 movement.

Cross-Cultural Ministry

Immigrants may have their own agendas for coming to America, but we believe that God is facilitating *his* agenda! He is doing it by bringing the people of the world to an area where they are free to make choices and are likely to encounter those who can share the gospel and their lives with them. At the same time, our nation benefits, as it always has, from the ideas, values, and diligence of new arrivals. They do bring change, but these changes are turns of the kaleidoscope of history—more a cause for rejoicing than for rejection, for delight rather than dejection! God has set amazing possibilities before the Christian community, and it's exciting to be a part of the action.

Join me on a visit to several communities where growing cultural diversity has brought changes. These are communities where Christian leaders and churches saw the changes as challenges and the obstacles as opportunities. Their response in ministry has helped ensure that the changes, like chips of colored glass in a kaleidoscope, reflect the glory and presence of God, not the collapse of our country, as some have conjectured.

New Life Community Church, Chicago

It's a Sunday in the late '90s, and I am on my way into Chicago with Ken Flurrie and his family. They have served as missionaries in Brazil and miss the lively, compelling worship in Latin America, so they are heading for New Life Community Church, even though it represents a seventy-five-mile round trip from Aurora. They are excited and so am I! This is my first chance to see the amazing things God has done through the ministry of Mark and Dee Jobe and the people they have discipled. Although everything about this dynamic ministry is attributable to the grace of God working through this couple, it had been the privilege of my wife and me to pastor this church in the '60s when it was a little storefront ministry called Berean Memorial Mission.

There were about thirty-five people in attendance when we began our pastorate. It grew to fifty while I simultaneously studied at seminary. People told me storefront churches never grew, but true to the promise of Jesus that he would build his church and the gates of hell would not destroy it (Matt. 16:18), the ministry continued. By the time Mark began his ministry there thirteen years ago, the membership had dwindled to eighteen. But today more than seventeen hundred people attend, and a number of the original believers are still involved as leaders and faithful servants.[15]

When we arrive at the auditorium of the Illinois Institute of Technology on Chicago's South Side, we find ourselves surrounded by exuberant people. In the foyer people are chatting together; some are picking up helpful tapes of past sermons, buying books, or signing up for retreats and workshops. The majority look Hispanic, most of whom are speaking English, and there are many Anglos and quite a few African Americans as well. The people are a cross section of Chicago's South Side in a city that has seen many changes in its relatively short history. Mark Jobe says, "In 1940, Chicago was 92 percent white and 8 percent black. In 1999, Chicago is 32 percent white, 37 percent black, 5 percent Asian and 26 percent Hispanic. At least seven neighborhoods in Chicago are so integrated they have no dominant racial group."[16]

Jobe says that New Life is now about 60 percent Hispanic, 30 percent white, and 10 percent black. It is also quite mixed in socioeconomic terms, but the majority are blue-collar workers, many from very difficult backgrounds.[17] It's interesting that, apart from the addition of African Americans, it reflects the same makeup of thirty years ago when, even as a small storefront, it attracted English-speaking Hispanics, Anglos of Polish descent, and Appalachian whites—the people living in the "Back of the Yards" area of South Ashland Avenue. Today New Life Community reflects the growth of the Hispanic population in particular and is a commentary on the second and third generations of immigrants to North America.

Ethnically homogeneous congregations who are concerned about the departure of their second generation from the life of the church should look at churches like New Life Community.[18] New Life represents the next step for ethnics who really want to be a part of the American mainstream, while not forgetting their distinctive cultures. New Life is not an ethnic church. It is an urban church that evenly reflects the people who live in the community. It is a place where the younger generation it targets is clearly a part of the ministry and authority structure. People of distinct ethnic backgrounds feel at home there because it looks like the face of the community at large.

As worship begins at New Life Community Church, the auditorium is packed. A competent and consecrated group of music and worship leaders guide the congregation in a contemporary style of worship. People clap and sing enthusiastically, while behind the scenes people who form part of a twenty-four-hour-a-day prayer chain lift the celebration in prayer. The worship celebration includes testimonies to changed lives, which underline the main reason for being in church in the first place— to experience a God who acts on behalf of those he loves in answer to their prayers.

A visitor to New Life quickly gets the idea that the pastor knows the people in this congregation. He may personally address them during the celebration, referring to their struggles and victories, and urging others to thank God for what he is doing and intercede for those who need it. Like people on Tejano (or Hispanic) radio stations in my home city of Dallas, Mark, who was raised in Spain by missionary parents, can switch easily to Spanish or even start a sentence in English and finish it in Spanish. This really communicates to second-generation Hispanics that he knows their situation.

Though the look and feel of worship at New Life is very contemporary, the church is old-fashioned in its commitment to disciplines like prayer and fasting, challenging biblical preaching, and a life of witness that God is blessing. Many of the people in this church fast a day each week. Many have fasted for a week at a time, and not a few, led by the pastor, have been on forty-day juice-only fasts, while they have prayed, studied the Word, and looked to God for guidance in their lives.

New Life asks for a high level of commitment from its members.[19] Most are in small-group Home Teams. Pastor Jobe extends his ministry by developing lay leaders who evidence the right character and gifting and seem called to lead the Home Teams. Many members of this congregation, averaging in age between twenty and forty, have come out of chaotic backgrounds. Even the more upwardly mobile have developed in an urban society that teaches them to trust no one but themselves. The fellowship, encouragement, and accountability structure of the Home Teams is a revolutionary element of their new life in Christ.

A part of the attraction of New Life is that it seems globally oriented. The world has come to America, and it thrives as a microcosm in this church. The church is not simply rooted in one location or orientation. A single vision guides it, but it exists in several satellite churches, as well as at New Life Central. Two of these satellites are Spanish-speaking only, ministering mostly to recent arrivals and older Hispanics. For the latter group, getting to the United States was the major goal of their lives. They came for their children. They may never be fluent in English, but their children speak English and attend the vibrant youth activities held in conjunction with New Life Central, where English is the language spoken.

New Life serves homogeneous "specialty" groups with a network of ministries, some directed to urban professionals, some to the gay community, others to where community development is needed. New Life Community Church is a highly *relevant* church, serious about following Christ in the city and enfolding the full spectrum of the kaleidoscope that is Chicago. We shall come back to New Life from time to time in this book to look at additional elements that make it such an exciting and effective ministry to a multicultural community.

International Students in the United States

Some years ago my wife and I were ministering in Japan. My translators, Koji Ishikawa and "Hank" Obari, had both studied in the United States. Koji had returned to pastor in Japan and is now a leader in the Christian movement there. He has remained a warm personal friend. Hank is a layman actively involved in his local church. While in this country these men were part of the more than 490,000 international students who are here in any given year.[20] Hank's case is one exciting example of how churches and believers in America can have a major impact on the colorful international student segment of the American kaleidoscope.

Hank (many internationals graciously allow Americans to call them by a name they can pronounce) came to the United States to study in Oklahoma. His parents were wealthy Japanese who for generations had owned a large liquor distillery. Hank's affluence permitted him to live well as a student, but he began to spend more time playing around than in the books. It began to look as if he would return to Japan as a failure, a shameful blow for his parents and himself.

Christians from a church near campus had a ministry of hospitality to international students. Hank was invited to spend weekends in American homes—an unusual opportunity since 80 percent of foreign students never spend a night anywhere else than in their dorm while in this country.[21]

Hank enjoyed the times spent in American homes, and his hosts enjoyed him. They would go to church together on the weekends, and as Hank listened to gospel messages and watched the lives of his hosts, God touched his heart and he became a believer. His life orientation changed; he settled down to study and returned to Japan with honor.

After his return to Japan, Hank sat down with his father and explained that when he, as the only son, inherited the distillery and distribution business, he would sell it because its product was wrecking the lives of thousands of Japanese. Surprisingly, his father agreed to sell, and they entered into the real estate business instead. They are still very comfortable economically.

All this was explained to me while I enjoyed the weekend of my life staying in the Obari's home in Mito City. (My wife was attending a women's conference and so did not accompany me on this visit.) The Obaris treated me like the proverbial king: hot bath, a robe of my own, a marvelous multicourse meal, a night's sleep on luxurious futons in a room sweet with the scent of cedar walls and tatami mats. The next morning, while I was immersed in the serenity of the peaceful garden, Hank came out and asked me if I was having a good time. "Yes," I replied, "This is one of the most wonderful experiences of my life!" Beaming, Hank responded, "I wanted to do this for you because staying in Christian homes in America meant so much to me, and I told God I would return the pleasure whenever I got the opportunity."

Ordinary Christians and churches in America can do a lot to minister to the multicultural kaleidoscope in ways as simple as hospitality, friendship, and the example of their lives. Churches around the country have experienced the satisfaction of outreach to international students. First Baptist of Atlanta began an extensive ministry to foreign students and their families in a program called Friends from Abroad. After the congregation moved to another location away from the nearby campus, one of their members stayed behind and maintains this highly effective outreach through West Meritt Baptist Church.[22]

International Students Inc. trains and links Christian families to foreign students on university campuses.[23] Joe Henriques, the coauthor of this book, heads up People of the World, a ministry that enables individuals and churches to reach out to students from overseas, the many international business families assigned here, and those who have settled in America to work.[24] We will learn more of these ministries in later chapters. The point to remember now is that internationals studying or working in this country constitute a significant ministry opportunity and a satisfying, enriching experience for those who get involved. In addition, many are already believers with a vibrant Christian life to share with us. They may come from societies with stronger family values and commitments than our own. We need to get in touch.

Faith Lutheran Church, Surrey, British Columbia

Visit Faith Lutheran Church on any Sunday and you will find that the faces inside the church reflect those who live around it in this incredibly diverse suburb of Vancouver, British Columbia. Besides the Anglo folks in the congregation who are from England, Scotland, Germany, and Scandinavia, you'll find Chinese, Korean, and Hispanic believers. Although worshipers usually attend services that are in their own language, Faith Lutheran is more than simply four congregations meeting under the same roof. It is a single church with a single board and budget, and they hold united staff meetings each week.[25] They have frequent combined worship celebrations and socials that involve and highlight all their cultures. A genuine sense of oneness permeates the congregation.

How did this multicultural arrangement come about? It is not simply the product of several ethnic congregations who asked the Anglo congregation for a place to meet. In the early 1990s, the leadership of Faith Lutheran looked around them and realized the community was changing. They did not need demographic studies to tell them what was happening, even though these were available.[26] More than anything else they wanted to be a church that really ministered to the surrounding neighborhood. If it was changing, then they would also change.

In the community Koreans were present in considerable numbers. Many of them were already Christian. In the early '90s many Chinese had moved to Canada, especially from Hong Kong, where there was growing fear of the consequences of that city falling under a possibly repressive regime after 1997. Since the '60s, Central Americans from war-torn El Salvador, Guatemala, and Nicaragua have found refuge in Canada, just as many have in the United States. Indo-Canadian Sikhs also form part of the community.

In 1998 eighty-two unreached people groups were identified in Canada. Some were groups that already existed in Canada, but many were part of the 2.5 million people who had immigrated to Canada in the previous twelve years. The movement of people from many nations represents a great opportunity for ministry, but researcher and missionary Brian Seim says that while 47 percent of Canadians, especially newcomers, live in urban areas, "We are largely running from the oppor-tunity of bringing Christ to the city and to the newcomer."[27] That was not the case, however, with Faith Lutheran Church.

When Faith Lutheran bought land in Surrey on which to build their church, they had intended to be a missionary church because of the var-ied cultures in that community. Their plan was to be a multicultural church, a true church of the community.

Under the original leadership of Pastor Carrol Dubendiek, Faith Lutheran invited a Korean pastor, Huang Soo Kim, to help minister to Koreans in Surrey. Then they obtained the service of a Chinese layman to lead and eventually pastor the Chinese congregation. This layman continued with his Lutheran studies and has since been ordained. Finally, a Hispanic pastor, who also assists with another Hispanic church, was called to minister to the Latin Americans.

I met all these leaders in a class on ministry in multicultural North America, which I taught at Associated Canadian Theological Schools (ACTS) on the campus of Trinity Western University in 1994. They did not get their idea to unite in ministry from me! They already had the idea when they came with leaders from fifteen other ministries in Canada to work on issues in multicultural ministry. As usual in these courses, I learned as much from them as anything they may have learned from me. Now in the year 2000 this dynamic congregation continues to grow, even in the face of issues that often come up when God is at work. Today Faith Lutheran is ready to occupy a newly constructed multipurpose building, capable of holding all the fellowships when they meet together.

What's the secret of diverse peoples thriving in the same congrega-tion? That's what this book will attempt to make clear, but above all it is the dynamic movement of the Spirit of God. Christians in all cultures have the same Holy Spirit (1 Cor. 12:1–6). This Spirit first showed him-self on the day of Pentecost as the one who understood and could give understanding among different cultures and languages (Acts 2:1–41). Those people from fourteen nationalities, which Luke enumerates with characteristic exactitude, were all affected by the Pentecost experience. They are found at the close of the same chapter in Acts, worshiping, enjoying fellowship and meals, and studying together in one of the most ideal manifestations of what we call the New Testament church (vv. 42–47). Is that not possible today? Should we not derive some clue from the activity of the Spirit of God at the church's beginning? He came in power to indwell believers as an international Spirit or a supranational Spirit. Harry Boer in his work *Pentecost and Missions* makes this clear:

> It is the Holy Spirit who effects the unity of the Church. The wonderful fellowship of the early Church was a direct outgrowth of Pentecost. . . .

the glory of Christ as the unifying power in the Church . . . lies at the heart of the gift bestowed on the Church at Pentecost.[28]

The God of the cultural kaleidoscope lives in each of us who believe and in the churches where we worship. Have we asked ourselves if we are truly letting him express who he is through us individually and in our local fellowship? Let's turn to some other examples of exciting multicultural ministry before moving along to discover what's going on in North America, where it will lead us, and what our response should be.

Common Grace Ministries, Dallas, Texas

East Dallas became the destination of thousands of Southeast Asians at the close of the Vietnam War in 1975 and during continuing hostilities in Vietnam, Cambodia, and Laos.[29] About ten thousand were initially settled in Dallas, and thousands more in other relocation settlements. They were desperately poor and traumatized by the experiences of war and life in refugee camps. Over the years, the various nationalities represented among the refugees resettled themselves in homogeneous clusters around the country. Some three thousand remain in East Dallas in an area known as Little Asia.

Like many immigrants, most Southeast Asians are very diligent, appreciating the opportunity to work and realize their ambitions in a free society. Many of the refugees now own their own businesses or have become teachers, police officers, and medical workers. But many remain abjectly poor. Average family income in Dallas's Little Asia is $8,500, a full $4,000 below the poverty level. Several factors account for this. Unlike Chinese from Hong Kong or Indians, Southeast Asians did not come to this country speaking English. Compounding the problem, many families had been torn apart by the wars in Indochina. A disproportionate number of the refugees were widows who, because of the trauma during the years of war, retain permanently damaged psyches and wounded spirits. These people need special care.

Throughout the area of East Dallas, some seventy faith-based agencies work to assist struggling minorities. Their workers are indefatigable saints, whether they see themselves that way or not. Charles Kemp is an expert in community health who has given his services freely for more than eighteen years in free clinics. Nurses he trains at nearby Baylor Hospital help in the clinics to serve their internships. Habitat for Humanity assists with low-cost housing, and a number of students and graduates from Dallas Theological Seminary minister in the area.

Martin Hironaga, Alison White, and Mike Maden worked among the Southeast Asians while students at Dallas Seminary. On graduating, they continued. As a Japanese American from Hawaii, Martin seems very much at ease among the people to whom he ministers. Alison, who earlier served as a social worker among Marshall Islanders in the Pacific, learned the Lao language. She and Martin formed the Asian Mission of Common Grace Ministries. At its inception Park Cities Presbyterian Church (PCPC) encouraged and helped to guide the work, and a Japanese American Christian businessman gave substantially to start and maintain it. Martin saw the need to develop ministry leaders in the context of service to the poor, so a link to Dallas Theological Seminary was forged, called Community Connection. Mike Maden mentors seminary students and neighborhood residents. Seminary students receive scholarships through the generosity of Common Grace Ministries and do service, field education, spiritual formation, and reflection on their studies right in the context of the community.

For ministry to be relevant in the new millennium, it must take into account the growing ethnic diversity in North America. Ministry is not simply a matter of refining the Christian understanding of white upper-middle-class suburbia. It is a question of becoming Christ's man or woman, serving as he served, and ministering to very diverse kinds of people. This will involve self-denial. In East Dallas, ministry among the poor, many of which are like the residents of Little Asia, involves *real* learning and is a significant ministry. Martin, Alison, and Mike have grasped this idea, and so have those who work with them. Taking ideas from Henri Nouwen, who believed in forming a community *with* and *of* the community in need, not just *to* them, the leaders of Common Grace Ministries are committed to this ideal.[30]

Spend a day with Martin, Alison, and Mike and you are likely to get up at 5.30 A.M. to meet for prayer with a number of new Christians from the community. They will meditate silently for quite some time, then tell each other their concerns for prayer. A relative died in California, and one brother has had to go out for the funeral. It has lasted a week as Buddhist monks chanted hour after hour in the home of the deceased. It felt strange and uncomfortable to this new believer who now has hope in God for the future. The group prays for him and the extended family.

Another believer was at home the previous evening when his eighteen-year-old sister tremblingly told their parents that she was pregnant though unmarried. Her parents' world and her own came crashing down. There were other concerns and praises lifted, and then they had breakfast together before the new believers headed off to work.

Within minutes, a young woman who had turned to Christ from Buddhism, burst in. She was terrified because spirits were oppressing her at home. Alison embraced her and assured her she was safe. Though demons may try to bother her, she is now free in the Lord Jesus and need not fear them. All of us went to her home and prayed, declaring that she is a child of God and nothing can harm her (Luke 10:19). She calmed down and set about her day's work.

We visited another woman who was cruelly beaten in the killing fields of Cambodia. She still can barely stand because of her experience. Common Grace is helping with her rent, but someone is harassing her, demanding rent she does not owe. Fortunately there is an Asian patrol officer in the Dallas Police Department who understands her language and predicament. He was called to help her.

Nearby, a free clinic held at the Vietnamese Catholic Church overflows with mothers needing care. Some are Laotian, others Cambodian or Vietnamese, and some are Hispanic. They will all get a high grade of medical and health assistance from Charles Kemp and his Baylor nurses in training.

Later on, at the Police Storefront Station, part police, part social service, you may find Shigeko Hironaga, Martin's wife. She has a Ph.D. in TESOL (Teaching English to Speakers of Other Languages), and she is mentoring student teachers as they help community residents obtain the indispensable skill of fluency in English. One cannot visit these community-assistance programs without realizing that they represent foundational answers to spiritual, health, housing, education, and employment needs. They also represent the many opportunities for established Americans to help others, perhaps as their own parents or grandparents were helped in another era.

Immigrants from areas where English is widely spoken have a lot less difficulty obtaining employment or the necessary education to move ahead in America. They come from countries like India, the Philippines, Hong Kong, or anglophone Africa. But getting established is still a challenge for them. Once again, the vigor and responsibility of new immigrants becomes apparent. Most immigrants want only a fair chance to live and work where their efforts will be equitably rewarded.

George Alexander has recorded the progress of Asian Indians in his book *New Americans*.[31] He shows how, since the Immigration Act of 1965, Indians have been able to immigrate to America more freely. In America many have shown their preference for work in the fields of medicine and hotel management. Their willingness to bear humbly with many obstacles and patiently work, putting off immediate gratification, studying hard, and qualifying for good jobs has resulted in growing prosperity. They are enjoying the American dream and contributing to America at the same time. Many rural towns and inner-city hospitals that seem unable to attract American doctors benefit from the services of an

Indo-American doctor. A number of these doctors have received prizes and recognition for their work, pioneering the development of hip replacement surgery and new treatment of AIDS.[32]

It's clear that though the early years may be difficult for immigrants, necessitating a helping hand from others, they can make it and form part of the amazing unity this country enjoys, even though it is made up of so many disparate pieces of the human kaleidoscope. During their transition to life in the United States, immigrants have normal human needs that call for the compassion and spirit of helpfulness Americans have shown historically and that certainly ought to be a part of the ministry of any local church.

First Baptist Church, Dallas, Texas

First Baptist, begun in 1885 and made famous by the lengthy ministry of Dr. W. A. Criswell, has been a church-planting church during its entire history. Fifty-five churches have been started at or by First Baptist. The Southern Baptist Convention (SBC) is highly committed to reaching ethnic America, and this commitment is reflected in the ministry of this particular local church. (Southern Baptists have more than 6,000 churches operating in 110 different languages across the United States. There are 26 ethnic associations in the SBC.)[33]

First Baptist has helped start twenty-one different ethnic churches that are now autonomous and meet in their own facilities. They have done this in two ways: They have invited small ethnic ministries that needed a place to get started to do it under their roof, and they have reached out into the greater Dallas area to start new ethnic churches.

Pastor of Missions Lanny Elmore says that, at the present time, there are six Spanish-language mission churches getting started off campus. A Chin (Burmese), a Japanese, and a Hebrew Messianic fellowship using mostly Russian language meet at First Baptist. A multicultural English-speaking fellowship, a Korean, Laotian, Chinese, and a sign language fellowship meet around the Dallas area. Each of these mission churches average fifty to sixty people in Sunday school and seventy-five in their worship services.[34]

I have had the opportunity to minister in several of the ethnic churches that were initially a part of First Baptist and are now fully established autonomous churches. Most remain Baptist, but some are not. Regardless, they are exciting, growing fellowships that continually reach out to their community. The Filipino American Baptist Church, which began and grew at First Baptist, outgrew facilities at another church, which hosted them in an area closer to where most of the members live. My wife and I were present two years ago when a building fund was launched to construct their own facility. This year they will move into the new building. They use English, as many are second-generation Filipino, and their faith and joy are so infectious that many non-Filipinos are joining them! Pastor Bal Gonzales welcomes them all.

First Baptist exemplifies a principle in multicultural ministry that needs our attention. A given church does not have to meet every need to have meaningful outreach to other cultures. Churches need simply to give the "green light" to what God wants to do. Ethnic fellowships need facilities and encouragement from existing churches, and God often places dedicated believers of diverse ethnicity in a community and arms them with a vision to reach their own people. Ninety percent of the churches started at First Baptist began that way.

Every church does not have to be multicultural. Taken as a whole, First Baptist in Dallas is a homogeneous Anglo church, but it has generously encouraged the use of its ample facilities to advance ministry among the varied cultures of the Dallas area, and it has been blessed by the presence of many diverse peoples meeting alongside them.

Summary

Do the ministries you've read about in this chapter excite you? They are only a few of thousands that could be cited, some of which we will introduce in later chapters. Local churches, Christian schools, businesses, and individuals could all be experiencing much joy by interacting with people from the diverse cultures that make up the United States and the North American continent. The ministries we have already cited give you an idea of how, at various levels and multiplied ways, Christians around the country are responding positively to our growing ethnic diversity. It's not a chore! It's an exciting experience! Culturally relevant ministry breathes life into churches, turning them from isolated igloos into red-hot crucibles at the crossroads of life in the new millennium.

Whether you are the leader of a flock, a cautious follower wondering whether your pastor's ideas for a more multicultural ministry are just plain madness, or a minister in training looking to make the most significant impact with your life, we invite you to continue reading. My wife tells others that I have read the first two chapters of every book on the market! Are you like that? I hope you will invest the time to keep going with this volume. Joe and I believe you will find a path toward a ministry that is both relevant and significant in our modern, incredibly diverse American society.

In the next chapter, we will deal realistically with the fears of Americans about increasing ethnic diversity and demonstrate that there's less to scare us and more to encourage us than some have claimed.

Kaleidoscope America! It may be different than it used to be, but it's still "America the beautiful." That's why so many keep coming to our shores. Are we going to put up "No Trespassing" signs now that the rest of us immigrants have settled down and found our slice of the pie? It hardly sounds American, does it? If we are "one nation under God," we have to remember that our God is an "international" God, and he has a plan for us in all our growing diversity. Let's find out what it is!

Discussion Starters

Many of the questions in the Discussion Starters sections are written with group discussions in mind, but if you are reading this book by yourself, not as part of a group, it would still be worth your while to think about the questions and formulate answers as they relate to your situation.

1. Divide your group into pairs and have each person do the following:
   - Tell your partner about any positive experience you have had with people of other cultures.
   - If you have heard about churches, schools, or organizations that have particularly effective ministries or that enjoy good relationships among people of different cultures, share it with your partner.
2. After ten to fifteen minutes, regather in the larger group. Have each pair recap what was said and suggest some factors you think contributed to the positive atmosphere in the cases shared.
3. Record the factors on newsprint in storyboard fashion or on overhead transparencies.
4. Discuss: Are these factors or characteristics found in our group, school, or church?

2

Clouds in Our Communities
Joseph Henriques

Susan, a white woman who is very loving and gets along with just about everyone, did a report in her class recently on the effects of the slave trade in America. Because she is white, she was harshly criticized for choosing this topic. Susan was saddened by this criticism because she sincerely believes in equality and has no problem discussing the subject. Her critics did not know her and assumed that, because of her race, she would be racist. Little did these people know that Susan is married to an African American. People who have nothing to do with the behavior of America's past seem to be blamed just because of their skin color. This too is a form of racism.[1]

Americans are not generally characterized as mean-spirited racists. In fact, as early as 1831, Frenchman Alexis de Tocqueville recorded his observation in *Democracy in America:*

When an American asks for the co-operation of his fellow citizens, it is seldom refused; and I have often seen it afforded spontaneously, and with great goodwill. If an accident happens on the highway, everybody hastens to help the sufferer; if some great and sudden calamity befalls a family, the purses of a thousand strangers are at once willingly opened and small but numerous donations pour in to relieve their distress.[2]

While the general state of interethnic relationships was not necessarily the focus of Tocqueville's observation, one point remains unchanged from his day until ours: It is not uncommon for Americans at large to generously provide for a successful assimilation of immigrants. This is in spite of predictable ongoing interethnic feuding that seems to accompany each successive wave of immigration. Any mean spirit of the 1831 dominant culture toward certain groups of immigrants would be no different than how some would feel today.

Consider the following examples of under-the-surface hostilities that continue to mar our otherwise positive image as a universal refuge, the land of the free:

- Jeanne O'Laughlin, or "Sister Jeanne" as she is known in south Florida, is a seventy-year-old Dominican nun who has been president for nineteen years of Barry University, a private school of eight thousand students in Miami. She put her reputation on the line in the Elian Gonzalez case, arguing that the six-year-old Cuban boy—who was rescued from the sea as a refugee—should remain in the United States instead of being deported to Cuba. She reminded Americans that the experiences of Miami's Cubans mirror those of her own people: "My ancestors who came over during the potato famine walked ashore with one shoe on and one shoe off and had to work in the quarries and live through 'No Irish need apply.'" People forget, she says, that Cuban Americans have, like the immigrants not so many generations ago, paid a heavy price for their status in America. How did many descendants of immigrants respond to her pleas? With e-mails that read, "Send him back and 100,000 Cubans with him."[3]
- A truck driver reports, "I did a lot of labor-type jobs, and I remember people making . . . incredibly racist comments . . . and saying these things in front of me. . . . In general, what I do is keep my mouth shut. Unless I feel very, very confident in a situation, I just keep my mouth shut. I don't have a job to do as far as race relations goes. It's not my job to straighten out the world. And so I'll sit and listen very often. It's very interesting. I drove a truck for a while. . . . And the other guy who worked on the truck with me was attending a Bible school. And he made some of the most incredi-

ble racist statements I ever heard anybody say. And he enjoyed doing it. He would sit in the cab of the truck with me as we drove down the streets of Minneapolis, and shout out these things."[4]

- After I spoke in his church about our unprecedented opportunity to reach out to the new foreign population in America, an elder confided, "You have a hard sell here." "Why is that?" I asked. He replied in hushed tones, "So many of our people have lost a good portion of their livelihood to foreigners who own companies in the same line of work. By law, minority business owners are given priority on bids that they and our people make on the same job. Even if minorities bid higher, they get the job. There are a lot of hard feelings."

"Those who wish to succeed must ask the right preliminary questions," said Aristotle. Over the course of fifteen years, I have engaged in hundreds of hours of frank discussions with both Christians and non-Christians alike. Certain preliminary questions emerge: Why is there such blatant, latent, or lingering negativism between peoples of various colors? Why do the otherwise nicest people socially distance themselves from those who are culturally different? Why do ethnic jokes, pejorative stereotyping, avoidance, and stuffed feelings of dislike hang over us like dark clouds, clouds that cause unrest in our communities? Dark clouds keep us from seeing the other side. What we do not see, we do not know; what we do not know, we do not understand; what we do not understand, we fear. When applied to people, it is hard to accept those we do not understand. This same principle applies to our relationship with God. "The fear of the LORD is the beginning of wisdom, and the knowledge of the Holy One is understanding," declares the ancient writer of wisdom (Prov. 9:10 NKJV). Respect for the Lord is the first step toward knowing how to live with the Lord. To know the Lord's way of thinking is to understand why he does what he does and how he desires for me to live accordingly. The parallel to interethnic relationships is clear.

Our American ideology, embedded in the Declaration of Independence and the U.S. Constitution, encourages us to believe that everyone has "inalienable rights" to equality, liberty, and opportunity. At the same time, America has sustained many policies that make it difficult for the ethnically diverse to enter into the mainstream of our society. A monocultural mindset in our business, ecclesiastical, and residential communities maintains practices that keep people out—encouraging some ethnicities to belong and others to remain apart.

Christian churches and individual believers also show a tendency to include some ethnicities and exclude others from their fellowship circle. This doesn't square with biblical teaching about mutual acceptance in the love of Christ. Scripture enjoins us to love our neighbor—the most famous example of being a loving neighbor is Jesus' parable of the good Samaritan (Luke 10:25–37)—but we often find it difficult when our neighbor is not like us. The point of Jesus' story was that true neighborliness transcends cultural differences. If we know this, why don't we do better?

This chapter focuses on three causes of negative feelings toward those who are not like us. Biblically speaking, the universal sinful propensity that contaminates relationships is at the root of this issue. This propensity mingles with responses that are part of our personal and national identity, and in and of themselves they are normal, legitimate, and common: ethnocentrism, nationalism, and traditionalism. When laced with sin, however, these three elements can really cloud our judgment when it comes to dealing with those who are different from us.

Identity Matters

To rephrase this all-important point, powerful forces that form our cultural identity are often at the root of intercultural and interracial negativism. We call these forces *ethnocentrism, nationalism,* and *traditionalism.* Experience has trained me to expect to see these elements as primary causes for Christians pulling back from fully embracing multicultural ministry. The desire that one's own culture be dominant is both strong and natural. It comes as no surprise, then, that people in homogeneous churches are concerned about the implications of other races and cultures assimilating into the mainstream of their church life, although most would not object to nonhomogeneous types attending church or participating in church events. The friction comes when culturally varied expressions and expectations meet like cars at the same intersection at the same time. What are the rules for who goes first?

For example, who has the right of way in the following situations? While the predominantly white congregation is having their worship service, the Vietnamese fellowship meeting at the same location is preparing in the kitchen for its fellowship dinner. Pungent garlic odors waft up the hallways and invade the main sanctuary. Should preparations be delayed so as not to offend the olfactory sensitivities of the white brethren (who are probably the landowners)? On a personal level, if your daughter wants to marry the Indian brother, should the wedding be held in India, where she is, in effect, obligated foremost to his family? Or should he bow to American expectations? Or, in the business arena, which value should receive the highest priority—time or money? For example, being on time (as in showing up at least ten minutes before the appointment) is important to a westerner. Being on time is also important to the Nigerian, but the actual time he shows up for the appointment all depends on the friends and family members he might greet along the way. To the American, time is money; to the Nigerian, time is relationships, a value that is shared by many Latin cultures.

To be sure, ethnocentrism, nationalism, and traditionalism are not the only influences that make us proud of those who are like us and prejudiced toward those who are not, but these attitudes are core to our cultural identity and foundational to our interaction with others. Whether that interaction is positive or negative depends on how these forces are used. If my motivation is kindness and my purpose is the well-being of another, then these forces can bring great good. If my motivation is arrogant pride and my purpose is to denigrate or deride another, these forces can bring great harm. Our motivation and our purpose determine whether the impact of these forces is healthy or unhealthy, beneficial or harmful.

Ethnocentrism, for example, can be used to build friendships of trust. Helping a foreign-born person understand that it is impolite in American culture to ask the hostess the cost of certain household items can save a foreign visitor or new immigrant great embarrassment. Similarly, the force of nationalism can be used to help immigrants understand important people and values of their new American homeland. Telling stories of our forefathers, such as Abraham Lincoln and George Washington—along with stories of the indispensable contributions of every people group, race, and culture to America's greatness—can give today's new immigrants a sense of pride in America and a vision of how they themselves can and should make their own positive contribution as good citizens.

Injury occurs, however, when we allow these attitudes to control us, making us feel that our culture, national heritage, and traditions are superior to any other. One church caused great harm by the unwise use of tradition. International students were pressured to raise their hands and walk forward at the end of a meeting to show their desire to believe on Christ. Church members—high on zeal, low on knowledge—forced conformity to the church's evangelical tradition, resulting in the group of students complying just to please their hosts. Making matters worse, the church's ministry leaders had assured university officials that no proselytizing efforts would take place at church socials held for international students. University officials banned this church, along with any other evangelical group, from hosting international students. Sin

can infect tradition when it is so misused, bringing about the conse-
quence predicted by Paul: "Sin simply did what sin is so famous for
doing: using the good as a cover to tempt me to do what would finally
destroy me" (Rom. 7:13 The Message).

Familial inclusiveness of foreigners was obviously what God had in
mind when he spoke to Israel about being a light to the nations: "When
a stranger resides with you in your land, you shall not do him wrong.
The stranger who resides with you shall be to you as the native among
you, and you shall love him as yourself; for you were aliens in the land
of Egypt: I am the LORD your God" (Lev. 19:33–34 NASB). Yet no law mandate can ever ensure heart compliance: Jewish society, as a whole, was
emotionally shut down to foreigners. Jewish hearts had crusty layers of
superiority, distrust, and resentment. Infected by religious leaders, who
viewed all Gentiles as odious simply because they were not Jews, many
of God's chosen people revealed the dark side of ethnocentrism, nationalism, and traditionalism.[5] They had minds to know God's law, but God's
love for foreigners was beyond their willingness to comprehend and
their ability to perform—so much so that Jesus' affection for such "sinners" infuriated the religious leaders of his day.

Of course, early Jewish Christians were not free from ingrained prejudices. It took an elaborate dream to convince Peter to enter Cornelius's
Gentile home and share with him the gospel (Acts 10). Until God
revealed the truth to him in his dream, Peter believed that Gentiles were
physically unclean and that no good Jew would intentionally touch anything or anyone that did not conform to the Mosaic law's standard of
cleanliness.

It is inescapable: As skin binds the body, so our culture, national origin, and traditions tightly bind each one of us into the uniqueness of
who we are. Let's examine these dynamics more closely.

Ethnocentrism

Ethnocentrism results from the socialization process we experience
while growing up in our culture. The essence of ethnocentrism is the
belief that certain things are right and good,[6] and that there is appropriate behavior that expresses those beliefs. Ethnocentrism becomes
the tendency in us to believe that our culture's values and norms of right
and good are absolute; this tendency uses our values and norms as the
standards against which to judge and measure all other cultures.[7] So
tightly bound are we by ethnocentrism that we assume that others, if
given the opportunity to do so, would naturally adopt our values and
norms since they are superior. Why do we believe them to be superior?

Because it feels right to think and behave as we do; this is the state of being we understand.

To validate our culture's belief system, we rely on people in our culture who agree with our beliefs and behavior. Our neighbors, family members, and colleagues at work and school provide us with an understanding of who we are within the context of our culture group. Such cultural identity and allegiance are core aspects of mental and emotional health. Without cultural identity and allegiance—ethnocentrism—Jesus could not have had a ministry in Israel. Knowing that others viewed him as a Jew (Matt. 1:1–17) and as a Nazarene (Matt. 2:23) gave Jesus a personal and cultural framework out of which he conducted his ministry. As a Jew, he was the embodiment of what it meant to live in perfect agreement with the laws of God as given through the prophets to the nation of Israel. As a despised Nazarene, he brought to the Jews a full understanding of God's intent to bestow the blessing of Abraham on all the nations.

Problems of Ethnocentrism

Each of the Americans in the following situations illustrates the problems inherent in ethnocentrism. In each scenario, a person believes what is right and good according to his or her cultural conditioning and acts according to those beliefs. He or she then judges others by how their actions measure up to those beliefs. The culturally different person being judged reacts negatively to that judgment, based on his or her own cultural conditioning—and so the predictable never-ending downward spiral continues, bringing with it misunderstanding and personal frustration. Place yourself in each situation:

- An Asian is leaving a social event and you try giving her a hug. She turns away. You are surprised, maybe even offended at her unfriendly response.
- Ham is served to an Arab for dinner. He sets it aside, never touching it. You think, *How ungrateful!*
- As you cross your legs, the bottom of your shoe points to the Thai person beside you. The conversation gradually turns cold. "How unfriendly!" you murmur to yourself.
- South Americans you invited for dinner show up two hours late. They offer no apology and carry on as if nothing has happened. By your actions, they perceive you are upset but do not know why.
- A group of Chinese international students gives an outstanding presentation of China's history. You then select one of them as the

outstanding presenter of the whole group. You have to literally pull him up front to receive the award. You think, *What's wrong with this fellow? He acts like I'm punishing him instead of rewarding him!*

- You are having a conversation with a Japanese businessman. He hardly says a word. You feel you have to carry the conversation. You think to yourself, *The least he could do is talk!*

How was ethnocentrism reflected in each scenario? Let's consider each one: Most Asians find hugging as a form of greeting unacceptable and uncomfortable. Religious beliefs prohibit Arabs from eating pork. Your crossed legs? Thai people consider the sole of the foot to be the most unclean part of one's body. Pointing it toward anyone is a non-verbal insult. Every culture is punctual. It's just that many South American (and other) cultures have a different sense of punctuality—the acceptable time to show up for an appointment. Doesn't everyone want to hear kudos? Sure, but remember that Chinese culture favors honoring the group rather than the individual. It is socially unacceptable to the group when one member alone receives praise. Craig Storti explains the last example: "While Americans feel a need to respond immediately to a question, Japanese believe it is polite not to respond immediately after someone has spoken, particularly if the person has made a proposal or suggestion. A pause before answering (up to thirty seconds) shows respect to the speaker, indicating that one is carefully considering what was said and is thoughtfully composing a reply."[8]

So who had the correct view of "right and good"—the American or his international friend? Obviously it is a matter of the perspective of one's own ethnocentrism.

Whether right or wrong, the nature of ethnocentrism can lead us to at least three assumptions about those in the community who are of a different culture: (1) Their culture is inferior to ours; (2) they need to see and do things as we do; and (3) there probably isn't that much difference between us anyway. Such assumptions suggest both ignorance and arrogance—ignorance because they reveal a lack of awareness and appreciation of the many beautiful ways that cultures can express themselves; arrogance because such assumptions presuppose one's own culture to be the universal standard.

The reflections of one Korean college student illustrate experiences with ethnocentrism fostered by ignorance: "Since I have been in the U.S.A., I have experienced fear each time I have attempted to communicate outside of my ethnic boundary. I have never believed that I could be the same as Americans. This belief has often held me back from reaching out to them. [In high school] I experienced this fear. I have a bad memory of being made fun of by classmates. I believe that it was my inability of defense and my limitation of communication that made me so frustrated. They probably thought I couldn't confront them to stop their actions. My frustration was that I felt I was not accepted. I couldn't go to them to stand against them because I knew I wasn't going to be able to win them over with my poor English. Although I was so mad at them, the only thing I could do was to just be a victim of racism."⁹

Fortunately, this kind of ignorance can be corrected by education and training. As the Venezuelan educator Luis Machado has said, "Stupidity is a curable disease." According to the renowned intercultural trainer L. Robert Kohls and his coauthor, Herbert L. Brussow, we need to be skilled in managing the power of ethnocentrism so that it doesn't interfere with good intercultural communication:

> It is this strong and magnetic force [ethnocentrism] that must be reduced if we are to make the essential point with which all intercultural training begins: *Although you are personally happy to have been born in your own country and into your own ethnic group, and although you feel very strongly that, for you, your own ways are the best, yet you must realize that other people feel just as strongly about their own cultures as you do about yours. For **them, their** cultures are the best. In this sense, one culture is not **better** than any other is—only different from the rest.* Simple though it sounds, this is not an easy message to get across.¹⁰

Cultural arrogance springs from failure to understand the binding influence of culture on values and norms. This failure is at the root of suspicion and intolerance among ethnic groups. Consider the well-publicized conflicts between the African American and Korean American communities in some of our cities. The 1992 Los Angeles riots triggered an eruption of volcanic proportions between these two ethnic groups. Korean stores were plundered and Koreans were killed, mostly by African Americans. This has taken place not just in Los Angeles but in other cities as well. Why such hostility? Why do Koreans stereotype blacks as lazy and blacks stereotype Koreans as rude? One probable cause is ethnocentrism—the inability to see the same event through the lenses of another's culture.

One Korean professor believes that ethnic tensions would greatly diminish if African Americans could understand just one important aspect of social interaction within the Korean culture. She writes:

> For instance, according to Korean tradition, they are not supposed to show their feelings or emotions in public, and not smile at strangers; direct eye contact is discouraged, especially to older people. When they accidentally

bump into other people on the street, Koreans do not say "Excuse me." Men in Korea are expected to be serious and engage in little "small" talk.[11]

To facilitate understanding between both groups, this professor is developing cultural exchange workshops for African Americans and Korean Americans. Both groups will mutually identify and explain insights into their cultural practices. Such encounters engender a greater appreciation for the powerful force of ethnocentrism and how it affects our behavior.

Adopting and Adapting

Robert Kohls suggests that reducing one's ethnocentrism is an obvious necessity for the individual living outside of his or her own culture. After all, it is the dominant culture that establishes the standard and expressions for what is right and good. The onus is on any individual living in a foreign culture to *adopt* the freedoms or restrictions of that standard. As an example, American female soldiers serving in Saudi Arabia during the Persian Gulf War were asked not to wear shorts and to make sure that their arms were covered while on base (even more so while out in the community). Likewise, South Americans living in the States should learn to adopt the American business norm of punctuality when keeping appointments (for example, meeting someone at 9:00 A.M. means arriving earlier not later).

An equally important suggestion is for individuals from the dominant culture to choose to reduce the expression of their own ethnocentrism for the benefit of the foreigner. In this case, the person in the dominant culture *adapts* to the cultural expectations of persons from minority groups. Such deference is a key factor in facilitating positive intercultural relationships. In other words, to achieve the greater value of unity we of the dominant culture choose to lay aside the right to use our own cultural expressions in order to accommodate the cultural norms of others. We refrain, for example, from hugging the Asian and from crossing our legs in the presence of a Thai. We tailor our compliments to address the Chinese as a group, and we learn to use silence as forcefully as spoken words. We plan to keep the food warm until our guests feel it is the appropriate time for arrival. In some cases, we lay aside our taste for ham and choose instead to serve lamb.

Naturally the need to use deference is in direct correlation to the potential offense of our words or actions. Sitting at the table instead of on the floor for dinner would most likely not greatly disturb a Japanese guest. On the other hand, if an American man chooses to greet an Asian woman with an embrace rather than her preferred handshake or bow, the Asian woman would be highly embarrassed by the inappropriate greeting.

For the sake of the gospel, we as Christians should first understand our own ethnocentrism. Second, we should understand that specific cultural expressions are important to the foreigner God brings across our path. Finally, we should adopt what I call Paul's Christian Bill of Rights of Intercultural Relations:

> Even though I am free of the demands and expectations of everyone, I have voluntarily become a servant to any and all in order to reach a wide range of people: religious, nonreligious, meticulous moralists, loose-living immoralists, the defeated, the demoralized—whoever. I didn't take on their way of life. I kept my bearings in Christ—but I entered their world and tried to experience things from their point of view. I've become just about every sort of servant there is in my attempts to lead those I meet into a God-saved life. I did all this because of the Message. I didn't just want to talk about it; I wanted to be *in* on it!
>
> 1 Corinthians 9:19–23 The Message

Nationalism

> It is an incontrovertible truth that the civil institutions of the United States of America . . . now stand in imminent peril from the rapid and enormous increase of the body of residents of foreign birth, imbued with foreign feelings, and of an ignorant and immoral character. . . . [because of] the suicidal policy of these United States . . . a large proportion of the foreign body of citizens and voters now constitutes a representation of the worst and most degraded of the European population—victims of social oppression or personal vices, utterly divested, by ignorance or crime, of the moral and intellectual requisites for political self-government. The mass of foreign voters . . . will leave the Native citizens a minority in their own land!
>
> The Platform, Native American (Know-Nothing) Party, 1845[12]

The Native American party's passion to stem the flow of immigration emanated from the second force contributing to our cultural identity—nationalism. The Know-Nothing party feared that unwise immigration policies were allowing an out-of-control tidal wave of un-Americanized immigrants to become naturalized citizens. They believed that Americans, and the values that America stood for, would be overwhelmed by foreign influence.

For many in the tradition of the Know-Nothing party, it is hard to conceive the following statement as also motivated by that same force:

Sam Donaldson [ABC News]: "[Native-born Americans] don't have any more right to this country, in my view, than people who came here yesterday."

Cokie Roberts [National Public Radio]: "That's right."[13]

The nationalism of the Know-Nothing party and of Sam Donaldson and Cokie Roberts is the same in that they are all concerned with the well-being of America—the country of their allegiance—its values and prosperity. Their difference lies in their view of immigration policies, the number of and kinds of immigrants allowed to come to America, and the perceived value of both to America.

According to Webster's dictionary, *nationalism* is "the national consciousness exalting one nation above all others and placing primary emphasis on promotion of its culture and interests as opposed to those of other nations or supranational groups." Originating in the root for nation, *ethnos*, nationalism implies loyalty to one's ethnic, or national, group.

At the heart of nationalism is patriotism, meaning, "love or devotion to one's country." Since *patri* means father or forefather, a patriot is one with deep loyalty not only to his nation but also to the Founding Fathers of that nation. If the nation's Founding Fathers are of his or her same cultural, racial, or ethnic background, the patriot's natural sense of loyalty runs deep. This is not to say that to be loyal or patriotic, a citizen must be from the same culture as the Founding Fathers. African Americans, Asians, Hispanics, and people from other ethnic backgrounds have all been patriotic U.S. citizens and outstanding examples of valor in military service.

Nationalism and patriotism are rooted in specific values as set forth by each country's religious beliefs or political ideology. Most Americans claim the constitution accurately reflects the timeless values and vision of our founders. Pledging allegiance to the flag is swearing allegiance to those values. When people speak of preserving or returning to "traditional values," they are speaking as patriots. In this sense, nationalism is healthy for any country, giving its citizenry a sense of unity and pride in their corporate history and achievements.

To patriotic purists, their nation's history, culture, traditions, and values must be protected at all costs. Any opposing foreign influence is considered a threat of corruption or destruction. The ideals of protectionism are thus rooted in patriotism.

Nationalism takes a negative turn when protectionism becomes isolationism. The natural tendency for those who fear the loss of that which is precious is to distance and even separate themselves from outsiders considered a threat to the stability and harmony of the motherland. The allegiance to America of immigrant settlers or sojourning aliens is often held suspect, at best.

Views on Immigration

What does nationalism and patriotism have to do with our view of the foreign-born peoples of our communities? Because more immigrants entered the United States during the '90s than in any other time in our country's history, immigration has become a charged political issue.[14] Many native-born Americans have low tolerance for immigrants whom they believe have come to America for what America has to offer, not because they love America or believe in the ideals of her founders.

Christians and non-Christians alike join the debate, falling at all points along the spectrum concerning immigration policy. More often than not, the view we take on a political issue is also the view we take on people who are involved in the issue. We tend to like those who agree with us and dislike those who do not. Since emotions dictate actions, our nonverbal communication will clearly tell immigrants whether we accept them or not. One Asian told me recently, "I just want to go to a church where I feel internationals are accepted."

On one end of the immigration spectrum, nativists demand that immigration be highly restricted. On the other hand, multiculturalists demand that even illegal aliens be given nearly full-citizen status, with free government benefits, including the right to vote in local elections. Somewhere between these positions are Christians like Pastor Stephen Rhodes who believe that the church should involve itself in practical action, not in the public debate over immigration. The real question for the church, he says, is ". . . not whether a nation . . . has a legal right to protect its borders or to determine whom it wants or does not want to let in . . . the real question for the church is, How shall we, as God's people, treat the foreigner, the alien, in this land?"[15]

Patrick Buchanan, who has launched three bids for the White House, has won both a loyal following for and a fierce opposition to his views of economic nationalism. The centerpiece of his message in his "proudly rebellious Republican presidential campaign" is "an economic nationalism that blames unfair trade practices for decimating the U.S. industrial and manufacturing base." Mr. Buchanan favors stringent immigration laws that protect America from those immigrants who are either unwanted or undesirable.[16]

While not every American sets forth the case against immigration quite as strongly as Patrick Buchanan or Peter Brimelow, they still acknowledge a validity in the rationale of their concerns. Here's what Brimelow has to say:

> There is a sense in which current immigration policy is Adolf Hitler's posthumous revenge on America. The U.S. political elite emerged from the war passionately concerned to cleanse itself from all taints of racism or xenophobia. Eventually, it enacted the epochal Immigration Act . . . of 1965. And this, quite accidentally triggered a renewed mass immigration, so huge and so systematically different from anything that had gone before as to transform—and ultimately, perhaps, even to destroy—the one unquestioned victor of World War II: The American nation, as it had evolved by the middle of the twentieth century. Today, U.S. government policy is literally dissolving the people and electing a new one.[17]

Brimelow continues his argument:

> The mass immigration so thoughtlessly triggered in 1965 risks making America an *alien nation* . . . not merely in the sense that America will become a freak among the world's nations because of the unprecedented demographic mutation it is inflicting on itself; not merely in the sense that Americans themselves will become alien to each other, requiring an increasingly strained government to arbitrate between them; but ultimately, in the sense that Americans will no longer share in common what Abraham Lincoln called in his first Inaugural Address *"the mystic chords of memory, stretching from every battlefield and patriot grave, to every living heart and hearthstone, all over this broad land. . . ."*[18]

Many Americans can sense kinship in the national mood as assessed by Linda Chavez:

> . . . there is also a sense that immigrants today may be less malleable than those who came early in the century, during the country's last large influx. The challenge of adding millions of new, possibly unmeltable ethnics seems to many Americans too heavy a burden to assume at a time when the nation is still struggling to define what constitutes an American identity and to include more than 30 million black Americans in the full social, political, and economic mainstream. . . . What's more, many native-born Americans say they feel lost in urban communities with large immigrant enclaves, where English is rarely heard on the streets or seen in storefronts.[19]

Because of the force of nationalism, feelings of hostility toward the foreign-born may be largely unspoken but can erupt by the slightest provocation. My aunt and her cousin, for example, have been United States citizens for more than fifty years. They speak English as fluently as their native Puerto Rican Spanish. But when two or more Puerto Ricans get together, they naturally revert to their mother tongue, as they did one day while shopping in Wal-Mart. A man snapped at them, "We speak English in this country!"

Our Dual Allegiance

In light of the issues and concerns that surround immigration, what should be the focus for Christians? No matter if the forecast of many comes true that by the middle of the twenty-first century no ethnic group will be large enough to claim to be the majority; no matter if your ethnic group will one day become one of many competing for scarce resources; and no matter if the color of tomorrow's American really turns out to be brown, the Christian must be a faithful citizen of both heaven and earth. This is no easy task.

As citizens of heaven, we find ourselves becoming more like Christ in our love for foreigners on the fringe of society. As citizens of earth, we live in a country subject to the ebb and flow of immigration. As citizens of a heavenly kingdom, we are working for a cause far greater than national preservation. Yet we remain citizens of earthly kingdoms and must work for their preservation as well. Our dual citizenship becomes our tension.

As American citizens, we must responsibly think through the national issues of the impact of immigration on America. We must ask, Do our immigration laws reflect what is right and good? Yet as Christians, we view life from the perspective of a citizen of God's holy nation. We must ask, Regardless of our laws, do I now know this immigrant because it is God who brought him or her here to learn the gospel through me? The same apostle who demanded, "Let every person be in subjection to the governing authorities" (Rom. 13:1 NASB), also declared, "Our citizenship is in heaven" (Phil. 3:20 NASB). Peter admits to the tension of our dual citizenship by anointing us "a chosen generation . . . a holy nation, His own special people" (1 Peter 2:9 NKJV), while simultaneously insisting that we, "submit [ourselves] for the Lord's sake to every human institution, whether to a king as the one in authority, or to governors as sent by him" (1 Peter 2:13–14 NASB). But how can we pledge allegiance both to our nation and to our Lord's kingdom while ministering to immigrants? Let us choose a particularly difficult situation on which to focus our discussion: What do you do with illegal immigrants?

Paul's dilemma with Onesimus, assuming that he was indeed a runaway slave, offers a potential model for us to follow. While in Ephesus, Paul had phenomenal success, as Luke records for us: "All who dwelt in Asia [Minor] heard the Word of the Lord Jesus, both Jews and Greeks" (Acts 19:10 NKJV). Philemon, a wealthy businessman from Colossae, was among the many who responded favorably to the gospel. He took his newfound faith with him on returning to his hometown of Colossae. Years later, one of his slaves called Onesimus ran away to Rome. By providential design, his wanderings led him to Paul, his master's spiritual father. Soon, like his master Philemon, Onesimus believed on the same Christ.

Paul faced a dilemma. As a citizen of Rome, he was obligated to national law, which demanded the return of the runaway slave to his master, or at least to the local authorities. He knew well the consequences for Onesimus if the latter action were taken. Perhaps Paul also struggled with the application of the Mosaic law that prohibited the extradition of a runaway slave (Deut. 23:15–16). And to complicate matters even more Paul had great love for Onesimus whom he described as "my son . . . whom I have begotten while in my chains" (Philem. 10).

Paul opted to send Onesimus back to his owner, but not without protection. Tychicus, Paul's trusted associate, escorted the fugitive back to his master with a personal letter from Paul. Leaning heavily on his personal relationship with Philemon, Paul lobbied for Philemon to receive Onesimus back, not as a slave deserving punishment, but as a brother who had proved himself profitable in Christian ministry. Paul put the responsibility on Philemon to model Christian maturity before a watching community of believers and unbelievers alike.

As we consider our posture toward illegal aliens, what principles can we glean from this story that enables us to be good citizens of heaven and earth?

First, be fully confident in God's sovereign activity. Paul allowed plenty of room for divine rule over human affairs when he told Philemon, "Perhaps he departed for a while for this purpose, that you might receive him forever . . . as a beloved brother" (vv. 15–16). We too must leave plenty of room for God's sovereignty, acknowledging that the influx of internationals in America is part of God's sovereign plan that we might receive them forever as brothers.

Second, Paul appealed for a best-case scenario in this conflict between the best interest of the nation and the best interest of the individual. Like Paul, we must appeal to the conscience of those involved to do the right and merciful thing. If a person is in violation of the law, we must argue for the best-case scenario on his or her behalf. This was Paul's main objective when he asked Philemon to accept Onesimus, "no longer as a slave but more than a slave" (v. 16).

Third, the decisions we make are not always clearly defined for us. Paul surely encountered internal tension as he dealt with the competing emotions of his personal ties to Onesimus, his allegiance to his brother and friend Philemon, and his moral obligations to both Roman and Jewish law. We can expect no less a conflict as we deal with similar issues.

God will provide ways for us to express our allegiance to the spirit of his laws and to the laws of our nation. How do we discover these ways? We must be vigilant and diligent to maintain a balance between and an integration of knowledge and zeal. We cannot disregard—or remain ignorant of—the laws relating to immigration, yet refusing to love the foreigner in practical ways is unbiblical. To disregard the law while seeking to meet the needs of illegal immigrants is to discard the laws of society meant for the common good. On the other hand, to strictly uphold the laws of society in complete disregard for the immediate needs of the illegal immigrants we know is to break the second commandment. We must be confident that God will ultimately provide "a way out" (1 Cor. 10:13) as we seek to apply the characteristics of wisdom found in James 3:17. We must be committed to the principle of due process as we seek to change bad laws or laws that treat insufficiently the concerns of illegal immigrants.

Traditionalism

The powerful and volatile nature of both ethnocentrism and nationalism is also found in the third force defining our cultural identity: traditionalism.

Tradition is to a nation what walls are to a house. Without a well-defined structure, community life falls apart. Take the story of Reb Tevya in *Fiddler on the Roof*. Tevya is a poor milkman who is also an important patriarchal figure in his hometown of Anatevka. An opening scene in the musical finds Tevya reflecting on the importance of tradition to everything precious in his small village. Tevya asks, "How do we keep our balance?" He then answers his own question with one bellowing word, "Tradition!" "Because of our traditions," he continues, "we've kept our balance for many, many years. Here in Anatevka, we have traditions for everything: how to sleep, how to eat, how to work, how to wear clothes. For instance, we always keep our heads covered, and we always wear a little prayer shawl. This shows our constant devotion to God.

You may ask, how did this tradition get started? I tell you . . . I don't know. But because of our tradition, every one of us knows who he is and," he adds, pointing emphatically upward, "what God expects him to do."[20]

Tradition encases our enduring values in the things we regularly do. Every society preserves and practices its values through personal and familial behavior as well as through community events. Veteran's Day parades, the placing of the hand on the Bible during presidential inaugurations, singing the national anthem at sports events, flying the flag at half-mast after a calamity, and Fourth of July fireworks are some of the public ways we show the values we believe in. Tradition perpetuates the customs and beliefs developed throughout a group's long, shared history.

Each family has its own traditions, such as celebrating birthday parties, sharing Thanksgiving dinners, watching the Super Bowl, and going to church on Sunday. Cultural traditions do not have written instructions. They are passed on from generation to generation, verbally and nonverbally, acted out in the daily routine of life.

Tradition and Change

Traditions are hard to change, and they should be. Traditional, predictable routine is a main source of stability to any community. But what happens when tradition stands in the way of a change for the better, when, because of tradition, we refuse to adapt our social structures to new needs and demands, when we resist eliminating unnecessary or outmoded ways of doing things? Adhering to tradition when obvious change is needed is like administering CPR to a lifeless status quo.

Today in our country immigration is changing the demographics— and thus upsetting the traditions—of many communities. Dominant-culture churches in those communities are faced with a serious challenge to their traditional ways of doing church. Will they remain a traditional white church, even with a dwindling white population? Will they continue promoting programs that traditionally met the needs of their members, even while the needs of the majority population in their community are now vastly different?

One pastor told me how he was answering these questions. He was leading his church to purchase property and build a newer and bigger facility farther out from its present location. The reason? The influx of African American and other minority groups into the area. This was his second move for the same reason.

Other churches see their ethnically diverse, politically varied, and economically mixed communities as opportunities for needed change and growth. Chapter 1 speaks of such churches.

Churches in rural areas—where local tradition often has the tightest hold—face an even greater challenge—an innate unwillingness and inability to unilaterally accept *any* person not already known to their local church community. As one pastor of a rural church once told me, "That is a great message you gave on reaching internationals, but it won't work here. We have a hard enough time accepting someone new from our own culture, much less someone from a totally different culture."

Some churches fear changing time-honored traditions because they equate such change with a change in values. This fear is unfounded. Values need not change when we change the way they are observed.

Many church leaders, for example, find it difficult to modify traditions of worship even for the sake of accommodating foreigners. I have encouraged some church leaders for years to make one simple change in their worship tradition: change "thee," "thou," and "thine" in the choruses they sing to "you" and "your." No one, to my knowledge, has ever made that change. For many in the older established churches, words from the old King James English conjure up a sentimental spirituality that is hard to let go (after all, many church leaders who are Baby Boomers and older used the King James as young people growing in their faith). Of course, to the nontraditional American, those very same words send them scrambling for the dictionary.

Traditions are to be cherished. God directed the Israelites to develop traditions that would help them remember what he had done for them. He meant them for good. But it was not long before their traditions became more important to them than God. We must never allow our traditions to interfere with our obedience to God. While being strong proponents of our tradition, we must be stronger proponents of doing what it takes to bring the good news message to those who have yet to believe. When our tradition hinders the advancement of the gospel, we become traditionalistic, taking on the demeanor of an overbearing, dominating parent who actively opposes any change in family custom that threatens the long-held interpretation of a stable environment. While remaining strong proponents of our tradition, then, we must be stronger proponents of the gospel.

The Negatives of Traditionalism

When tradition persists in its opposition to new ways—even with evidence that the new custom or belief is harmless or even potentially positive and good—then we have become traditionalistic. The Pharisees were traditionalistic in the worst way. In Jewish theology, tradition referred to the oral teachings of the elders. These traditions were reverenced by Jews along with the written teachings of the Old Testament and were regarded by them as equally authoritative on matters of belief and conduct. The crossfire dialogue, as recorded in Matthew 15, is but one example of charges made by the Pharisees against Jesus for transgressing "the tradition of the elders." Jesus countered with a charge of his own, "Why do you also transgress the commandment of God because of your tradition?" (v. 3 NKJV).

In Jesus' discussion with the Pharisees, we see his concern with the issues of the heart. These must be acknowledged and attended to, no matter the personal cost. It is a grievous matter, Jesus warned, when tradition hinders or prevents the work of God in the human heart. He had reason to give strong admonitions. Traditionalistic thought greatly hindered the ability of the Jewish people of the first century to minister to the ethnically different. As observed earlier, teachings of the rabbis forbade a Jew to have contact with anything touched by a Gentile. He could not enter a Gentile's home, much less touch him or eat his food. Centuries of domination by the Greeks and Romans had ingrained into the Jews a hatred for all Gentiles. According to the Roman historian Tacitus, "They regard the rest of mankind with all the hatred of enemies."[21]

Jesus demonstrated a wholly different attitude toward Gentiles. Mark tells us that "from there He arose and went to the region of Tyre and Sidon" (Mark 7:24 NKJV) where he had an encounter with the Syro-Phoenician woman. Although she lived only 50 miles from where most of the Twelve had grown up, hers was an entirely different culture, dominated by Greek influences and populated almost exclusively by Gentiles.[22] Through the story of Jesus' encounter with this woman of a different culture, Scripture immediately takes the reader from theory to practice. Jewish religious tradition strictly forbade such an encounter but Jesus breaks out of the mold, shocking even his disciples. They wanted him to heal her daughter and send her away as quickly as possible. Jesus did not yield his agenda to their demands. He prolonged the conversation, refused to send her away, and ultimately showed her the same favor shown to the Jews—he healed her daughter. In Jesus the caste system of the traditionalistic Jew was shattered forever.

As the church assimilates immigrants into its church life, new hybrid traditions will take the place of those that once served an important purpose in the church's life and ministry. Take the guitar, as an example within our own culture. As a young person, growing up in the folk song era of the Kingston Trio, Peter, Paul, and Mary, and Bob Dylan, I remember the difficulty of introducing the guitar in church as a legitimate instrument for spiritual worship. While in college I sang with a group called The House of Theophilus. We were on the "cutting edge" as we employed the new sounds of a bass fiddle, guitars, a banjo, and gut-bucket to sing the old verities of the faith. After a chapel performance, a venerable senior saint spoke to me, sternly warning me of the danger of going the way of the world.

But adapting the new does not mean disdaining the old. After Jesus had taught new truths about God's kingdom to his disciples through parables, he asked them, "Have you understood all these things?" When they said yes, that they had, he spoke yet another parable, one with special application to church leaders who are the official stewards of their congregation's traditions. "Therefore every scribe [scholar of the Old Testament] instructed concerning the kingdom of heaven is like a house-holder who brings out of his treasure things new and old" (Matt. 13:52 NKJV). The treasure (values) remains the same. The new and old, by way of application, are the different norms by which those values are expressed. The gatekeepers of tradition have the task of blending new ways with the old. For this reason, many churches have a traditional service and a contemporary or blended service. We are recognizing that both the new ways and the old ways are meant for mutual benefit. The same principle applies to cultural expressions of faith.

Church leaders of today have a threefold role in multicultural ministry: They are to be *sustainers* of their cultural traditions that promote and help God's work, *breakers* of those traditions that hinder, and *blenders* of the traditions of the cultures represented in their church. Just as a rain forest with its varied plant and animal life draws us to its beauty, so, when allowed to grow and flourish, the varied cultures of a local church will draw others to the beauty of the Lord's kingdom.

Reb Tevya, a patriarch in his own right, recognized the need to coura-geously face the changes his country was experiencing in turn-of-the-century czarist Russia. Centuries-old traditions were being challenged, and his heart was filled with painful conflict as he realized his inevitable need to embrace the new ways. By wisely traditionalizing new customs anchored in unchanging values, he responded well.

Summary

We have considered the forces of ethnocentrism, nationalism, and traditionalism in light of our challenge and opportunity to minister in a new multicultural society. While a healthy cultural identity is indis-pensable, the forces of ethnocentrism, nationalism, and traditionalism have divisive and destructive potential, which constitute clouds in our communities. Our minds must be open to new ways of expressing timeless truths.

1. Every church must ask the same question Paul asked when Christ challenged him to a deeper understanding: "What would you have me do, Lord?" We must be asking the same question in a different way: If Jesus were our pastor, what would he do to include the culturally diverse people of our church family? What does he want us to do? With that knowledge we must set forth a well-planned process to develop the next model of how our church can become involved in the King's command to make disciples of all nations.
2. God is calling us to skillfully understand and exemplify what he is doing at this time in our nation. Our nation is looking for institutional models of successful intercultural integration. Each church could become such a model. But we must become like the sons of Issachar, "men who understood the times, with knowledge of what Israel should do" (1 Chron. 12:32 NASB). Daniel was given skill to understand God's plan for how Israel should relate to other nations. Why? Because he humbled himself and dedicated himself to the process of understanding that which he did not know (Dan. 10:12; 9:2, 3, 22). We can do the same as we seek to relate to the culturally diverse people of our communities.
3. "There is no evolution without roots," so claimed his majesty Sultan Qaboos bin Said Al-Said of the Sultanate of Oman as he articulated his political and social policy for the future.[23] We who are willing to accept the change and challenge of a demographically diverse society are also willing to allow our identity to evolve. Our growth will be rooted in what we know to be right and good, in our loyalty to our nation, and in our traditions. These natural and historically stabilizing forces must not, however, stop us from reaching out in a Christlike manner to newer, ethnically different Americans.

Discussion Starters

The terms *ethnocentrism, nationalism,* and *traditionalism* are just three of the many terms used to describe issues, feelings, and concerns germane to life in a multicultural society. In the following exercise, you will explore both what needs to be done to prevent clouds forming in your community and what positive steps can be taken to create healthy relationships with the culturally diverse of your community.

1. Divide into small groups. Assign two or more of the terms and definitions listed below to each group.
2. Take several minutes to browse through your assigned terms: Underline what you consider to be concepts and definitions with important meaning for multicultural ministry. Place a check mark by phrases that remind you of an interethnic experience you have had yourself or observed in others, either negative or positive.
3. Discuss your thoughts with your small group. Talk about how negative attitudes between ethnic groups can be eliminated. Speak about positive behaviors that could be easily adopted by one ethnic group to reach out to another.
4. Reconvene as a large group. Share your thoughts as described in the directions above. Answer these questions: What do we need to do to break down barriers between culture groups in our church? How can we fully utilize the beauty and strengths of the cultures represented in our church?

Discrimination: Differential, negative, and unequal treatment of a group or a person belonging to that group.

Ethnic group: A social category of people who share certain unique historical and social experiences such as culture, religion, values, foods, language, norms, and history. Groups of such people may be called *ethnics*.

Ethnic identity: A group's common national or cultural origins based primarily on how the group defines itself in the present. Portuguese Americans, for example, have their national and cultural roots in Portugal. This does not mean that all people identifying themselves as Portuguese Americans have even been to Portugal. While important, the similar social and cultural bonds are not the major factor of their group's cohesiveness; rather, the history of their sojourn experiences in the United States is what binds them together. A group sense of identity may increase if it perceives itself as marginalized or oppressed by the dominant culture or threatened in some way by other minority groups.

Minority: A group of people who are singled out from others in society because of their physical or cultural characteristics. No one achieves the status of minority. This status is ascribed, that is, inherited at birth. It is based on who one's parents are. Some believe the designation *minority* is used by the powerful to subjugate certain groups and restrict their access to resources and positions of influence. According to this belief, a minority person is perceived as being distinct from the larger society, usually in a disadvantageous way. The general usage of the term *minority*, however, simply refers to a group that is smaller than the dominant group or—in the case of apartheid in South Africa—the group that holds fewer positions of power and influence.

Partiality: The term Scripture uses to describe favoritism shown to certain groups based on their socioeconomic, religious, or cultural status. Partiality looks up to, admires, and speaks favorably to the highly regarded ones. Those holding positions of power and symbols of wealth are given preferential treatment. Partiality also looks down at, disregards, and "talks at" those to whom social value is not given. The poor, disadvantaged, and powerless, therefore, are not given treatment equal to what others receive. Under no circumstances, said James, should the brethren "hold the faith of our Lord Jesus Christ, the Lord of glory, with partiality" (James 2:1; see following verses). Other key passages include Lev. 19:15; 2 Chron. 19:7; Job 34:19; cf. Deut. 10:17; 15:7–10; Prov. 24:23; 28:21; Matt. 22:8–10; Acts 10:34–35; Rom. 2:11; Eph. 6:9; Col. 3:25; 4:1; 1 Peter 1:17.

Prejudice: A negative attitude that prejudges and misjudges others. The basis for this attitude is frequently defined along racial and ethnic lines. A Hispanic who dislikes a white for the reason that he or she is white is prejudiced. Prejudice is a belief about someone or something that is unreasonable, not based on known fact.

Race: Ethnic groups are often associated with the idea of "race" because of certain biological characteristics. Yet race is a socially constructed category, as defined by people of a society. For example, how is a black person defined? Is it a person who has one drop of "black blood" (as defined in some southern states) or is it a person who has a certain skin tone? To complicate matters, consider someone like Tiger Woods. He is of Asian American and African American parentage. Is he black or Asian? Many Asians are lighter skinned than Europeans. Does their skin tone determine their race? If so, what race are they? Children of black and white parents are hard-pressed to identify themselves as either black or white.

The question arises then as to who defines race, on what basis, and, most important, for what purpose? Hitler defined the Jews as a race to solidify the perceived superiority of the Aryan "race" (white-skinned, blond, tall, blue-eyed people). When they first arrived in America, the Irish were defined as a race, separate from the white race. Some believe that the singling out and differentiating between people simply on the basis of physical or cultural characteristics is nothing but an effort of the most powerful group(s) in society to rule and control scarce resources.

Racism: Combining both prejudice and discrimination—whether in attitudes, actions, or policies—with the intent of oppressing, causing harm to, or dehumanizing another group. Overt racism is easily identified. Covert racism is subtle. Avoiding interaction with others out of disdain for their cultural group is racism.

Stereotype: A picture of a group of people that describes what we feel is true about the "typical" member of that group in their behavior, attitude, or values. These beliefs are oversimplified and often negative. Examples of statements that stereotype are: Asians are overly ambitious; blacks are lazy, loud, and good athletes; Poles lack common sense; Italians are emotional with connections to the Mafia; the Irish drink and argue; Middle Easterners have a low view of women; and Hispanics are in the United States illegally.

3

Catching the Idea of Kaleidoscopic Change

Michael Pocock

When evening comes, you say, "It will be fair weather, for the sky is red," and in the morning, "Today it will be stormy, for the sky is red and overcast." You know how to interpret the appearance of the sky, but you cannot interpret the signs of the times.

Jesus (Matt. 16:2–3)

"It's a big blue marble!" That's how one astronaut described the earth seen from space. NASA soon made those beautiful pictures available to the public. Then, to everyone's delight, in 1974 Harry Fownes inaugurated one of the most successful and widely acknowledged children's T.V. programs and called it *Big Blue Marble*. It introduced children to thinking and acting with global perspective.[1]

There's something transfixing about the view of earth as a whole planet seen from space. On a sea-blue globe, white clouds swirl across emerald plains and sandy deserts. This sphere throbs with life! It's alive, dynamic, and for better or worse, we are all on it together! This fascinating view has affected not only astronauts and children but theologians also. Early in the era of manned spaceflight, Paul Tillich wrote an essay, which he called "The Effects of Space Exploration on Man's Condition and Stature."[2] He understood that once we looked back on ourselves from space, our view of ourselves would change. He was concerned that we would become a society in which scientists and the physically fit would become new gods—elite people who could master both the technology needed and the fitness to endure space travel. Tillich was concerned that this would lead to greater human fragmentation. His was one of the earliest recognitions that we live in what is now termed a "global village." Activity in any part of the globe has an effect on the rest of the world. This definitely has implications for how we view change in North America, including the accelerated cultural diversification of this continent.

The movement of peoples across the face of the earth mirrors the swirling clouds we see in pictures of Earth, and on the weather channel every day. Some days these clouds appear to be in motion, moving and changing into beautiful formations. Other days the clouds seem quite static, with no perceptible motion. But we know one thing as a certainty—weather changes, and it does so because fronts move along, pushed by various dynamics that are beyond our discussion here. We welcome sunny days but we know we need periodic rain. In short, we see weather changes as normal and necessary, a part of being on this "big blue marble."

People are part of this grand creation scheme. They tend to move in ways similar to the weather patterns, and no wonder! People, Earth, and the atmosphere were all created by the same God. They have assigned roles, which we read about in the creation account of Genesis 1–2. It is not unusual in Scripture to see similes and metaphors comparing people to the weather, tidal movements, sand, and rocks. The rich are "like a wild flower. For the sun rises with scorching heat and withers the plant; its blossom falls and its beauty is destroyed," says James (1:10–11). In Isaiah we read: "The wicked are like the troubled sea, when it cannot rest" (Isa. 57:20 NKJV). God told Abraham that his offspring would be like the sand and like the stars, uncountable in number (Gen. 22:17).

Many Scripture passages assert that God controls the weather. Jesus amazed people, causing them to remark: "Who then is this, that even the wind and the sea obey Him?" (Mark 4:41 NASB). This same God commanded that people multiply and spread out over the earth (Gen. 1:28; 9:1) The history of humankind, especially after the Babel incident, bears record to the constant movement of peoples. When we consider the migration of people to America, we need to realize that it is part of God's plan, even though many of the immigrants themselves may be unaware of it. We shall reflect on this more in the next chapter.

In this chapter we will consider what made America into the place it is today from the point of view of its people. The weather is changed by forces interacting on a global scale. In a similar way, certain influences affect the movements of people, pushing or pulling them to where they are. People respond to these forces voluntarily, as immigrants, or involuntarily, as captured people, refugees, slaves, or convicts sentenced to penal colonies. We are in a fallen world. Much of what causes people to move is heartbreaking. This is not what represents God's hand so much as his sovereign ability to bring good out of it all. We need to understand the movement of peoples as ordinary, constant, and one for which God has an overall design; then, perhaps, we shall be more at ease with the developments in our own nation and respond more creatively.

> God is working his purpose out,
> As year succeeds to year;
> God is working his purpose out
> And the time is drawing near . . .
> When the earth shall be filled
> With the glory of God
> As the waters cover the sea.
>
> A. C. Ainger[3]

Migration as a Normal Pattern in History

We tend to believe that people belong where they have historically lived. We apply this to ourselves as belonging to America even though we know our forefathers came from some other country and continent. For example, the Celts are from western Europe; Scandinavians come from Sweden, Norway, Finland, and Denmark; and, of course, the Chinese live in China and the Zulus in South Africa. The reality is, however, that all of these and the other peoples of the world have been on the move throughout history.[4]

Scandinavians, for reasons that are still only conjectured, suddenly exploded from their traditional homelands as Vikings in the sixth century, displacing Celts in Britain and moving along the Atlantic coasts of Europe and through the interior of Europe. They became the palace guards in Constantinople and sacked cities around the Mediterranean.

They even established settlements in North America that flourished briefly around A.D. 1000.

Peoples of east Asia apparently spread to North America across the land bridge that existed twenty-nine thousand years B.C.[5] From there they spread throughout our whole hemisphere, eventually forming great peoples like the Iroquois confederacy in North America and the Mayans and Incas to the south.

Mongolians under Genghis Khan exploded west after conquering China in A.D. 1215. They rode their horses to the gates of Vienna. Look in the eyes of eastern Europeans and you will often see traces of that great movement from the Orient.[6]

Zulus, a Bantu people of southern Africa, originated in the sub-Sahara regions around what we know as Nigeria today. They were still arriving in their present homelands when Europeans arrived at the Cape of Good Hope in the 1500s.[7]

My own home country of England has been peopled by Celts, who became Romanized Britons about the time of Christ.[8] They were subdued by Anglo-Saxons from the area of Germany as Rome left in the early fifth century, and then were invaded and occupied by Danes. Finally, the Normans came from France in 1066. The 900-year-old church near my mother's village in Wiltshire has a list of every rector who has served there, and the first dozen have French names! Recent visits to England confirm that change is still underway. Immigration from Commonwealth countries after 1950 added 1.6 million ethnics who had grown to more than 5.5 percent of the population by the early 1990s.[9] When our family emigrated to America in 1955, I, as a thirteen-year-old, had never seen a person of color in my entire life.

What we have noted briefly and selectively about the historical process of migration elsewhere has been true of North America in the past five hundred years since the establishment of permanent settlements by Europeans. Just as Native Americans had moved around the continent, Europeans moved in on them when they had the means and opportunity to do so. To describe the population of America at any one point is simply to take a snapshot of what is in reality a very dynamic and changing situation. The America we have grown up with is only one version of the America that existed before, and the picture will continue to develop.

The migration of peoples, which we earlier pictured as a reflection of other natural forces like wind, weather, and tides, has a tendency to stall for periods. This gives the impression that "this is the way things are." But soon people begin to move again. Some years ago we heard about El Niño, the Pacific current which, when it moves, affects weather and consequently the lives of millions throughout the hemisphere. Just as we were accustomed to it, the reverse effect called La Niña took effect!

Each meteorological change has both fortunate and unfortunate complications. We can adapt to it and we can benefit from it, but one thing we cannot do is stop it. King Canute (d. 1035) of England struggled with his advisors about his claim to absolute power in the realm. His nobles took him and his throne to the shore. They sat him down and invited him to forbid the tide to come in. He did, but it came in anyway, and he was dissuaded of the notion that kings have absolute power! It was with illustrations like this that they taught civics and the rise of constitutional monarchies when I was in school. It's also a lesson about our inability to stop natural processes, let alone the hand of God.

How have the hand of God and natural processes formed the America we know today? What are the lessons to be learned, the pitfalls to avoid? That is the subject to which we now turn.

How We Got to Be the Way We Are

Ellis Cose has shown that what we look like as a country at any particular moment is in large part determined by the immigration policies in effect at that time.[10] This means that even though migration is a practically unstoppable force, it can and has been selectively controlled by the government, but only to a degree. Legal treaties with Native Americans did not stop the encroachments of whites on their lands. But we can distinguish broad movements of people and see correlation between these and the immigration policies that existed at the time of these movements. There is also a distinction between what we can call the wide-angle picture and the smaller snapshot.

For purposes of condensation, we will divide our photos into two, one very wide-angle from 1500 to 1965, and the other a snapshot of 1965 to the present. There is no doubt that the look of America was quite different after 1965. Let's go back and examine the situation more closely.

America Prior to 1965

America has always been a mosaic, even before the arrival of Europeans. Early European explorations were carried on by the Spanish, Portuguese, French, Dutch, and British, but these were all Europeans, so the mosaic was very pale. The governments of these countries encouraged trading with native peoples and settlement. Each country was in fierce competition with every other and could not afford to allow another country to establish dominance.

Native Americans were of course a part of the early mosaic. They were far more numerous in Central and South America, perhaps numbering twenty million, but only one million are estimated to have lived in North America at the time Europeans arrived for permanent settlement. Today there are 2.3 million American Indians in this country.[11]

African slaves formed a large part of the early American mosaic. The tragic importation and exploitation of black slaves began within fifty years of the arrival of the first Europeans to this hemisphere. Negroes constituted a third of the population of the southern states at the outbreak of the Civil War. Living in America in 1860 were 3.9 million slaves and an additional 488,000 free blacks. A total of 10 million are documented on the cargo manifests of ships docking in the Colonies (and later in the United States) from the inception of this nefarious trade.[12] Even more tragic is that 15 percent to 20 percent of each cargo of slaves died en route to the New World.[13] This was a shocking loss, but the mortality rate for all passengers and crews on ships moving between Europe and America averaged 8 percent before the end of the nineteenth century. Marilyn Baselar summarizes the impact of Europeans and Africans coming to America in this way: "The Anglo-American societies that emerged on the coast of North America did indeed offer Europeans more economic opportunity and freedom than could be found in the Old World. But the promise of America was built, to a significant extent, on African slavery."[14]

Later we will expand on how the events that brought each group of migrants to America and their reception and circumstances when they arrived imprint their legacy. This legacy must be taken into account in any relationships with them or ministry among them.

Although other nations like France and Spain were present and making their mark in North and South America, Great Britain had the greatest lasting impact in the north. This was owing to its growing imperial strength and the sheer will and ability to place people in or draw them to its possessions and to provide an administrative and military presence. In many ways, the dominance of Great Britain has paid dividends. Even though England, prior to 1776, was not democratic, it had constitutional limits of power on the monarchy, and proto-democratic ideals were being espoused.

Religious Freedom

Protestant Christian movements like that of the Puritans, Separatists, and Quakers had within them the seeds of democracy. They believed in the dignity of the common man and his position before the Lord as a person capable, with the Spirit's help, of understanding the Bible. They believed in the necessity of reading and studying Scripture on their own, and this led them to widespread literacy and a belief in general education. These were liberalizing elements that were not all welcomed in their native land. Many risked all to come to the New World, which offered a freer atmosphere in which to develop and to live out these ideas. People from other European countries, who had similar beliefs, joined them.

North America may have seemed like a good place to send dissident people, but that was not primarily how European powers viewed it. Rather, they wished to ensure that no enemy in Europe would gain control of so great an area. They also wished to enrich their own government and merchant class. Settlements on this continent were at first exclusively crown entitlements. Immigration was encouraged, but "licensed" under patents. This was the case for both the Jamestown and Massachusetts settlements. Once patents were obtained, the leaders secured and expanded their areas by encouraging further immigration.

The search for religious freedom was a major motive of early settlers, and it has had a lasting impact on this country. Americans are still very religious in comparison to citizens of other countries. Forty-two percent attend church weekly in America versus 6 percent in England.[15] Freedom of religion was neither the only nor the singular motive of early settlers, however. The Plymouth colony certainly desired religious freedom, but their mercantile sponsors wanted profits. To repay the cost of making the move to the New World, the settlers at Plymouth had entered into a business contract with their carriers, one that took twenty-eight years to clear.

Individual people came to America by a variety of means. Some were free citizens coming on their own volition and paying their own way. Others purchased their passage by becoming indentured servants, usually for seven years at a time. England dealt with its orphans and poor children by sending them to America as indentured servants and apprentices, and even far less desirable types, such as convicted felons, were sent here to serve on an indentured basis. More than fifty thousand such convicts were settled in America.[16] It was among these that John Wesley had his early ministry as a chaplain.

The Colonies desperately needed more workers and more inhabitants who would be loyal to England, even if they were not themselves British. French Protestant Huguenots, who had endured much persecution in France, were encouraged to immigrate beginning in 1679. German and Swiss Protestants also fled to seek refuge in the New World. Many were highly skilled craftsmen and artisans. On arrival in the Colonies, the king granted them the same rights as Englishmen, in effect making them citizens.[17] Peter Salins has noted that timely conferral of citizenship on immigrants is one of the most effective ways America has promoted the assimilation of newcomers. "Citizenship has always served as an indispensable proof to immigrants and nations that they are part of the same national family."[18]

America has always struggled with conflicting ideals in regard to immigration policy. This may reflect the fact that English immigration policies from the time of Elizabeth I through the parliamentary period and the restored monarchy showed little coherence. However, Oliver Cromwell, a parliamentarian, was very favorable to his counterparts (British Puritans) in the Colonies, sharing their spiritual and civil commitments. After the revolutionary period, the U.S. Congress was faced with making its own immigration policy. George Washington put his approach in these words: "I have established it as a maxim neither to invite nor discourage immigrants. My opinion is that they will come hither as fast as the true interest and policy of the United States will be benefited by foreign population."[19]

This sounded like a "hands-off" policy as far as government was concerned. It seemed to assume that the rate of immigration and the kind of people coming would in fact always be beneficial. Perhaps he meant that some unspecified dynamic would make immigration self-regulating. But Congress had already begun to make the rules.

"The first U.S. naturalization law [passed during the second session of the first Congress in March 1790] reserved naturalization for those 'aliens being free white persons.'"[20] It required a two-year residency and an oath to support the constitution. This clearly kept citizenship away from both American Indians and blacks, and it showed the preference, which would always be present until 1965, for Europeans as immigrants.

Push and Pull

As each wave of immigrants arrived, they had been *pushed* by events in their homeland and *pulled* by the possibilities in America. Germans came in the 1700s, pushed by decades of European wars, pulled toward peace, security, and prosperity. The Irish came in the 1840s, pushed by a devastating potato famine and confiscation of their farms. They were pulled by the lure of survival as free men, of land, and of jobs. Irish labor was used to complete the transcontinental railway from the east to Utah following the Civil War.

Chinese were pushed by drought, famine, and warfare with Great Britain over Great Britain's insistence on trading opium in 1839, when war broke out between the two countries.[21] In 1849 the California gold rush attracted many Chinese, and they later became the principal work force building the western segment of the transcontinental railway, which was completed in 1869.[22] In spite of this great contribution by the Chinese, when a financial crisis caused the panic of 1873, anti-Chinese sentiments became evident. Even other immigrants turned against the Chinese. Dennis Kearney is an example of this phenomenon.

Kearney is a perplexing example of those who, though immigrants themselves, turned against other newcomers. Kearney was born in Ireland and settled in San Francisco in 1868. He had worked on steamships and began a heavy hauling firm in his new hometown. He considered himself a common man who had pulled himself up by his own bootstraps.

Kearney held eastern big business responsible for the panic of 1873 that threatened his own business. He also believed it was unfair exploitation of cheap labor, like the Chinese, that threatened the jobs of other working men.[23] Instead of directing his wrath at the powerful eastern establishment, he directed it at the Chinese. He formed the Workingman's Party of California. At one of its rallies, he incited a riot that led to the sacking of San Francisco's Chinatown. The Chinese were made scapegoats for the economic depression All kinds of irrational and hateful statements against the Chinese can be found in the West Coast newspapers of the day.

Kearney's campaign eventually led to passage of the Chinese Exclusion Act of 1882, which prohibited Chinese immigration. This act remained in effect until 1943 and was not truly remedied until 1965.[24] Although it seems so irrational—that people who were immigrants would turn against newer immigrants—examples of people reacting as Kearney did can be found each time the country experiences economic hard times. In spite of being a nation of immigrants, we still turn on the newest arrivals, even though they may be filling a very real need in this country.

In 1924 the National Origins Act was passed requiring that 82 percent of all immigrants be Europeans.[25] This continued to reflect the sense that non-Europeans were undesirable and it probably set the stage for the treatment Japanese Americans received during World War II. Although the hysteria against the Japanese Imperial Forces may have been understandable in the light of their activities in Asia and at Pearl Harbor, it was not justified to direct it against Japanese who had lived here for generations. They experienced similar or worse treatment during World War II than the Chinese had in the last century. In spite of the fact that many Japanese had been here for decades and were loyal Americans, they were interned and lost a great deal of their property.

This was not done to the German Americans, who had also lived in America for many years, even though we were at war with Germany.[26]

Many people think that a cultural trait of Asians like the Chinese and Japanese is being quiet and minding their own business. In fact this trait is as much bred by hard experience as by culture. They have learned that it doesn't pay to stand out and be different. So, even though a disproportionate number of Asians yearly find their way to valedictory honors in graduations from high schools and colleges around the country, Asians as a group are unlikely to emphasize it. In reality their accomplishments demonstrate the solid contribution to our country that newcomers and minorities have been making throughout our history.[27]

There is plenty of evidence to show that individual Americans, communities, and churches have welcomed and assisted newcomers throughout our history. And in some cases government policy has sought to rectify mistakes. All of this we will later show. But we have to accept the fact that elected officials have presumably reflected what Americans wanted. These legislators have been a picture of our own inconsistencies. America, by government policy until 1965, was kept a primarily European-based community and looked quite different than it does today.

America after 1965

The mosaic we call America is continually changing, and that is why we chose the kaleidoscope as the metaphor that best pictures our country. In 1965 an act of Congress had a major impact on the ethnic design of America today. This is not something to lament, but we do need to understand the phenomenon. We have assumed a new kind of diversity simply by dropping the provisions of the National Origins Act of 1924, which codified national preference quotas. How did this happen?

John F. Kennedy, a descendant of Irish immigrants, wrote a book in 1958 called *A Nation of Immigrants*. It was as if he wished to right the wrongs of almost a hundred years earlier, perpetrated by Dennis Kearney, whose actions Kennedy would have seen as thoroughly un-American. He believed that existing quotas, keeping out certain kinds of immigrants on the basis of their origin or race, were wrong. Presidents Truman and Eisenhower had also been concerned, so this was not simply a partisan issue. Kennedy argued for the passage of a new immigration and naturalization bill, but he died before it could be enacted.

Cose writes, "To the surprise of much of America . . . [President] Johnson took up the immigration reform banner, along with the rest of Kennedy's unfinished business."[28] He fought for passage of a bill eliminating national origin as a consideration for immigration. In 1965 the new Immigration and Naturalization Act became law. It limited immigration from Western Hemisphere countries to 120,000 annually and 170,000 from everywhere else. No country could have more than 20,000 in a single year. This bill, as Cose says: "repudiated more than eight decades of legislation whose principal purpose had been to keep outsiders [meaning non-Europeans] away."[29]

This landmark bill also specified that people with skills were to be given priority along with the reunification of families.

Critics have assailed this bill and other local legislation as the beginning of the end for America as a First World country.[30] Various commentators note that Edward Kennedy, in his arguments for passage of the bill, assured the public that this bill "will not flood our cities with immigrants. It will not upset the ethnic mix of our society,"[31] Lyndon Johnson, on signing it at the Statue of Liberty said, "It does not affect the lives of millions. It will not reshape the structure of our daily lives. . . . it does repair a very deep and powerful flaw in the fabric of American justice . . . and will make us truer to ourselves both as a country and as a people."[32]

The question is why, if they did not think it would change anything, they argued for it in the first place. They were right to redress the wrong, which they correctly observed existed. They were wrong to assure Americans that nothing would change. The very point of the bill was elimination of racial and ethnic quotas. Why would it *not* have meant that a greatly more variegated pattern of immigration would develop, and that eventually this would change the ethnic or cultural fabric of the country?

The 1965 act and others that followed in 1973, 1986, and 1990 really did change the face of America. Recall the push-pull dynamic. Apparently neither Kennedy nor Johnson foresaw the impact on the country of circumstances in which they both participated. The Vietnam War, its aftermath in Southeast Asia, instabilities in the Caribbean and Central and South America, the collapse of the Soviet empire, and exploding populations in developing nations would push people from the affected areas to the United States. The image and reality of America as a prosperous, secure nation pulled them.

Emma Lazarus in her poem at the Statue of Liberty proclaims what we as a nation *think* we have been, and for many thousands, what we truly *have* been. She says:

> Give me your tired, your poor,
> Your huddled masses yearning to breathe free,
> The wretched refuse of your teeming shore.

Send these, the homeless, tempest-tost, to me,
I lift my lamp beside the golden door![33]

Lazarus's poem codifies our desire, and what some have called our myth, that we are an asylum for the suffering and persecuted. Although it is "not policy but poetry," as someone has said, it expresses a deep sense of what we *ought* to be. It speaks of a greatheartedness, which, even if we have been inconsistent, we nevertheless retain. Did any other nation offer to rebuild Europe as happened with the Marshall Plan at the close of a war we did not start? In spite of all the animosities felt toward the Japanese because of World War II, this country pursued an enlightened policy of national reconstruction in Japan under General MacArthur, which the Japanese have built on for their own and everyone else's benefit in the ensuing years.

An Influx of Refugees

The Korean War in the '50s, the Soviet repression of its eastern satellites, and the Vietnam War produced hundreds of thousands of casualties and refugees. Simple humanitarian concern demanded that the United States do something to help. Because America partnered with certain national movements in Southeast Asia that were defeated with the United States forces, it seemed only natural that we would find a place for our allies who lost everything and for whom life was untenable in their homeland.

When President Kennedy, Edward Kennedy, and President Johnson argued for passage of the 1965 bill, they were part of a country that had never known defeat in war. Experience told them that whatever the United States decided to do, it would succeed in doing. War in Vietnam and later Somalia would prove them wrong, and with defeat came a sense of responsibility to people who had been displaced by war.

More than three hundred thousand boat people from Vietnam and Cambodia set out into the China Sea in 1975. These masses of people were picked up at sea or arrived at Hong Kong, Taiwan, and the Philippines, and others fled by land into Thailand. Thousands lost their lives to storms and pirates. Because of the horrors of the killing fields in Cambodia and the trauma of even surviving, many bore scars in their souls as well as their bodies. Ministry among them requires a special tenderness and patience in dealing with such existential horror.

Congress appointed a Commission on Immigration and Refugee Policy in 1978 in an attempt to put a coherent plan in place to determine who qualified for refugee status. Respected theologian and educator

Theodore Hesburgh of Notre Dame was asked to lead this effort. The commission formulated a definition of refugee that became the guide for determining who would be admitted with refugee status: "Anyone who fled because of a well-founded fear of persecution due to race, religion, nationality, political opinion or social group membership."[34]

This paved the way for the Refugee Act of 1980, which opened the doors to 50,000 refugees annually, more recently set at 85,317 in 1999.[35] With no more discriminatory quotas against them and a desperate need to find refuge, thousands of Southeast Asians began to arrive in the United States.[36] They were settled in scattered areas of the country, many finding assistance through churches that had humanitarian concerns and, in some cases, had previously conducted extensive missionary work in Southeast Asia. This was especially true of the Catholic Church, which predominated in those areas, but smaller denominations like the Christian and Missionary Alliance assisted magnificently.[37]

Ministry to Immigrants and Refugees

The impending return of Hong Kong to the People's Republic of China, which took place in 1997, spurred the immigration of many worried Chinese to the United States, Canada, and other countries. This wave of immigrants, unlike Southeast Asian refugees, was uniformly well educated and prosperous. They brought immense resources in funds, education, and technology. Refugees, on the other hand, have experienced excruciating pain and loss and need greater assistance on arrival in the United States. The Hong Kong Chinese, however, generally knew English and could easily cope with a highly developed social system, not unlike that of Hong Kong. But the enormous changes in the lives of these newcomers gave them greater openness to spiritual as well as national reorientation. Chinese churches in the United States and Canada reached out to these newcomers, and a great many have become believers. In fact Christianity is probably growing faster among the Chinese than any other ethnic group.[38]

The implications for ministry among the two different kinds of newcomers—refugees, such as Southeast Asians, and immigrants, such as Chinese or Asian Indians, differ, because of the kind of assistance each group needs. Southeast Asian refugees faced horrifying brutality, have had fewer opportunities for education, are less likely to speak English, and have lost everything. They need housing, financial assistance, ESL (English as a second language) classes, counseling, extended patience and understanding, and the love of Christ. Chinese or Asian Indians are more likely to speak English, have marketable skills and professions, and a greater likelihood of friends, relatives, and churches ready to help them. In all events, some period of settlement and assimilation will have to occur, but the immigrants will be able to contribute to the community more quickly than the refugees as they have fewer obstacles to overcome.

In 1997 George Alexander added a chapter to our understanding of a lesser-known group in America, Asian Indians. Alexander speaks authoritatively and compassionately about his people. He understands that the 1965 Act is what has made the difference in Asian Indian migration to America, and he salutes those who worked to pass it. "It is to America's enduring credit that unlike many nations which have not only made profound mistakes, but continue to perpetuate them, it chose instead to reverse its stand."[39]

The result of lifted quotas was that by 1979, five hundred thousand Asian Indians had come to the United States.[40] This grew by an average of thirty-eight thousand annually, from 1995 to 1998.[41] The overwhelming reason for migration from the Indian subcontinent has been the growing density of the population, now numbering a billion people, a sixth of the world in an area one-third the size of the United States.

According to Alexander, Asian Indians in America have been particularly interested in two occupations: hotel-hospitality and medicine. The aggregate value of hotels owned by Asian Indians was twenty-two billion dollars in 1997. They also "constitute the largest group of foreign born doctors in America," numbering 23,547.[42] Although India is predominantly Hindu, some areas, like the southern state of Kerala, are 20 percent Christian. But those who come to America from that region are 85 percent Christian. They are interested in forming Indian congregations. This provides opportunities for American congregations of whatever established ethnicity to partner with them, providing facilities in the early stages and reaping the benefits of association with those believers from another culture.

What we have said of Asian Indians is also true of Koreans. Koreans, however, have enduring struggles with English because their homeland is very monocultural, and English, though taught in schools, is not widely spoken. In India, English is the second national language after Hindi. South Korea is about 34 percent Christian. Several of the largest churches of the world are located in Korea. When they immigrate to America, Koreans often bring a dynamic Christian presence with them.

Naturally not all immigrants come bringing firm commitments to Christianity. Uncertainties, violence, and lack of economic opportunity have drawn many Asian and Middle Eastern peoples to North America. Many of these people are Muslim or Hindu. They expect to continue with their religious commitments here and in fact work to expand their spiritual movements. But in the United States they live in a neighborhood with many Christian families, something that would not have been the case in their home countries.

As we look at the heightened presence of very diverse cultures and peoples in America, it is worth remembering that, overall, Christianity is stronger in numbers and vitality outside the West.[43] Even non-Christian cultures at this point may have stronger families and higher morals and work orientation than many in the West. These values transfer with the newcomers, bringing needed vitality to Western cultures. Immigrants who are already Christian are eager to begin new congregations among those of their own culture. They simply need the encouragement and facilities that existing American churches can provide.

In many cases, churches in North America have been salvaged and rejuvenated by ethnic newcomers. This was certainly true for First Presbyterian Church of Jamaica, Queens, New York. This church dates from 1662, founded by the Dutch. After near collapse, it now thrives with Caribbean, Central and South American, African, and Anglo believers.[44] Another vibrant example is Culmore United Methodist in Fairfax, Virginia. There, pastor Stephen Rhodes turned a dwindling congregation in what had been a predominantly white area into a totally multiethnic church with a significant ministry to its community and members.[45] In both cases, the positive results are due to intentional, committed ministry by seasoned Anglo pastors and the response of immigrant Christians hungry for fellowship with other believers.

Hispanic Immigrants

What about the growing population of Hispanics in this country? They now number thirty-one million, 40 percent of all immigrants to the United States.[46] In North America the southeast was part of Spain and the southwest part of Mexico, and Spain before that. Hispanics have therefore been at home in these areas since before other Europeans. In spite of this, the vast majority of Hispanics began arriving in the United States in the late 1930s when agricultural workers were needed. Migration steadily increased for the rest of the past century, at first primarily from Mexico, which still provides the vast majority of Hispanic migrants, later from other South and Central American countries.[47]

The original and continuing push from Mexico has been underemployment and low wages. The initial pull was the need for "braceros" (literally "arms"), or workers. American farmers needed agricultural workers in the southwest and citrus workers in the central and southeastern states. Now the construction trades and services, including domestic help, draw the majority of workers. Established Hispanics have also entered into the professions, education, medicine, and government; in short, they are an integral part of mainstream America.

Non-Mexican Hispanics first came in numbers following the Communist revolution in Cuba under Castro in 1959. It was Castro's policy to target intellectuals, putting such pressure on them that thousands fled to the United States. In the decade 1960–70, Ellis Cose says, Cubans in Dade county, Florida, increased from 29,500 to 224,000, 85 percent foreign born.[48] Some of my friends were among those Cubans. Even though they were medical doctors and teachers, they had to take very low-paying jobs until they had acquired English and the necessary licensing. Today the Cubans who first fled Castro are the best-educated and most-affluent of all Hispanics.

Later, during the presidency of Jimmy Carter, Fidel Castro allowed thousands of poor, blue collar workers to leave Cuba if they wished. They departed in every imaginable boat or floating device from the port of Mariel. They are known as the Marielitos. Eventually 125,000 left before Castro closed the door.[49] Cubans already in the United States did what they could to assist these desperate newcomers, and the government helped the rest to settle in various parts of the country, trying not to impose an undue burden on any particular area. The Marielitos were in a different category from the earlier Cubans. They were less educated and had generally more difficulty assimilating into the North American system.

Cuba was not the only source of instability pushing refugees northward. Haitians, driven to desperation by the violence, injustice, and poverty under the Duvalier regimes, began to arrive first in small boatloads, later by the thousands. In spite of indications that many Americans believe Haitians are not a benefit to U.S. society, they are clearly trying hard to succeed in this country.[50]

Civil wars in Guatemala, Nicaragua, and El Salvador pushed many thousands out of their homelands. Some of these conflicts went on for decades. Today there is a fragile peace. But some countries, like Nicaragua, remain in economic ruin. Peru has overcome a long-running insurgency of the "Shining Path" guerrilla movement, during which approximately one million Peruvians fled the country. Colombia continues to struggle with leftist guerrillas who in 1999 controlled more than 40 percent of the country. Drug trafficking combines with the guerrilla movement to destabilize the country. All these factors put pressure on Latin Americans to seek a more stable situation. Many have given up the struggle to exist in their own country and take repeated phenomenal risks simply to get to this country.[51]

Although the forced migration of refugees often means that they begin with practically nothing, it is astounding that Hispanics in the United States have buying power of 452.4 billion dollars annually, an increase since 1990 of more than 118 percent.[52]

It is a matter of grave concern that about 50 percent of the annual influx of Hispanics is undocumented and therefore illegal, but it is also a measure of their desperation. The Immigration and Naturalization Service (INS) returned 179,672 people to their home countries in 1999. In spite of this, there were approximately five million undocumented immigrants, and the number is growing by 275,000 each year.[53] They are desperate to provide for their families and the future of their children.

Inez, a Mexican, is a typical undocumented worker who risked his life to work here because of his depth of commitment both to being here and to the survival of his family. Chased by dogs and the border patrol, Inez crossed the border several times and paid ruthless "coyotes" to help him find his way through the blistering hot deserts of Arizona, New Mexico, and west Texas. The jobs he so desperately wanted paid minimum wages, a significant part of which he sent home to his family. Inez and many like him are willing to suffer the hardships of being undocumented immigrants in the United States to provide a better life for themselves and their families.[54]

We Need Them

Sometimes lost in the discussion of why people are so desperate to come to America is the fact that we need them. Both a push factor and a pull factor are at work. The people who struggle so hard to be here are not irresponsible. Once here they do the work we need them to do. My father was a skilled woodworker who, before we came to the United States as legal immigrants in 1955, made about twenty-four dollars a week in England. When he obtained a job in his trade in the United States, his pay immediately jumped to one hundred dollars a week. My sister's pay went from fifteen dollars as a medical secretary to sixty dollars as a legal secretary in America. In both cases it was a 300 percent increase. My father eventually went on to win medals for his woodworking, some of which is in the White House, U.S. Capitol, and the National Presbyterian Church of Washington D.C. He did well, as do the majority of those who are given an opportunity to settle and work here.

In a sense, it is the newcomers themselves who have made America a beacon of hope. Every one of their stories is a testament to people back home that America is the land of opportunity, security, and freedom.

Sometimes those who have been here for generations tend to believe that *they* have made the country outsiders now want to enjoy. That is partially true, but *they* are actually *we,* the conglomerate of "newcomers" who make up America and those who came generations earlier.

In this new century and millennium America is continuing to develop. It *is* different than it was even a generation ago, far more diverse in culture and color. Some have called it a sea change, meaning a fundamental transformation. Perhaps they are right, but there are many positive elements to this change, more to be welcomed than feared. Immigrants are the new human resources we need to help us on our national way. What will be the shape and color of the national kaleidoscope?

Summary

In the year 2000 the United States had a population of 281 million. The U.S. Census Bureau shows that 75 percent of us are non-Hispanic white, 12.5 percent Hispanic, 12.3 percent black, 3.6 percent Asian, and .9 percent American Indian.[55] That is just a snapshot. The picture is continually changing. But becoming culturally different is not a problem for our country!

Newcomers will be changed by their experiences in America, as the entire history of our country has proved. But they will each remember where their parents came from, the things they held dear, and the food their people like. They will remember that from which they fled and that for which they dreamed. They will still have individual and community identity, but they will have the sense that they are a part of a single great nation, and those who are believers, part of an even greater family of God.

Besides the economic benefits to the United States that newcomers represent, many bring vibrant spirituality, strong family values, and an unquenchable desire to do well. Their vitality serves not only themselves but us all. Many are Christian believers when they come. Others are from areas where the gospel is not well-known. If current levels of immigration represent a rising tide, let us think of it as a wave of opportunity, bringing the nations, which we have previously gone out to reach, right to our doorstep.

Discussion Starters

1. Briefly tell each other in your group the story of how your family came to America, even if it was generations ago.

2. Was your family welcomed to this country? Did they have struggles with those already here?
3. Do you think that today most newcomers get a fair shake when they arrive?
4. How do you or your group feel about being a part of a continually evolving society? Does it help to know that all societies are in flux?
5. Have you, your group, or your church done anything to welcome a newcomer to America?

4

The Compass
for the Journey

Michael Pocock

Your word is a lamp to my feet and a light for my path.

Psalm 119:105

Voyageurs National Park sits astride the Minnesota and Canadian border. Wooded green islands are scattered across the surface of a thousand lakes, a great place to shed the cares of the world and get back to the wilderness. In the summers, clear days and crisp nights make canoeing, fishing, and camping a delight. But beware of the weather! Clouds and mists can quickly develop, making any attempt to distinguish the islands from the shoreline impossible, and you will quickly lose track of where you are. Robert Service's poem reminds me of this place:

> Pines and pines, and shadows of pines,
> As far as the eye can see . . . [1]

Finding your way in the wilderness is impossible without a compass and a map. The same can be said for those navigating North America's diverse cultural waters. We need help. Since we are considering ministry, the best place to start is with Holy Scripture, the map and compass pointing to the Creator who providentially sustains the world and longs to bless its peoples.

Scripture: The Compass for Multicultural Ministry

Why Scripture? Why not sociology, cultural anthropology, or linguistics? All these provide helpful insights for ministry in our global world and in the culturally diverse climate here in North America. For years missionaries have been drawing on the sciences for their work abroad. Eugene Nida, Louis Luzebetak, Charles Kraft, Paul Hiebert, and Sherwood Lingenfelter are just a few who have integrated science and Scripture to enhance cross-cultural ministry. The work of these and others has resulted in an entire discipline, called missiology, used to prepare missionaries and intercultural workers for their assignments.[2] But as evangelicals address themselves to any enterprise, it is important that Scripture take precedence over science.[3] Ministry must be rooted in the Word of God and the very life of God.

Stephen Rhodes, who led the transition at Culmore United Methodist Church in northern Virginia to become a church that truly reaches and represents its diverse community, says this about the relationship of the Bible to multicultural ministry: "Unless a multicultural congregation locates itself with the story of God's salvation of humanity, it has nothing more to offer than its own particularity, however interesting that may be."[4]

Scriptural and theological reflection is integral to any Christian understanding of the world, its men and women, and the cultures in which they live. Every phenomenon in the world can be traced to the creative word and act of God. Even though the creation has been marred by the fall—attributable to Satan and our primal parents—nothing can be properly understood without reference to God as revealed in the Scriptures. William Dyrness has said: "Culture is what we make of creation."[5] Culture is an amalgam of innovative patterns of human understanding and interaction with the environment. It starts with the "givens" of creation and builds a pattern of meaning and actions deemed helpful for a particular group. But what do I truly know of creation without revelation?

For a Christian, Holy Scripture is indispensable. How do I know that ministry to others is needed, or the nature of that need, its roots, its solution, if I do not reference the Scriptures? I may see a person hungry and, from compassion or logic, feed him. From history, sociology, meteorology, or economic theory, I may discover what gives rise to this man's hunger, but I could not address or change his personal human condition of sin, or that of others, that has also led him to this point. I could not work for the good of humanity if I did not know its central problem and the solution to it. I need to accept the truths of Scripture as my guide.

Dyrness observes, "When Christian philosophy [or ministry] has borrowed its methods from arguments not shaped out of biblical materials, it has left itself vulnerable to serious attack."[6] We seem to need regular reminders to get back to the Bible in facing challenges today. Roland Allen jogged mission leaders in the last century with his *Missionary Methods: St. Paul's or Ours?* Speaking of a tendency to discard the Bible as either mythological or unrelated to the modern world, he said:

> It is impossible but that the account so carefully given by St. Luke of the planting of the churches in the Four Provinces should have something more than a mere archeological and historical interest. Like the rest of Holy Scriptures it was "written for our learning." It was certainly meant to be something more than the romantic history of an exceptional man, doing exceptional things under exceptional circumstances—a story from which ordinary people of a later age can get no more instruction for practical missionary work than they receive from the history of the Cid, or from the exploits of King Arthur. It was really intended to throw light on the path of those who should come after.[7]

Allen referred to a key point made by the apostle Paul in 2 Timothy 3:16–17, establishing the nature and value of the Word of God. Paul asserts, "All Scripture is God-breathed." The Authorized Version reads, "given by inspiration of God." He would have been referring to the Hebrew Scriptures of the Old Testament, the canon of which had been fairly well established prior to 100 B.C.[8] Paul goes on to state that this Scripture is "useful for teaching, rebuking, correcting and training in righteousness, so that the man of God may be thoroughly equipped for every good work."

All of this is in addition to the value of the Word of God for making the reader "wise for salvation through faith in Christ Jesus" (v. 15). In this way Paul linked the authoritative and applicable nature of the Old Testament to events in the New. He lived at a time when Israel and the Mediterranean world experienced an incredible intermingling of nationalities. He reflects on this fact and its implications for the church, even citing difficulties that leaders like Peter had in adjusting to the work of God as it advanced among all cultures, not just the Jewish culture.

The books we call the New Testament are equally authoritative and helpful for multicultural ministry. The Gospels had only begun to appear in written form in the last decade of Paul's ministry.[9] But the writer of Hebrews says the revelation of Jesus, which we have in the Gospels, is a product of the same God who spoke to the prophets in the Old Testament (Heb. 1:1–4). Paul says the idea that the people of the nations would be linked together with the people of Israel in sharing in the promise of Christ Jesus was a mystery revealed by the Spirit to the apostles (Eph. 3:4–6).

Peter endorses Paul as a Scripture writer, referring to "all his letters," (2 Peter 3:15–16). By these assurances and many others within the New Testament, we can be confident that these Scriptures are indeed the Word of God, a trustworthy and authoritative guide to Christian life and work today. No wonder Laird Harris concludes, "The Church came to a very high degree of unanimity on these matters in the very early years [of its existence]."[10]

We can confidently draw insights for multicultural ministry today from both the Old and New Testaments. Far from being remote commentaries of a bygone era, they were produced by the Holy Spirit working through men who lived in continual interaction with other cultures. This same Holy Spirit was present at creation (Gen. 1:2), and the sign of his coming at Pentecost was the believers' knowledge of the languages of all who were present at that event—fourteen different languages (Acts 2:1–12).

Today we find ourselves in what has been termed the postmodern era, and people of every culture are delving into the occult. Author Clinton Arnold has shown that Paul had knowledge of "principalities and powers." The gods of the era in which he lived had very similar characteristics to entities worshiped today. In Paul's day, people worshiped and served principalities, powers, authorities, and dominions (Eph. 1:21). They worshiped the "powers of this dark world" (6:12). Today these powers may be Gaia, the earth goddess of neopaganism, and nature religion (wicca), or the planets and the zodiac in astrology. Paul's understanding of his first-century world fits the twenty-first century as well with its openness to occult powers.[11]

There is every reason, then, to use the Scriptures as the compass and map for ministry in multicultural America today. But what parts of it are particularly helpful? A study of selected passages from both Testaments will show their significance for understanding and ministering in culturally diverse communities today.

Our treatment of Scripture bearing on multicultural ministry will be relatively brief. Biblical theologies of mission developed for the guidance of foreign mission work are far more complete. George Peters's

Biblical Theology of Missions and the more recent reader *Perspectives on the World Christian Movement,* edited by Winters and Hawthorne,[12] are well worth further study. For our purposes, we will take five Scripture contexts with clear application to today's culturally diverse ministry arena.

The Creation Account

Genesis 1–3 establishes the fundamental realities on which the Judeo-Christian peoples base their worldview. Truths found in these early chapters help us understand the distinctives of the Christian faith in a spiritually diverse environment. In particular, we gain insights about the nature of God, ourselves, and the purpose God has for us and all humankind.

Although we realize we live in a culturally diverse world and that every culture is valuable, evangelicals are not pluralists. Increasingly, pluralism does describe the direction of North American culture, meaning that people tend to believe that the varied claims for truth found in different and competing spiritualities all have equal validity. A pluralist does not believe in absolute truth, only personal or group perceptions. This understanding was practically codified in Canada by Prime Minister Pierre Trudeau in 1971 when he defined a policy called multiculturalism.[13]

This belief in no absolute truth is increasingly the approach adopted by public policy makers in the United States. In distinction, Scripture teaches absolute truth. It establishes that God is one God existing in three Persons, and he is the unique Creator of the heavens and the earth. This is the first point made by the author of Genesis. God precedes all that we speak of as "the creation." He is not the projection of his creatures seeking meaning and order but the originator of them all. "In the beginning God created the heavens and the earth" (Gen. 1:1).

As our society has become more culturally and religiously diverse, some claim that the God of the Bible is simply one of many deities, or that he is identical with those of other religions. The general tendency, for the sake of peace and harmony, is to stay away from controversies and avoid evangelism, or proselytism as it is pejoratively termed.

The creation account of Genesis proclaims that God is universal, worldwide (not Western), and distinct from his creation. The principal difference between most religions originating in Asia and Christianity is that the former tend to be monistic, they believe that all existence is of one essence. Christians believe that God is everywhere present, and that in Christ, he is *in* all believers (Col. 1:27). Christians hope to be godly, but they will never become God, nor will they in a higher state of consciousness realize that they *are* God as New Age advocates, following a form of Hinduism, believe.[14]

The creation account establishes the responsibilities of people to multiply and fill the earth (Gen. 1:20–28) and exercise a stewardship over the environment (2:15). These are repeated in 9:1 and 9:7. These passages give the clear idea that the earth is capable of sustaining large numbers of people and that they should spread out and live throughout the earth. So *movements* of people, all over the earth, are to be the normal pattern for humanity.

Human beings were created "in the image of God" (1:26–27), a statement repeated in Genesis 9:6 even after the fall. We bear a likeness to God, even though we are *not* God. The very creativity of God was transferred in relative fashion to people, so they get from God himself their desire to make something out of creation. It is what man makes of creation that we call culture, according to Dyrness.[15] Man tills the ground, raises crops, builds homes and communities, and learns to live in relation to others. He builds a culture, "the more or less integrated system of beliefs, feelings and values, and their associated symbols, patterns of behavior and products shared by a group of people."[16] When men and women make arrangements to live in community, they are also reflecting the interrelatedness of God himself who exists in a Trinity ("Let *us* make man in *our* image"). The social nature of people flows from the nature of God in whose image we have been made.

Cultures in themselves are not evil. They proceed initially from the design and provision of God. Cultures are innovative group approaches to problem solving. The ability to see cultures around us that differ from our own as beneficial rather than as threats enables us to respond more positively to them than would otherwise be the case.

But the fact that culture flows from the nature and mandate of God does not mean that every aspect of everyone's culture is correct and acceptable. The creation account of Genesis 1 and 2 leads to the fall in Genesis 3. The fall clearly affected relationships between God and man, and between people and their environment. The perception and judgment of humans became mortally affected by sin. The solutions they developed to cope with the reality around them showed their sin nature. Envy, murder, polygamy, and debauchery appeared. Nevertheless people continued to be intelligent and innovative. They made tools, musical instruments, cities, and cultures, but they did not use these for the glory of God. Every person and group showed a mixture of wonder and woe, the former seen in Noah, the latter judged in the deluge and at Babel.

How could a person or society have discerned the right path in those days? Or what can we use today to discern right and wrong in a culture? In those early days they had their conscience, the presumed wisdom of fathers passed on to children, and the testimony of creation to the reality of God, as Paul indicates in Romans 1:18–32. The Scriptures go on to explain themselves as the guidance needed, providing the lamp for the feet (Ps. 119:105) and the correcting everyone requires (2 Tim. 3:16–17), regardless of culture.

From the creation account, we understand, then, that all people and cultures proceed from God. Every person, regardless of culture, is related to us and distantly to God. In a culturally diverse society such as our own, every person and group is valuable and deserves our respect and appreciation, even though there may be some aspects of their culture we cannot approve. It is equally possible that my own culture may fall short in God's eyes.

Babel: The Beginning of Linguistic and Cultural Diversity

One of the real challenges faced in motivating or mobilizing people for ministry in a multicultural setting is dealing with differences. Moses, by the inspiration of God, provided a map and a compass for the people of God in the wilderness during the days of the exodus. The whole Book of Genesis is a foundational explanation to the Israelites about who they were in reference to God and the many different peoples who surrounded them. One can well imagine someone asking Moses, "Moses, what are we supposed to make of all these tribes and nations around us? We know about the Egyptians, and we've heard rumors about the Mesopotamians and all the people in between. How did there ever get to be so many languages? We've been slaves, nobodies. Do we have any kind of pedigree?" Genesis, particularly following the call of Abraham, answered these questions.

The hypothetical questions of the Israelites are not too different from issues that come up today when a congregation begins to be surrounded by people very unlike themselves. Scripture has the answers. Moses showed the people that the multiplicity of nations was no surprise to God. He had meant there to be many nations. The different languages and migration to every part of the world were part of what had advanced the program of God. Genesis 10 and 11 are the heart of the explanation.

Genesis 10 contains a list of seventy nations with their founders. Logically there were less then than now, when authorities like Wycliffe Bible Translators list 6,165 separately identified languages.[17] Moses wanted his readers to understand that all the nations are known to God. To know a name implies a relationship, or even control of the person or group named. Imagine the sense of security when God tells Israel later on, "I have engraved you on the palms of my hands" (Isa. 49:16).

Allen Ross and others have observed that in Genesis 10 and 11, the phenomenon (the dispersal of the people to form many nations with many languages) and the cause (the tower of Babel and God's judgment) are reversed.[18] Usually the causative event comes first, then the result. Babel actually precedes the emergence of the nations. Babel is a major turning point in Genesis from the general history of humankind to the particular history of Israel beginning in chapter 12.

The account of Babel in Genesis 11:1–9 deserves special consideration because it is correctly thought of as a judgment, and some have then concluded that distinct languages and cultures are therefore a curse. This view was actually explained to me by a fellow student in language school when we both were studying Spanish. I didn't need any discouragement! So I took a closer look at the event in question.

According to this passage, people had multiplied since the deluge, but while they had moved somewhat (on the plains of Shinar or Mesopotamia), they had stayed together as one people (11:1). They had a common language. They showed ingenuity, creativity, and building skills, but they used what they knew to subvert the basic plan of God for humankind expressed in Genesis 1:26–27 and 9:1. They had been told to spread out and populate the earth, but motivated by pride, the desire to be people of renown, they stayed together and embarked on a single enterprise—"a city, with a tower that reaches to the heavens." This was expressly to avoid being scattered over the earth (11:4).

Ross's detailed description of the event is well worth further study, but we will summarize it here.[19] Even though the builders intended to reach heaven, God, ironically, came down to see what they were doing (11:5). God was displeased with the negative use people had made of their intelligence (11:6). God's judgment put an end to the building process by making communication between the builders impossible. The confusion of their understanding, or of their language, led to their scattering "over the face of the whole earth" (11:8–9).

Babel is undoubtedly a judgment, but the resulting phenomenon, separate languages and cultures, is not a curse, even if many would-be language learners think so! Babel, like any judgment of God, is not simply a destruction or punishment, it establishes righteousness, or "rightness." Judgment gets things back on an intended track, just as the threatened judgment of Ninevah secured their repentance under Jonah's preaching. As Walter Elwell says, "Judgment is bound up with the notion of justice and righteousness, and it is foundational for biblical religion."[20] And Leon Morris writes:

The judgment of God is not impersonal . . . it is a strongly personal notion. It is closely linked to the thought of God's character of mercy, loving kindness, righteousness, truth. . . . It is the working out of the mercy and wrath of God in history and in human life and experience. Thus the judgment of God can bring deliverance for the righteous . . . as well as doom for the wicked.[21]

The outcome of Babel was the facilitation of the will of God. Just as God knows the names of all the nations, he knows their languages also. The masses of nations and languages are not chaotic; they are an outworking of the purposes of God. It should not surprise us, then, to learn that at Pentecost the Spirit knew and could give understanding to all the languages of those present on that occasion. Paul is able to tell his pagan listeners at Mars Hill:

The God who made the world and everything in it is the Lord of heaven and earth and does not live in temples built by hands. And he is not served by human hands, as if he needed anything, because he himself gives all men life and breath and everything else. From one man he made every nation of men, that they should inhabit the whole earth; and he determined the times set for them and the exact places where they should live. God did this so that men would seek him and perhaps reach out for him and find him, though he is not far from each one of us.

Acts 17:24–27

It certainly sounds as if Paul was familiar with the Genesis account and particularly chapters 10 and 11. He makes the point that God intended both the unity of humankind in Adam and the dispersion of humankind into nations as means to facilitate people finding the Lord. Have we truly grasped that people were *meant* to move to the ends of the earth and that is why they and we are here? The presence of people anywhere is known by the Lord and even engineered by him for salvation purposes! That is Paul's interpretation of Genesis 1–11.

Some two hundred years following the Babel incident, Abraham, like his father Terah, responded to God's call to move (Genesis 12). He went out, as the writer of Hebrews says, not knowing where he went and living as a stranger in a foreign country, "for he was looking forward to the city with foundations, whose architect and builder is God" (Heb. 11:8–10). Abraham stands as the epitome of righteousness that comes by faith, but let's not forget that Abraham became the friend of God in the context of migration. He does exactly what the pre-Babel people would not. He responded to the command of God. By his movement, *in* his travels, he discovers God and becomes the man God wants him to be, the founder of a great people and the channel of salvation through the promised Messiah. Does this make you feel any different about migrants and internationals in your neighborhood? Their presence may be an appointment of God!

The fact that people are migrating all over the earth, including to America, is part of God's plan. We need to welcome those who are on the move, even as we or our fathers were welcomed to America. God seems to communicate with people on the move, and he places people where they are to help them find him.

The Magnetic Attraction of the Presence of God: The Temple at Jerusalem

God promised Abraham he would make him a great nation and bless all the nations through him (Gen. 12:1–3). As God led the patriarchs around, their families increased. They were both blessed themselves and a blessing to the nations. God used Joseph to save Egypt and the Hebrews from famine. Centuries passed while Israel served in Egypt, then departed and settled in the Promised Land. God's sovereign hand was with them. In spite of many failures, the nation grew, realizing the height of its glory under Solomon. One of Solomon's greatest achievements was the temple he built at Jerusalem. Understanding the magnetic attraction of the temple is instructive for multicultural ministry.

Solomon was no isolationist. He interacted with the nations around him. The assessment of his wisdom in 1 Kings 4:29–34 is that it surpassed that of numerous other sages in surrounding nations. The result was that "Men of all nations came to listen to Solomon's wisdom, sent by all the kings of the world, who had heard of his wisdom" (v. 34). Once again, the people of God, in this case the king of Israel, fulfill the promise of God to make Israel a blessing to all nations. Solomon must have understood that nations would come to the temple he built and pray there. This is expressed by George Peters, who observed the centripetal pattern of missions, also seen at work in the Old Testament.[22] In general terms this means people in the Old Testament came to Israel to observe the glorious acts of God in Israel, whereas in the New Testament God's people were sent out to the nations in a centrifugal pattern of missions.

As Solomon dedicated to the Lord the completed temple in 1 Kings 8:22–53, he spoke of its intended role for those of other nations:

> As for the foreigner who does not belong to your people Israel but has come from a distant land because of your name—for men will hear of your great name and your mighty hand and your outstretched arm—when he

comes and prays toward this temple, then hear from heaven, your dwelling place, and do whatever the foreigner asks of you, so that all the peoples of the earth may know your name and fear you, as do your own people Israel, and may know that this house I have built bears your Name.

verses 41–43

Although the temple had certain restrictions for foreigners, it was open in most respects to them. It was to be as Isaiah said it would be prophetically: "a house of prayer for all nations" (Isa. 56:7). We usually think of the program of God centering on Israel in the Old Testament, but the nations of the world remain in focus, for condemnation or for blessing, throughout it. God's plan is always to bless the nations through their interaction with the people of God, and it is this principle that applies in the New Testament as well.

The church, while not identical with national Israel, is clearly the people of God (Gal. 3:26–29; Eph. 2:1–3:6; 1 Peter 2:9–12). We are the fruit of the promise to Abraham. Christ was the promised seed, who would be the transcendent blessing to all peoples by virtue of being the *author* of their salvation. But the people of God, also called seed or offspring of the promise, are the *vehicle* of salvation, the disseminators of the Good News about Christ.

Christian churches today should be fellowships that attract people from all nations. Our house of worship may not look as grandiose as the temple, but that does not matter. Solomon himself said in his dedication that he knew God lived in heaven, and it was from there that he would respond to the prayers of all people (1 Kings 8:43). The attraction of a fellowship of believers ought to be that God is central to them, and fervent, effectual prayers are offered and answered in its context. In that sense the people of God today are like the temple of old. Paul actually calls both individual believers and the collective church, "the temple of the Holy Spirit" (1 Cor. 3:16; 6:19).

Perhaps the first thing we need to establish in the hearts and minds of non-Christians from other nations who live in our communities is that God hears and answers prayer. Then, like Cornelius in Acts 10, they will be prepared for the message of Christ.

Jesus: A Man for All Peoples

Jesus is rightly called the Messiah of the Jewish nation. That was how John the Baptist presented him (Matt. 3:1–17), how his disciples like Peter understood him (Matt. 16:13–18), and how he presented himself when directly questioned by Pilate (Luke 23:3). Since the Great Commission, directing the disciples to all the world, occurs near the end of each Gospel, some may think that the evangelization of the nations was plan B, following Christ's rejection as Israel's Messiah, something not quite intrinsic to the plan of God. In fact Jesus never took his eyes off the world at large. Jesus did not wait to discover the attitude of Israel before disclosing his plan for all peoples, but he faced a tremendous challenge in getting either Israel or his disciples to be interested in anyone who was not like them. He faced a kind of xenophobia, which can sometimes be found in our own communities today.

When Matthew records Jesus' first preaching in Matthew 4:12–17, he makes it clear that Jesus was fulfilling a prophecy from Isaiah that Galilee of the Gentiles would see a great light that would dawn on them. Luke 4:14–27 records a more extended account of this sermon in which Jesus reminded his hearers that they were not the only ones God loved. He told them that while there were many widows in Israel in Elijah's time, only one, a non-Hebrew, received help from the prophet, and that in Elisha's time there were many lepers, but only Naaman, a Syrian, was healed. There was a strange and violent reaction to the facts of which Jesus had reminded his hearers. They immediately tried to kill him!

Why should it have disturbed the people to hear Jesus remind them of God's ministries to foreigners in the Old Testament? The answer is that in the four hundred years between the Testaments, the Israelites had become xenophobic. Foreigners were anathema to them. In the preceding chapter, we pointed out that the indigenous population of a country takes a more jaundiced view of foreigners in hard times. This happens in times of war or economic trouble or under occupation by an outside power. It has happened in America, and it happened in Israel prior to and during the time of Christ.

In 605 B.C. the inhabitants of Jerusalem went into captivity in Babylon, and they were there until 539 B.C.[23] Other parts of Israel, Judah, and surrounding nations were taken into captivity or made subject to the Babylonians around the same time. The captivity came about because Israel and Judah had become chronic idolaters, embracing the religions of the nations around them. Polytheism became more common than monotheism, and so God's people were subjected to some very hard lessons in captivity (2 Chron. 36:15–21).

The Jewish people began to return, some in 587 B.C., others in 539 B.C. By that time, they had shed their tendency to polytheism and had become monotheistic, as the Books of Ezra and Nehemiah attest, but now they seemed angry with foreigners and the sin of intermarriage with them (Neh. 13:23–27). Israel enjoyed only about two hundred years in their homeland before the military campaigns of Alexander the Great delivered them into the control of another foreign power, the Greeks. The Greeks imposed their culture, hellenizing the whole region. The Jewish clan of the Maccabees overthrew the Greek rulers in 165 B.C. but after a relatively brief time had to submit to the Romans whose strength and administrative network were growing. By the time Jesus' ministry began, Israel's rulers were simply national administrators approved and controlled by Rome. This explains the antiforeign attitude of the people and why it was so hard for them to think in terms of God blessing the Gentiles.

Although Jesus told Nicodemus about God's love for the whole world (John 3:1–21), spoke to a Samaritan woman in John 4:1–42, resulting in the conversion of many Samaritans, and ministered to a Roman centurion in Luke 7:1–10, it was still hard for Jesus' hearers to understand that he had "other sheep that are not of this sheep pen" (John 10:16). No wonder it took time and even supernatural visions to convince Jesus' own disciples, like Peter in Acts 10, that they should reach out to Gentiles, people who were not like them.

In America we are surrounded by internationals. At one point or another in our history we have been at war with the British, Spanish, Germans, Japanese, Italians, and many others. The more distant the hostilities, the less they are felt today—and the less likely Americans are to distrust those who were once our enemies. More recently we have had hostilities with Iran and Iraq. The terrible trauma caused by the September 2001 attacks on the World Trade Center and the Pentagon, attributed to al-Qaeda, a coalition of Middle Eastern Muslim radicals, will influence for years to come the way many Americans feel about Middle Eastern people. Yet through these events, we have learned much more about the area, the people, and Islam.

Harsh experiences with some national or religious groups often grow into dislike and distrust of everyone from these groups, yet we know in our hearts that this is stereotyping, overgeneralizing, and not really Christian at all. How would Jesus respond? Even as his enemies betrayed and killed him, he prayed, "Father, forgive them, for they do not know what they are doing" (Luke 23:34). St. Paul echoed this when he said, "Bless those who persecute you" and "Do not be overcome by evil, but overcome evil with good" (Rom. 12:14, 21).

The New Testament Church in a Multicultural World

The Book of Acts is a veritable toolbox for multicultural ministry. It presents ministry at a point that Paul calls "the fullness of the times" (Gal. 4:4). This was a time when God had fully used the Law to show that righteousness according to its requirements could never be achieved apart from the grace of God shown in Christ. In another sense, the time was fully ripe for expansion of the gospel among all peoples, as they were mixed throughout the Mediterranean region, while at the same time all speaking koine Greek. The church was called into existence in this context.

The Book of Acts demonstrates how the people of God can and did reach out and incorporate those of very different cultures into their fellowship. That's why Acts is a textbook for ministry in multicultural communities. There are at least three main contributions Acts makes to our understanding of multicultural ministry in North America today:

1. Acts identifies the basis for success in multicultural ministry—the Holy Spirit.
2. Acts demonstrates how to resolve tensions in a multicultural church.
3. Acts shows how an older generation can incorporate a newer generation.

The Holy Spirit's Role

Jesus told his disciples in Acts 1:8 that after the Holy Spirit came on them, they would be his witnesses in an ever-widening geographic expansion of the gospel. The coming of the Spirit was what we might call the "Great Condition" of missions and multicultural ministry. Luke, the writer of Acts, never wants us to forget that every advance depicted in the book is based on the presence and power of the Spirit.

"How," asks Harry Boer, "are we to understand that the Spirit *came* at Pentecost?"[24] He is correct in understanding that the Holy Spirit had always existed, so the only question was in what *way* the Spirit was to be present after Pentecost. Jesus had earlier told the apostles that the Holy Spirit was *with* them and would be *in* them (John 14:15–17). The new reality beginning at Pentecost was that the Spirit would do his work chiefly *in* and *through* people. The Spirit had worked selectively in people for special tasks in the Old Testament, enabling craftsmen to do their work on the tabernacle, judges to lead God's people, and certain kings and the prophets to fulfill their callings, but he was not *in* all believers before Pentecost.

In the Book of Acts the Holy Spirit filled believers, took away fear, provided guidance, and even prevented the apostles from going to places he did not want them to go. The Spirit enabled these believers in the early church to be effective in culturally diverse communities.

The first manifestation of the Spirit at Pentecost was when the apostles and others gathered together spoke the languages of fourteen different nations (Acts 2:5–12). God, through his servant Luke, wants us to know that the Spirit is an "international Spirit." To have the Spirit is to be empowered and capable of ministry to other cultures. Believers, in the Spirit, can transcend the challenges of other languages and cultures. This is the Spirit's first interest. This does not mean that every intercultural worker will instantly master the language of the people to whom he or she is sent! Missionaries can testify to that! It certainly *does* mean that successful intercultural outreach is desired and made possible by the Holy Spirit. This is so because his role is to glorify Christ and make him known (John 15:26–27; 16:14–15).

Penetrating other cultures with the gospel and securing repentance, belief, and regeneration requires a miracle of the Holy Spirit. This makes all ministry dependent on supernatural power. If we feel that reaching others who are not like us is difficult, we are right. But it is absolutely possible in the Spirit. Now let's look at how the Spirit works to resolve the inevitable tensions that arise in intercultural ministry.

Resolving Tensions

Let's face it—any social group will have tensions, but combining people of different cultures only makes group dynamics more complex. During the New Testament era, there were many who were not ethnic Jews who became attracted to the Jewish religion. These were known variously as "devout" people, "God-fearers," and "proselytes." They reflected various levels of integration into the Jewish community or participation in their customs.[25] Many of these came to faith in Christ, like the Ethiopian eunuch of Acts 8 and Cornelius in Acts 10. Some of those gathered at Pentecost were also in this category, and of course there were Gentiles with no prior identification with Jewish life and religion. So the New Testament church was made up of a variety of ethnic groups.

The first recorded controversy in the early church pitted one cultural group against another in Acts 6. Apparently there were destitute widows of various cultural backgrounds who received assistance in the church. Those who had a Hebrew background complained that they were being neglected, that there was an inequitable distribution of food. The tensions threatened the peace of the assembly and the ministry of the Word. Something needed to be done.

To their credit, the apostles took the women seriously. They did not wish to stop attending to their main work of teaching, so they asked the believers to choose seven men, "known to be full of the Spirit and wisdom" (Acts 6:3). The leaders did not choose these administrators, the people did. From the names of those chosen, it is clear that some were of a Hebrew background, and others were not. In other words, the ones chosen to solve the problem were representative of those who had the problem.[26] The new leaders administered the assistance program to the satisfaction of all the parties and the church grew. What can we learn from this approach?

1. It showed all the people, Jews or Greeks, that they were significant.
2. The choice of administrators from both sides by the laity showed trust.
3. The equitable distribution of food secured a sense of justice.
4. The primary ministries of the church were not interrupted.
5. The gospel spread and the church grew.

The rule is that for a mixed group to succeed, every person must feel significant and that his or her concerns are taken seriously. Every person must feel trusted and that leadership does things in an equitable, just way. The ministry of the Word and prayer must continue, and if these elements are present, the group will thrive and extend itself.

Assimilation

As the early church grew, incorporating people from many different cultures, it was probably inevitable that the original group of believers from Jewish backgrounds would ask themselves how much they could accommodate other cultures in the church. They most likely felt that the Jewish culture was the standard by which true spirituality could be measured. New people were welcome to the degree that they could conform to Jewish culture. This was generally how the Jews had dealt with people from other cultures prior to Christ. Jewish Christians were the older or original generation in the early church; people from other cultures were the new generation, like second-generation children of immigrants in ethnic churches today or the newcomers in any congregation.

The farther away from Jerusalem that the early churches flourished, the less pressure they felt to retain Jewish culture. It seemed clear, as Paul preached, that salvation came to all, Jew and Gentile, on the basis of grace through faith in Jesus, not by obeying the Jewish law. In the Syrian town of Antioch, a thriving multiethnic church had formed (Acts 11:19–30). They were a generous church, with a preponderance of Gentile believers. When some older generation believers from Jerusalem, who were Jewish in background, visited the church in Antioch, they were offended that the believers there were not living according to Jewish culture. Specifically, they were not requiring Gentile believers to be circumcised (15:1).

The attitude of these older believers caused a great deal of consternation, and the whole issue was taken up by church leaders in Jerusalem, the location of the "mother" church. Certainly this incident had to do with whether salvation comes by grace or by the law (vv. 10–11), but the issue could be stated another way: Must the younger generation fully adopt the culture of the older generation, or must Gentiles become Jews to become Christians?

When the council met in Jerusalem, they were clearly pleased that the gospel was spreading among other ethnic groups. Actually only a portion of the believers in the Jerusalem church had any problem at all with the believers in Antioch. Although Peter himself had some problems with the issue, he presented the case of the Antiocheans clearly and faithfully. His main points were that God had shown that he accepted Gentiles on the same faith basis as Jews and proved it by giving them the Spirit (v. 8). He added that salvation is a matter of grace in every person's case (v. 11). Since salvation does not come through adherence to the Jewish law, it was pointless to put "on the necks of the disciples a yoke that neither we nor our fathers have been able to bear" (v. 10).

After considerable discussion, James, apparently the elder spokesman of the Jerusalem church, put it this way:

> It is my judgment, therefore, that we should not make it difficult for the Gentiles who are turning to God. Instead we should write to them, telling them to abstain from food polluted by idols, from sexual immorality, from the meat of strangled animals and from blood. For Moses has been preached in every city from the earliest times and is read in the synagogues on every Sabbath.
>
> Acts 15:19–21

The elements of James's solution were:

1. Do not make life unnecessarily difficult for believers from other cultures.
2. The new generation (or culture) should not do things that would disgust the older generation or culture.

James's decision represented a reasonable compromise, not on doctrine but on practice. Gentiles would not be required to adhere to the entire body of the law, more than six hundred commandments, including circumcision, but they should not blatantly disgust Jews on four points, compromise with idolatry, immorality, strangled animals, and blood. It sounded reasonable. He directed that a letter be sent out to the churches informing them about the decision. The result in Acts 15:31 was that wherever it was read, the hearers were encouraged, and churches grew (16:4–5).

Summary

Settling intergenerational and interethnic conflicts in a reasonable and spiritual way makes churches thrive. One rarely sees a book promoting sound decision making and equitability among Christians as bases for church growth, but Manuel Ortiz makes these very points in his observations of Bethel Temple Community Church, a multiethnic church in the Philadelphia area. It sounds very much like the situation in the Book of Acts:

> Bringing people together from diverse backgrounds inevitably causes conflict. The staff at Bethel Temple is committed to working on personal conflicts. These conflicts are handled through the intervention of a multi-ethnic staff. . . . This, as I see it, is an intentional ministry. . . . This church is fleshing out the gospel of reconciliation both vertically and horizontally. . . . Justice and justification are two very important biblical themes in this ministry.[27]

In my own experience I recall a time when we lived in west Chicago. Ten or a dozen young people began to attend our Bible church in what, for most of us, was very outlandish attire. They would have been called punkers then. Today they might be called goths. They wore black clothes and had spiked and colored hair, tattoos, pierced lips, eyebrows, and noses, and multiple earrings. They were quite a sight!

To the credit of all the regulars, no one criticized the newcomers, who usually sat on the front row. They were as interested as anyone in the messages and sometimes even took notes. Many of us got into conversations with them and discovered that their spiritual interest was real. God was doing a work in their hearts. These newcomers stayed and grew. As time went by, they moderated their appearance a bit, and they added spontaneity, reality, and joy to our fellowship. Punkers in the pews might be a shock to some, but this is the kind of mutual acceptance needed if multiethnic, multigenerational ministries are to succeed.

WWJD—What would Jesus do? the bracelets ask, reminding us to get back to the pattern of our Lord and Savior Jesus Christ. How can we know what he would do without reference to the Word of God? That is why we must make the Scriptures the map and compass of all multicultural ministry.

Discussion Starters

1. Does it help you to be more receptive to newer cultures in your community when you realize that God may be at work through this process of migration? Review Genesis 10 and Acts 17 to understand this point.
2. Would you say your church is attractive to those of other cultures, as Solomon's temple was to the nations around Israel? What could you do to enhance your church's appearance, worship, fellowship, or programs in the eyes of people from other cultures?
3. Can you identify anything that may cause hostility between your culture and others in the community? Have there been unfortunate incidents that make you or your culture dislike the peoples of other cultures moving into your area? Do you see parallels with the situation of the Jews in Jesus' time?
4. Can you identify any perceptions of inequities felt by visitors or members from other cultures in your church? Is it possible that a newcomer would feel he or she had to conform to your culture in order to be welcomed in your church? What should you do about it?

5

Colliding Cultures

Joseph Henriques

> All good people agree,
> And all good people say,
> All nice people, like us, are We
> And everyone else is They:
> But if you cross the sea,
> Instead of over the way,
> You may end by (think of it!) looking on We
> As only a sort of They!
>
> Rudyard Kipling, "We and They"

In the world of organizational development, it is understood that change will occur only when there is a high correlation of two variables: a sense of urgency and a consensus to change. The same principle holds for individuals. For example, a first-time dad may feel high anxiety when his wife tells him, with certain excitement, that she just felt her first labor pain. His sense of urgency makes him want to go immediately to the hospital. But his wife's doctor and her mother (who has had six children) calm him down, saying that the contractions need to get far more intense before it is time to move on from the living room to the labor room. The group's lack of consensus to change diminished the influence of the urgency to change.

It is probable that most evangelical homogeneous churches are similar to the majority of those that I have worked with over the years. When it comes to reaching the people of the world here in America with the gospel, they have either a consensus to change or a sense of urgency. (Some have neither!) But rarely can one find these two variables both present and present at equally high levels in any homogeneous church. Why is this so? Let's generalize from the smallest unit to the larger group. Use yourself as the example. Looking back over the first four chapters, you read about churches that are effective in multicultural ministry, you thought through our proposal that three powerful forces keep culturally diverse people apart, you compared the changing demographics of today with the historical pattern of immigration in America, and more than likely you nodded in agreement throughout our discussion of biblical reasoning for bringing Christ to the nations. Does this knowledge create in you a sense of urgency to reach out to people who are not members of your cultural group? Do you have an inner consensus that you will do what it takes to reach them? Just as individuals may or may not respond to a need for action, so churches will vary in their response when presented with the same need.

The focus of this chapter is to address the question, Why do many Christians and churches still find it difficult to commit themselves to serving the Lord in a multicultural setting? Essential to this discussion is the understanding that cultural diversity can give another dimension to what would ordinarily be a standard ministry of the church. (For example, in a culturally diverse church, the music should be representative of the various culture groups.) People are reluctant to "cross the sea," as Kipling suggests we do, when they are asked to leave the comfort zone of their own culture.

Culture is like a house made of glass; both those outside and those inside can see each other. They live in the same neighborhood, work in the same office, talk with each other every day, yet they continue to live separate from each other. Permission to enter either world is by invitation only.

Consider, for example, one large church with which I have interacted over a long period of time. Throughout the years I have encouraged the church's leaders to form and train a team to lead the congregation's outreach among the ethnic entrepreneurs and professionals of its metropolitan community. The church is perfectly situated in the town center, has a membership that interacts with other nationalities on a daily basis, and demonstrates its commitment to world missions by dedicating a full 50 percent of its budget to sending the gospel overseas. It has recently started an ESL program in which a handful of members are involved. As important as this outreach is, it doesn't begin to tap the full potential of what the church could do if it opened its doors wide to other culture groups.

Another excellent evangelical church is located a few blocks from a major university that has 1,700 international students. My repeated attempts to convince its pastor and members to form a team to minister to those students have failed.

In one neighborhood hardly anyone, including one dedicated Christian family, speaks to the Indian, Vietnamese, or Japanese families living there. The Christian family in this neighborhood mirrors many others who prefer to stay within the predictability of their own world.

So why is there such a deficiency of multicultural ministries? The reason, again, is bondage to our own culture. Culture-bound people are a primary reason for the lack of involvement in a multicultural setting. The good news is that we can choose to be free from our culture to serve others. Each of us has the power to open our culture's sliding glass doors at will. This freedom is precisely the intent of Paul's declaration:

> Though I am free and belong to no man, I make myself a slave to everyone, to win as many as possible. To the Jews I became like a Jew, to win the Jews. To those under the law I became like one under the law (though I myself am not under the law), so as to win those under the law. To those not having the law I became like one not having the law (though I am not free from God's law but am under Christ's law), so as to win those not having the law. To the weak I became weak, to win the weak. I have become all things to all men so that by all possible means I might save some. I do all this for the sake of the gospel, that I may share in its blessings.

> 1 Corinthians 9:19–23

What will enable us to move beyond the cultural distinctions that keep us from multicultural ministry? We must begin by respecting the truth that all people without exception are shaped by their culture. Second, we must appreciate that a person's identity is defined by his or her culture. That, in turn, leads to the understanding that a person depends on culture for communication. Finally, we must recognize that prejudice may be hindering our urgency and consensus to change. As our understanding develops, it will be clear why we naturally tend to keep our doors shut to those on the outside. Only with this understanding will we feel secure and free to finally open those doors.

All People Are Shaped by Culture

"Real culture" consists of the patterns of actual behavior and the thoughts of the people—what, in fact, they do and think.

Paul Hiebert

Question: What is like all others, like some others, and like none other? Answer: We are.

All human beings are made in God's image; we are "his offspring," as Paul said to the Athenians. This explains the similarities between the needs and desires of John Doe in the United States and Ching Chung-ying in China. *We are like all others*. On the other hand, we Americans have certain rituals that people from other cultures would have trouble understanding. *We are like some others*. Taking the comparison one step further, each person is like a snowflake, uniquely shaped by his or her experiences and personality, having no equal. *We are like none other*.

At this point in our discussion, which will focus on the uniqueness of culture, its differences, and its potential barriers between people, it is tempting to make the erroneous assumption that culture is to be credited for all human behavior. We must remember that culture has its place but also its limitations in explaining differences between people.

Not all behavior is cultural. There are many things people do and say that are neither caused by nor related to their culture. If all human behavior were put on a continuum, that part related to culture would fall in the middle, between universal at one extreme and personal at the other. . . . Universal behaviors are those which apply to everyone regardless of culture, what is usually referred to as "human nature." All people in all cultures eat regularly; eating is not French or Indonesian or Kenyan. . . . At the opposite end of the behavioral continuum from the universal lies the personal. While the shared assumptions, values, and beliefs guarantee that people from the same culture will be similar in many ways, personal experience guarantees that no two people from the same culture will be identical. To put it another way, each of us is in part a product of culture (and to that extent similar to others from the same culture) and in part a product of our own unique life circumstances (and to that extent like no one else anywhere.)[1]

Our culture instructs us in our thought and behavior patterns, and it also colors our view of how those outside our culture should behave.

We are most adept and comfortable operating within our own cultural ways. Naturally, we prefer that people from other races or cultures who enter our cultural environment act like we do. We want them to speak with the same accent, have the same values, see the world in the same way—in short, to have the same culture.

This strong preference for the culture that shaped us can be positive in that it ensures the future stability of a people. Such preference, though, can also be a hindrance to proactively welcoming and assimilating other culture groups. Many people groups view any outsider with suspicion or disdain. Thomas Sowell, senior fellow at the Hoover Institution at Stanford University, has observed that a nation that has a primary "homogeneous group can afford to be secure in its liberalism toward outsiders"[2] is true only for nations such as America whose culture is rooted in a biblical notion of equality among people. What is true of a nation is true of a church: A secure dominant culture can actually facilitate peaceful coexistence with minority cultures.

What does this knowledge about the strength of culture mean for us as we consider multicultural ministry? It means we must be aware that those who are of the dominant culture are prone to dismiss their responsibility to enter the cultures of immigrant settlers. For example, Christians, irritated by my suggestion that we should learn about the cultures of others, have said, "Why do we have to learn about their culture? Weren't they the ones who decided to come to America? Let them learn about us!"

Christians are uniquely positioned for brokering and modeling intercultural reconciliation. Only the Lord's people are shaped by what Manuel Ortiz calls in his book *One New People* the "Christ Culture."[3] Since his people were meant to be distinguished "from all the other people on the face of the earth" (Exod. 33:16), God calls us to demonstrate the power of Christ to bring oneness to groups that are normally fractured by hostility.

Paul's words regarding Jews and Gentiles have direct application in this regard:

> For he himself is our peace, who has made the two one and has destroyed the barrier, the dividing wall of hostility, by abolishing in his flesh the law with its commandments and regulations. His purpose was to create in himself one new man out of the two, thus making peace, and in this one body to reconcile both of them to God through the cross, by which he put to death their hostility. He came and preached peace to you who were far away and peace to those who were near. For through him we both have access to the Father by one Spirit.
>
> Ephesians 2:14–18

I will never forget the day when the Christ Culture was so clearly evidenced in the International Christian Church I founded in Cascais, Portugal. During the Sunday morning worship service, a white South African man stood to give this testimony: "I want to testify of God's grace and power to change lives. Today I am sitting in church worshiping with people from many nations, including black brothers and sisters. A black sister is playing the organ, another black sister is teaching my children in Sunday school. This would have never happened in my country. Jesus Christ has changed me and has given me such love for those for whom I had no love before." The South African personified a key concept of the Christ Culture, namely, when I know that "by the grace of God I am what I am" (1 Cor. 15:10), I am willing and able to extend that same grace to others. Christ and his culture reigned supreme on that day, and the Lord's people rejoiced.

Multicultural ministry provides a wonderful opportunity to be living examples of God's culture, the standard by which all human cultures are measured.

Identity, Meaning, and Cohesiveness

Culture is the underlying influence that shapes our thought processes, our perceptions, our everyday activities, and our patterns of interpersonal interactions. It penetrates to the very core of the individual; it is the imperceptible force that directs thought and behavior. Even when the driving force of culture is raised to a level of awareness, cultural behavior is resistant to change. Once a people group acquires a certain cultural configuration, it is completely absorbed by that culture. According to Thomas Sowell, the most obvious fact about the history of racial and ethnic groups is how different they have been—and still are—even when over time people are removed from their original roots.

> One may repudiate one's roots and still exhibit them unwittingly. The *conversos,* Fifteenth-century Spanish converts to Christianity from Judaism, in many cases promoted anti-Semitic policies, but nevertheless worked in the same kinds of occupations and with the same kinds of success as when they had been Jews. . . . Conversely, people who have in fact lost contact with their cultural roots, and who have shared little or none of the social experience of their group, may not only "identify" with their group, but even do so in a highly vocal and exaggerated way.[4]

The examples Sowell gives demonstrate the powerful grip that culture has in the continuation of ethnic differences, even after a lifetime of living together with other cultures under common institutions, as in the United States. As Sowell calls it, the "messages"—distinctive cultural patterns—of a people group continue to influence the behavior of its members for generations.

The comprehensive nature of culture's defining role is well expressed by the following experts:

Marvin K. Mayers: "Culture is everything that is a part of one's everyday life experience. It includes: tangibles such as food, shelter, clothing, literature, art, music, etc.; and intangibles such as hopes, dreams, values, rules, space, relationships, language, body movements, etc."[5]

Edgar H. Schein: "Culture is a pattern of shared basic assumptions that the group learned as it solved its problems of external adaptation and internal integration, that has worked well enough to be considered valid and, therefore, to be taught to new members as the correct way to perceive, think, and feel in relation to those problems."[6]

Donald K. Smith: "The core of a culture is not a miscellaneous collection of beliefs and values. Instead, it provides a large consistent interpretation of life."[7]

Edward T. Hall: "When I talk about culture I am not just talking about something in the abstract that is imposed on man and is separate from him, but about man himself, about you and me in a highly personal way."[8]

Every culture is like none other. Yet, as has already been determined, the image of God in us links us to all others. We can view Abraham Maslow's proposed hierarchy of needs (physiological, security and safety, love and belonging, self-esteem, self-actualization) as a list of basic needs resident in all people at all times. All people everywhere know the experience of striving for sustenance and shelter, of longing for love and acceptance, and of desiring esteem and fulfillment. A major part of a group's identity is how its culture defines what constitutes achieving these needs.

One Out of Many

Church leaders have asked me at times, "Do you think it is really possible for a church to experience unity with people who come from various cultural backgrounds?" Assuming that English is the common language, my answer has been in the affirmative.

Wanting to explore this question from the aspect of how a worship service reflects the culture of its people, I decided to use the Fourth of

July as my day of observation. I attended two services, one in a traditional American church (made up of people of predominantly European descent) and the other in a multiethnic church (a large percentage of whom were recently arrived immigrants, mostly from non-European countries). Would there be a contrast between a traditional American service and a multiethnic church on this, the greatest of all American holidays?

At my first stop, the American church service started right on cue. Pulsating patriotic fervor set the tone for the hour of celebration. In this ceremony for honoring American history and values, the congregation was fully engaged. As the theme songs of the various military branches sounded forth from the professional band and orchestra, the congregation clapped while past and present members of the armed forces took their turns standing. From button-down shirts and Dockers to Giorgio Armani suits, from Fords to Jaguars, this was mainstream America at its best. No one in attendance could doubt that the American dream was alive and well for those who claim it and work to bring the vision to pass.

Sprinkled throughout the predominantly white crowd were other skin colors and facial features, representing nontraditional Americans who had achieved the right to fit in with the best of suburbia, located in one of the richest areas of America. Quite frankly, so stimulating and uplifting is this celebratory service, I try to attend every chance I get on the Fourth of July. You can count me in when it comes to being an unashamedly proud, flag-waving American. My immigrant parents taught me well the high privilege and responsibility of living in the land of the free, the country of opportunity.

Riding high on patriotic emotion, I left the first church for my next service at an urban multiethnic church. I arrived about twenty minutes late but was soon aware that in this church the concept of lateness was fluid, as members continued coming in, nodding and waving greetings to fellow parishioners as they took their seats. The congregation was a vibrant variety of skin tones and ethnic-specific styles of clothing, dyed in a wide spectrum of shades, from bright to subdued. Individual accents could be detected as the voices joined in worshipful singing of the great hymns of the faith. There were fervent prayers for the nations, and the people were exhorted to believe in God's faithfulness. At the close of the service, participants were invited by rows to walk up front to receive communion from the hands of the multinational pastoral staff.

Each community was living in its own reality, and it was clearly reflected in the church services. In the multiethnic church, not a word in the bulletin, not a song in the service, not a comment in announcements, not a phrase in a prayer was dedicated to America. When compared to the attention the first church drew to America and her history, it appears that the second church was lacking in patriotism. Could they be patriotic but from a different perspective?

Any people with a common connection to the past feel solidarity. The basis for their common connection is the myths that unite them. Myths are stories that illumine the nature of how we as a people came to be who we are. The new citizenry of America and the traditional citizens have different myths that unite them. Having nothing in common with the Boston Tea Party, George Washington and Valley Forge, or the Statue of Liberty and Ellis Island, the beginnings of the new immigrants have more to do with refugee camps and the Red Cross, Silicon Valley and graduate school, and the Immigration and Naturalization Act of 1965.

Once a national fountain where students drank in knowledge of America's past, many public schools may now fail to emphasize the American metanarrative. In the past, immigrant children learned the story of the nation to which they had moved. The trend in current education is to provide equal time to teaching the history of the nations from which the students came. Traditional Americans would say, "If our goal was to begin forming a new United States of the World, then this trend would make sense. But our goal is to forge a citizenry of a new America dedicated to its past and committed to its future." They would agree with Paul Greenberg, in his article "The Power of Myth in Shaping Destinies," where he observes, "When we lose our connection with a common past, we no longer have a common future. When we no longer revere the same heroes or respect the same words, we lose the thread of our story. The mythic tie is broken, and our future unravels. We no longer have a narrative to act out."[9] The challenge for all Americans is to learn how to appreciate and blend the myths of the past and of the present to preserve *e pluribus unum*.

Differing Concerns

The multiethnic congregation I visited was composed largely of new immigrants and their children. So, then, was it a serious oversight for the leaders not to lead the congregation in prayer for America? Unquestionably. All Christians in America should celebrate God's faithfulness in granting to America historical roots in biblical thought.

Besides the surface difference in patriotism, there is also the difference in economic prosperity and cultural proficiency between the two churches. The urban multiethnic church reflected a membership of people whose lives focused on meeting physiological and safety needs: adequate housing, jobs, official immigration papers, work visas, safe places for their kids in unsafe neighborhoods, language acquisition, and learning to navigate in a strange culture. Their sensitivity to these issues was clearly evidenced in the prayer list in their bulletin. Every prayer item was for specific members of the church who had concerns in these areas. In addition, intercessory prayer was requested for family members in the Sudan, the Philippines, El Salvador, and other countries around the world that were also facing similar needs. Gratitude for God's faithful provisions was also a prominent theme on that Fourth of July.

The culture of the traditional American megachurch reflected the middle to upper class of people that it focused on reaching and retaining. This church was concerned with such issues as getting involved with the community, touching lives with the love of God, balancing professional life with family life, growing in a personal relationship with God, becoming part of a small group, and using biblical principles in raising children.

These concerns of the traditional American church are certainly concerns of believers in the multiethnic church as well. Yet when members of the multiethnic church lack economic freedom and facility in navigating in the dominant culture, their primary concerns become very different from those of the traditional church.

Could these two groups experience unity? If so, how would their worship service reflect the values and needs represented in the unified church?

Suppose that churches were forced to submit to the same standards applied to government agencies and schools. By law, government agencies must demonstrate that in their hiring practices they are giving equal employment opportunity to members of all cultural backgrounds. In schools there is a societal expectation that all students be successfully socialized as proactive and responsible members of the institution. Part of the strategy for fulfilling this expectation includes celebrating the cultural diversity of its student body and utilizing a variety of methods to do so.

If churches were subject to these same expectations, could they become healthy multicultural entities that worship together? Would multiethnic church members be of mutual benefit? Is it possible that the combined multifaceted issues and concerns could be addressed and met? Or are the disparities of culture and socioeconomic levels too great to overcome? Is the Christ Culture powerless to overcome human differences?

Any church that chose to pursue a wide range of cultural diversity in its membership would fulfill many of the principles and teachings of Scripture regarding relationships between diverse groups:

I am obligated both to Greeks and non-Greeks, both to the wise and the foolish (Rom. 1:14).

For there is no difference between Jew and Gentile—the same Lord is Lord of all and richly blesses all who call on him (Rom. 10:12).

Though I am free and belong to no man, I make myself a slave to everyone (1 Cor. 9:19).

For we were all baptized by one Spirit into one body—whether Jews or Greeks, slave or free—and we were all given the one Spirit to drink (1 Cor. 12:13).

There is neither Jew nor Greek, slave nor free, male nor female, for you are all one in Christ Jesus (Gal. 3:28).

My brothers, as believers in our glorious Lord Jesus Christ, don't show favoritism. . . . have you . . . discriminated among yourselves? . . . If you really keep the royal law found in Scripture, "Love your neighbor as yourself," you are doing right. But if you show favoritism, you sin and are convicted by the law as lawbreakers (James 2:1, 4, 8–9).

In the last passage James indicates that partiality in a socioeconomically diverse congregation was a deviation from the norm of community life that God intended. This suggests by silence that a mixed congregation could indeed be a normative experience for believers.

All People Communicate through Culture

Communication is essential to meaningful community life, and without culture, communication is incomprehensible. Famed anthropologist Edward T. Hall showed that people communicate using ten "primary message systems":

1. *Language*—gestures, words, written articles
2. *Social relationships*—how people of different age, gender, kinship, status, and roles relate to each other
3. *Individual functions*—daily routine, life cycle
4. *Learning and thinking patterns*—the way people learn and process information
5. *Religious activity*—beliefs and rituals
6. *Personal preferences for living*—care, clothing, dwelling, food, and travel

7. *Political systems*—how people govern and defend themselves
8. *Fine art*—artistic expression and recreation
9. *Economic system*—how money is used and exchanged
10. *Values*—the varying degrees of importance of each of the above systems in relation to each other[10]

These primary message systems suggest that communication is always a complex and multifaceted phenomenon. Words are only one part of everyday communication.

Communication Is Demanding

Communicating with others is the most important, most natural, and yet most demanding of our daily tasks. Senders and receivers understand each other through cultural codes. For example, the sender of the message *encodes* his or her ideas by choosing from a wide assortment of available communication expressions; the receiver has to then *decode* the message accurately. The most competent *encoders* and *decoders* are those who know well the meaning of cultural cues, such as, the sounds of a voice, the possible meanings of a word, and the unspoken rules of nonverbal communication. Nonverbal communication occurs through gestures, touch, smell, facial expressions, silence, choice of clothes and colors, verbal inflections and nuances, status symbols, space, and the use of time. And you thought communication was easy!

An interesting passage in the Bible reveals how Moses' years of experience had honed his decoding skills, surpassing those of a much younger Joshua. As the two came down from the mountain, Moses carrying with him the two tablets of the Testimony, Joshua heard the noise of the people shouting, and he said to Moses, "There is the sound of war in the camp." Moses replied, "It is not the sound of victory, it is not the sound of defeat; it is the sound of singing that I hear" (Exod. 32:17–18). Indeed, the people were participating in a great orgy of celebration before the golden calf.

Stephen Rhodes tells of one church that learned the importance of accurate decoding the hard way. One night during choir practice, the choir director said something that offended three Asian women. "They turned to each other, and one asked, 'What did he say?' The other replied, 'I think he just called us stupid.' The three women left rehearsal and eventually left the church." The incident caused so much internal turmoil in the church that the choir director soon left for a new position. Those who investigated the incident, by way of a tape of the rehearsal, discovered that the director had actually used the word *stufe,* a German musical term for degree.[11]

The potential for such conflict could cause even the most committed enthusiast to think twice about ministry in a multiethnic environment. Some might say, "I want my church to be multicultural, but then I know I would have to be concerned about what other ethnic groups are thinking. Sunday morning would become more complex for me. All that effort of encoding and decoding cross-culturally is work I can live without. I don't have to come to church; I do have to go to work, to the grocery store, to the doctor's office, where I have to deal with others who are different. I put up with rules of civility all week long with people I don't understand. But church is purely voluntary. I come here to relax, to worship, not to occupy my mind with multicultural complexities."

As married couples, who work through their problems, wind up glad they didn't divorce, so those who persevere in building a community of multiethnic Christians are glad they did not give up. The rewards of commitment are greater than its cost. These rewards are as varied as are the members of the community. The sensational tastes of diverse cuisine, fascinating insights of how cultural behaviors and attitudes are changed by Christ, praise to and thoughts about God expressed in new configurations and intonations, and the deep satisfaction of mutual burden bearing with brothers and sisters of different color and culture are but some of the rewards.

Noise Can Disrupt Communication

Anything that distorts or interferes with one's message is noise. This interference ranges from *physical noise* (traffic on a busy street) to *psychological noise* (bias and prejudices) to *semantic noise* (heavy accents, technical jargon, or highly emotional statements) to *spiritual noise* (the conflict between right and wrong). As all participants in a communication process spontaneously receive, transmit, and give feedback, they are simultaneously influenced by various kinds of noise in their environment.

As an example, it took a while for me to become accustomed to the "noise" created by some of the members of our Portuguese church. While I was in the process of developing the next point of the sermon, they would be discussing among themselves the point just made. In our international church, an elderly British gentleman suddenly started tapping his cane in the aisle and calling out, "Here! Here!" I stopped the sermon, thinking that he had dropped something of value on the floor, had located it, and was asking for someone to pick it up for him. I soon discovered that he was just expressing his version of "Amen!"

People Communicate in Many Cultural Ways

Symbols and Signs

Symbols and signs are other means of nonverbal communication. Being made in God's image means we have the ability to "substitute signs and symbols for ideas, actions, and other phenomena, thereby giving them cultural significance . . ."[12]

- Think of the many different costumes people wear as symbols of their occupations.
- What symbols have people collected to symbolize victories or achievements in their respective fields?
- What are symbols that stand for military rank, wealth, religious beliefs, social affiliations?
- Consider the symbols God and his people have used to represent abstract truth about him.

Anthropologist Paul Hiebert claims that symbols are the link between physical things and abstract ideas that make human thought and communication possible.[13] Misusing or misinterpreting symbols will cause miscommunication. We must not underestimate the significance of signs and symbols in a multicultural setting. For example, it is not unusual for hosts of multicultural socials to make a critical mistake when using flags as decoration. Their intention is to create an international motif. Usually no one pays attention to the flags being used, no one, that is, but the international guests. Chinese international students have been upset when a Taiwanese flag and a Chinese flag are both displayed. To them this symbolizes the host's commitment to two rival countries. On the other hand, if the Taiwanese flag is missing while the Chinese flag is present, Taiwanese students could interpret this as symbolizing the host's belief that Taiwan should be a part of China.

Here is another example. Consider the signals we give during a meal:

> Did you know you can also send subtle signals with your Western eating utensils? For Americans, to signal we have finished eating we normally place knife and fork in parallel across the plate. For the Swedish, placing the utensils criss-crossed atop one another on an empty plate does *not* mean they are finished but instead signals they would like another helping. Among Egyptians, it is impolite to eat everything on one's plate.[14]

In some cultures, eating everything on your plate sends a signal that the hostess has not fed you sufficiently and you have room for more.

Signs and symbols create a picture in our mind of how we should interpret what is going on around us. Smoke coming out the windows of the house next door conveys certain information to you, which in turn will determine your behavior. In every culture there are certain signs and symbols that carry meaning peculiar to that culture and that evoke an emotion or action. Such symbols include arrows, certain flowers for funerals or marriage ceremonies, highway markers, the colors on light signals, barber poles, and rice at weddings.

We must be cognizant of the action we are suggesting or the emotions we are evoking by the signs or symbols we use. Perhaps the time has come for every Christian home to have quick-reference books on culture. When questions surface at the dinner table about the meaning of signs or symbols used by culturally different acquaintances, we should be able to do instant research. Such books that are both educational and entertaining include Roger E. Axtell's *Gestures: Do's and Taboos around the World* and *Do's and Taboos of Hosting International Visitors*.

The experience of an American professor in Italy could very well happen to anyone involved in a multicultural ministry here in America. The professor was very happy to receive his first invitation for dinner at the home of an Italian colleague. Having heard that Italians enjoy receiving flowers from their guests, he purchased a large bouquet at the local market. With a Texas-size smile, he presented the flowers to his colleague's elderly mother, who greeted him at the door. He was puzzled that he did not see her the rest of the evening. Only much later was he told that in Italy the flowers he offered (chrysanthemums) were a sign of death, used exclusively at funerals!

Words

Language forms culture; culture forms language. The relationship of words in their context, the symbols and rules they convey, and the variety of tones utilized in verbal communication are often complex even for a native user of that language. It is easy to understand the impossibility of becoming a full participant in any culture without sufficient language skills. Consider how those unfamiliar with our language would shake their head in bewilderment at the following two-headed headlines that turn the "blandly literal to the sublimely absurd."[15]

Grandmother of Eight Makes Hole in One

Quarter of a Million Chinese Live on Water

Chinese Apeman Dated

Doctor Testifies in Horse Suit

Iraqi Head Seeks Arms

Caribbean Islands Drift to Left

S. Florida Illegal Aliens Cut in Half by New Law[16]

Surely the last headline would catch the attention of those contemplating slipping into America through Miami!

When speaking to nontraditional Americans who may yet be unaccustomed to Americanisms, slang, or metaphoric expressions, the words you use should be simple and straightforward. Speak clearly. Beware of running words together like, "Hi, jeetyet?" instead of "Hi. Did you eat yet?" Make sure that a point you make is understood. When doing so, put the burden on yourself with statements like, "Sometimes I speak too quickly. Shall I go over that again?" On the other hand, don't speak loudly and draw your sentences out as a technique for making your message clear. If you speak slang or use colloquial expressions such as "That car is as ugly as a toad" or "He'll wait for her 'til the cows come home," always make sure that people are understanding your main point. In short, apply the Golden Rule by talking to others with the consideration that you would desire from others, if you were in their country.

Body language

GESTURES

Many anthropologists believe that 60 percent, and maybe even 75 percent, of all communication is nonverbal. Gestures and body language, which are part of every culture, are powerful communicators, adding color and life to daily interactions. They are both so much a part of our culture that each of us uses them instinctively and spontaneously, either as a substitute for words or as an embellishment to what we are verbally communicating.

Communications expert Mario Pei once estimated that humans can produce up to 700,000 different physical signs. Birdwhistel estimates that the face alone is capable of producing 250,000 expressions. Researcher M. H. Krout identified 5,000 distinct hand gestures that he believed had verbal equivalents, while another researcher in kinesics, G. W. Hewes, has catalogued 1,000 different postures and their accompanying gestures.[17]

The vocabulary of gestures plays a powerful formative role in any culture. Dr. Donald Smith believes that enculturation—personally assuming the core beliefs of culture, along with the other layers of traditions, values, and customs—is accomplished during babyhood, mostly by the use of gestures. According to Smith:

> They are almost entirely learned non-verbally, from observation and listening, from rewards received for acceptable behavior and punishment for what is unacceptable. . . . Two-thirds of an individual's knowledge is gained this way, by the time the child is seven years old. This includes fundamental knowledge about the nature of reality, God, humankind, and the world—mostly learned nonverbally.[18]

The problem, then, is obvious for anyone who participates in but did not grow up in a particular culture. For instance, suppose you, a woman, see a group of Filipino men talking together during an international gathering at your church. What would be your first impression if one of them glances in your direction, puckers his lips, and lifts his chin toward you? You would probably look away, thinking that a message is being sent that you do not want to acknowledge. The truth is that people from certain cultures will purse their lips and lift their chin to point toward a certain direction. This is their way of saying to each other, "It's that way" or "Over there."

Facial Expressions

With facial expressions alone people are able to communicate a variety of emotions, such as happiness, surprise, fear, anger, sadness, disgust, contempt, bewilderment, determination, repentance, love, and worship. Context influences the interpretation of facial communication. For example, if someone is smiling at a person with a sullen expression, you might think the one smiling is gloating. If, however, the same person is smiling at another who is frowning, you might interpret the smiling face to be peaceful, friendly, or helpful. It is apparent that all cultures have some facial expression that are universally interpreted the same way. For example, it was found that "people in Borneo and New Guinea, with little contact with Western cultures, were able to accurately match emotions with pictures of facial expressions of Westerners."[19] Americans, likewise, were able to interpret accurately the facial emotions of people from Borneo and New Guinea. On the other hand, facial expressions combined with other nonverbal expressions can have different meanings. A smile on a Korean coupled with covering his mouth with his hand is probably not a smirk but, rather, an expression of embarrassment.

Eye Communication

Eyes are powerful communicators. Scientific observations confirm that eyes are the most important nonverbal message system. Eye communication provides feedback (your reaction to the message you received), indicates who should speak next, reveals how people feel about each other, and brings psychological closeness, even though people may be physically apart.

Be careful about how you check the eyes for feedback in a multicultural environment. Cultures vary in the way people are taught to use their eyes. In some cultures, prolonged eye contact signals a message of intimacy. Arab cultures prohibit a man from even looking at a woman. In the American culture it is very important for a subordinate to look at an authority figure as a sign of respect, hence the admonition, "Look at me while I'm speaking to you!" In some cultures the opposite is true. Out of respect to your superior, you look down when he or she is talking to you.

The true story is told of a boy who grew up in Brazil and Suriname. He learned the hard way that two cultures don't always see eye-to-eye. When he tried to avoid eye contact with his Brazilian grandmother, she would slap him in the face and say, "Look me in the face." As with Americans, making eye contact with an elder was a sign of respect in her part of the world. Thinking that he had learned his lesson well, he visited his Surinamese grandmother and looked at her straight in the face to show respect, whereupon she slapped him too. In Suriname no respectful kid makes eye contact with an adult.

What is the lesson for us? When speaking to culturally diverse individuals, we can let their eyes guide our gaze. If they look away, we should also look away. If they look straight at us, then we can feel free to do likewise.

Touch

Touch is probably the first sense a baby develops. As a child grows, he or she begins to explore the world through touch, and the world around the child teaches culture through touch. Touch can communicate many things: our positive emotions toward another, our intentions toward playfulness, our demand for compliance, our signal of greeting and departure, or just simply the act of carrying out some function (for example, checking someone's forehead for fever or helping someone out of a car).

Cultures vary widely on the conditions of touch. Some cultures seek bodily contact and others assiduously avoid it. Same-sex touching in the Middle East is extremely common. Men often walk hand-in-hand or with their arms on each other's shoulders. Roger E. Axtell in his book *Gestures* says that he would have committed a major faux pas if he had jerked his hand away when his Arab business contact and he were walking along the streets visiting customers.[20] He realized later that in this country the act of taking a person's hand was a sign of great friendship and respect. The scale below is one that Axtell offers as a kind of geographic measuring stick of where "touch" or "don't touch" could apply.[21] (Because of their cultural diversity, Axtell did not generalize on African nations.)

Don't Touch	Touch	Middle Ground
Japan	Middle East countries	France
United States and Canada	Latin countries	China
England	Italy	Ireland
Scandinavia	Greece	India
Other northern European countries	Spain and Portugal	
Australia	Some Asian countries	
Estonia	Russia	

We could say touch is a touchy issue. Some Americans have felt insulted when Korean merchants place their change on the counter, clearly avoiding any physical contact and refusing to look at the customer. One Korean explained on national television that in his homeland they are taught to avoid physical contact of any kind or direct eye contact. In Korean cultures such actions can have sexual connotations.

I was a guest at a party honoring a man who had invested a considerable amount of time and energy helping people of other cultures assimilate into American culture and to know Christ. At one point in the evening's program, he was giving a gesture of appreciation for a multicultural group of friends by offering each one a hug. When he put out his arms toward the next person in line, a Chinese woman, she quickly ducked. Although he was probably embarrassed, it was somewhat comical to see him hugging the air! If you or your culture are prone to giving hugs, be familiar with the touch customs of others. Never assume that your expression of greeting will be understood or appreciated. Even this man—a dedicated worker who was more culturally sensitive than the average person—found himself out of touch with the rule of touch.

Space

Space, like touching, is another aspect of the silent language that communicates ideas and feelings. Sometimes personal space is known as someone's "bubble" of personal space. Space bubbles are culturally and personally determined with subconscious awareness. Trespassers crossing the line are not welcome. Edward T. Hall claims that the American's personal space requirement is 18 to 30 inches. This seems accurate and is reflected in the expression "she held him at arm's length," a way of saying she wanted him to stay out of her personal space and its inherent intimacy. The Japanese have a personal space requirement that drives them even farther apart in general business or social situations. In stark contrast, Latinos and Middle Easterners sometimes stand toe-to-toe when speaking with others.

A good strategy is to allow others to be your space adjusters. If you are talking to a Costa Rican and find yourself doing a slow tango backward, force yourself to stand still, allowing your Latin friend to adjust personal space to his or her level of comfort. On the other hand, halt any forward movement when your Asian friend backpedals away from you.

Time

How people groups use time, react to time, and value time is as varied as the people in the world. Some people groups view time as exact; others see time as approximate. When researchers LeVine and Bartlett checked the accuracy of clocks in different cultures, they found considerable variation.[22] Who had the most accurate clocks? The Japanese. In which country were clocks the least consistent? Indonesia. When the speed of pedestrians in those cultures was measured, who do you think walked the fastest and the slowest? (By the way, England, Italy, Taiwan, and the United States fell somewhere between those two extremes.)

In terms of planning social times with internationals, the subject of time is probably one of the most important to understand. Since all people live in time and in space, one would assume that there would be widespread agreement among cultures as to the meaning of being on time. Discard such thoughts immediately. A misunderstanding of how others view time can lead to unpleasant experiences for all involved.

Question: Do all cultures place a premium on punctuality?

Answer: Yes. The problem is that each group defines punctuality differently!

For an American, punctuality means five minutes before a business appointment or right at the appointed time for a dinner appointment. A Nigerian plans to arrive around the appointed hour, but unexpected events may affect this, such as meeting his cousin on the way and spending time discussing the issues of the day.

Check the on-time chart[23] below to see how punctuality could differ between the Egyptian Arab world and the American world.

Time	Arab Time	American Time
5 minutes before appointed time	Servants on time	Everyone on time
5 minutes after appointed time		Mumbled apology advisable
10 minutes after appointed time	Servants late	Slight apology necessary
15 minutes after appointed time		Mildly insulting

20 minutes after appointed time		Full apology required
30 minutes after appointed time		Rude
1 hour after appointed time	Equals on time	Very insulting
1 hour, 15 minutes after appointed time	Equals late	Unforgivable

When inviting someone from another culture to your home or when announcing a social event for your international ministry, do not hesitate to talk about the concept of being on American-style time. Be sure to present this in a kind, lighthearted way, not in military briefing style, such as "We expect everyone to fully cooperate by being here exactly at 6:00 P.M.!"

Why not adopt the Galatians 4:4 "fullness of time" view of being on time? Your social event begins as your first guests arrive until the time everyone is finally present. Remember: You are serving others. Watch *their* clock. Cultural concepts of punctuality are greatly influenced by a culture's philosophical perspective of time.[24]

Colors

Cultures attach different meanings to colors, and this exerts great influence on people. The American culture abounds in color symbolism. When we are in debt, we speak of being in the *red;* when we make a profit, we are in the *black*. When we are sad, we are *blue;* when we are healthy, we are in the *pink;* when we are jealous, we are *green* with envy; and when we are happy, we are tickled *pink*. To be a coward is to be *yellow* and to be inexperienced is to be *green*. When we talk a great deal, we talk a *blue* streak, and when we talk to no avail, we talk until we are *blue* in the face. When we go out on the town, we paint it *red;* and when we are angry, we see *red*.[25] Color idioms are generally a way of speaking and not necessarily a guideline for life. My wife does not wear a blue dress when she is feeling discouraged. But, upon the birth of our grandchildren, she did buy a blue outfit for our grandson and a pink dress for our granddaughter. Asking the people in your multicultural fellowship the meaning of certain colors in their culture could reveal important, useful information. In the case of the Chinese, knowing that red is the primary color used in joyous and festive occasions, it would make sense to use red during any celebration that includes Chinese.

Readers may be tempted to throw up their hands at the impossibility of ever communicating with those of other cultures—but in reality it is easier than it sounds, as long as we each maintain the attitude of a learner. People of all cultures are very forgiving when they realize you simply don't know the rules. Gradually you become more aware of others, and interaction becomes a pleasure.

The aspects of culture we have reviewed help us understand that a person's culture is not a passing fad, but rather the very fabric of his or her life. As with a piece of fabric, we cannot pull out any single thread—such as pulling out a person's belief system in the attempt to insert Christianity—without destroying or disrupting the orderly arrangement of all other threads. Every facet of an individual's life is inextricably woven into his or her group's basic beliefs about God, the nature of man, and the meaning of life. In light of these irrefutable realities, it is clear why Harvard professor Oscar Handlin wrote: ". . . men are not blank tablets on which the environment inscribes a culture which can readily be erased to make way for a new inscription."[26] Any person who works with culturally diverse people must have a profound respect for culture.

The Reality of Partiality

It isn't people that we don't like, it's their behavior. We understand our culture and what constitutes normal behavior for us. Culture is our life simplification system, our shorthand way of interpreting the varied demands of life. But when we move into the realm of another culture, we experience the tension of trying to interpret others. If familiarity breeds contempt, so can unfamiliarity.

I once spoke to a businessman who strongly resisted the idea of working with people from other cultures. He did not understand their accents and social behavior or why they enjoyed certain foods. If his company had a job opening, he would automatically discard any résumé that was not from a white applicant. Many people would rightfully object to this behavior, saying, "You can't do that! It is against the law!" But let's not be too quick to judge. We need to ask ourselves if the deepest thoughts of our own hearts harbor prejudice toward others of certain ethnic groups. In the most secret recesses of our mind, do we assess ourselves as superior to others? Do we avoid those of a different skin color or custom?

Could partiality be the reason that many of God's workers are immobilized, refusing to work in the abundant foreign harvest fields in America? Were not Jesus' last words, "You will be my witnesses in Jerusalem, and in all Judea and Samaria, and to the ends of the earth"? If it were not for partiality, would we not be overjoyed that he has brought the remotest part of the world, Samaria, and Judea, to our hometown Jerusalem?

A disparity seems to exist between our desire that the world know Christ and our consensus and urgency to reach people from the nations who live among us. Partiality contributes to this disparity.

According to the second chapter of James, there are always two sides to partiality: the upside and the downside. We look up to certain people and look down at others, speak up to some and speak down to others, admire and view one group highly and disdain and view another group with low regard.

James did not choose cultural diversity as his example of partiality. He chose instead to reveal that partiality existed in people's view of different socioeconomic classes within the same culture. Both the rich man and poor man attended the same gathering of the church.[27] When the rich entered, believers gushed forth words of welcome. "You, sir, won't you please have a seat right here in a good place?" The good place was a more comfortable place, a place of honor. The assembly halls sometimes had benches around the outside wall and a couple of benches in front. There were a limited number of good seats; these seats were the ones that Christians offered to the rich. But when the poor man came in dressed in his shabby, dirty clothes, the Lord's people would speak in a demeaning voice, "You, you stand over there, or sit on the floor."

Partiality in any context can assume similar patterns of negative words and demeanor. I was taken aback when one of the most congenial people one could know said to me: "I don't go to our local grocery store. There are too many foreign people there. I drive farther and go to the one down the road. Just our kind of people shop there."

If James were writing his words in chapter 2:1–9 to the church today regarding our issues of division caused by diversity, perhaps he would say something along these lines: "Partiality causes you to be divided about the faith you profess. Jesus Christ came to abolish distinctions that keep people apart. Yet you allow the evil in your heart to make wrong judgments about others. You profess that Jesus Christ came to demolish class distinctions but even among the brethren—people with whom you have a spiritual bond in Christ—you promote class distinctions and social discrimination. You perpetuate what Jesus came to destroy. You bring upon yourself a double mind, causing you to be at odds with yourself. No wonder there is envy, bickering, and divisions among God's people of different cultures."

The conclusion of the matter, James says, is to consider God who knows only impartiality in his view of people. He may choose one class or group for a specific purpose, but his favor extends to all. We who are bound to God's royal law of love are to do likewise.

Summary

Knowing how our culture so powerfully forms us helps us understand the common human experience of preferring the comfort and stability of one's own group. It is reasonable that culture is a natural divider among people. The pressure of decoding the schematic of other cultures is one that we would like to avoid. This we have called the problem of colliding cultures. Another factor that enters into the collision is our character, our sinful attitudes that precipitate collision.

Partiality is the potion brewed when pride is mixed with culture. Isolation and negative feelings toward others are created inwardly and exhibited outwardly. Culture is preference, but partiality is prejudice.

If we choose not to live by God's royal law of love, we are headed for a collision, a collision of what we say we believe because it's in God's Word and how we actually live. If we say that we love the African in Africa, whom we have not seen, and we send missionaries to show Christ's love to him, why don't we show the same love to Africans whom we see in our community?

This glaring flaw places many of God's children in a moral quandary. How can we fervently proclaim his love for the people of the world while virtually ignoring the very people from those faraway lands who unexpectedly show up as our neighbors? We must follow Jesus, our example, who infuriated his own people by ministering to outsiders, whom most Jews were not interested in reaching at all.

Cultures may collide like cars in our community. Why can't the church be the "body shop" that puts things back in shape?

Discussion Starters

1. We have seen that a high sense of both urgency and commitment is needed before any organization will institute change. Divide into two groups and discuss the topics of urgency and commitment.

   Group one: Discuss the level of urgency that presently exists in your community or church to meet the needs of different cultures.

   Group two: Discuss the current level of commitment in your church to reaching the ethnically diverse people of your community.

   After 20 to 30 minutes, return to the large group and share your findings.

2. When different cultures intersect in the same community, some tension will be evident. This is the result of colliding cultures. As you reflect on your own response to those who are different, can

you identify attitudes that you admit are not Christlike? These may be "character collisions." What will you do with them?

3. In Christian circles we often speak of "callings" to one ministry or another. Even the apostles had somewhat different callings. Do you think your church needs a special calling to intercultural ministry in your own community? Are you excused from responding to changing community needs if you don't feel called?

6

Choices for the Journey
Joseph Henriques

The best way to predict the future is to create it.

Peter Drucker

"A marathon? You're going to run a *marathon?* Which one? The Boston, New York, or Marine Corps?" Most people expect that a declarative statement of intent will be followed shortly by qualifying descriptors. If a neighbor says she is changing jobs, you would expect her to reveal what the next job will be. You would probably consider it unusual—if not unwise—for her to continue by saying, "I plan to take whatever job opening comes up in a conversation tomorrow." I have received calls from young men asking if I would perform their wedding ceremony. Each prospective groom, without fail, could identify a certain young lady who had already agreed to marry him. No one has yet to tell me, "I am just looking this week for whoever seems to be ready for marriage. Are you available this Friday night to do the wedding?" From a wide selection of possibilities, people typically undergo a process to determine their best choice.

The same expectation applies to involvement in multicultural ministry. It may be a starting point to declare, "Our church is going to start reaching out to the internationals in our area," or, even to say, "We are going to have a Hispanic ministry." From that point of declaration, however, a process must be identified by which a group decides exactly whom they intend to reach, how that group will be reached, and why this group was chosen instead of another. Usually there are steps to take, from simple to more complex, before we can reach a major objective.

The first part of this chapter deals with alternative models and strategies for intercultural interaction that are available to our society. We then explore somewhat corresponding choices facing the church as it seeks its niche of ministry in a culturally pluralistic society. Suggested guidelines for determining one's choice of multicultural ministry are provided in chapter 10.

Two Models of Plural Societies

Most if not all societies in the world today are culturally plural. Japan and Korea are rarities with more than 99 percent of a single ethnicity. In other words, a society that consists only of members that claim the same ethnic origin, language, and religion is almost nonexistent. Globalization, increased mobility, economic factors, educational pursuits, war, political factors, and the search for freedom have all contributed to the makeup of any modern nation—people of many cultural backgrounds living together.

A plural society must analyze and define the intercultural relations between its dominant (core cultural group) and nondominant groups to begin to benefit from and improve the interactions between these groups. Basic to the analysis is an understanding of how the society views cultural pluralism. Cross-cultural psychologist John Berry identifies two contrasting models of plural societies: the mainstream-minority model and the multicultural model.[1] The mainstream-minority model encompasses one dominant society and various minority groups that remain on the margins of the mainstream society until they are assimilated into the larger society. The multicultural model consists of a national social framework of institutions that accommodates the coexistence of numerous cultural groups. "The mainstream-minority view is that cultural pluralism is a problem and should be reduced, even eliminated; the multicultural view is that cultural pluralism is a resource, and inclusiveness should be nurtured with supportive policies and programs."[2]

The Mainstream-Minority Model

The mainstream-minority concept was prevalent in this country throughout most of the twentieth century, beginning with the first great wave of immigration (1901–1910). Immigrants were expected to assimilate and become Americans. The American national identity was embodied in the nature of American Protestantism, which had given rise to the universal principles in the Declaration of Independence and the constitution.

Current proponents of assimilationist policy advocate a renewed emphasis on our unifying English language and common American culture. State-sponsored affirmative action, bilingual education, and multiculturalism are seen by some to promote tension, divisiveness, and conflict among ethnic groups, resulting in a fragmented society.[3] Francis Fukuyama points to the inability of any multicultural society in history to maintain separate cultural identities, believing that assimilation is essential to a unified nation with a common identity.[4]

> It is wrong to argue that multiculturalism, as seen in today's public schools, is a necessary adaptation to the growing pluralism of our society. The New York City public school system at the turn of the century was incredibly pluralistic. New York was the point of entry for all of the Southern and Eastern European immigrant groups that, at the time, were regarded as foreign and bizarre as are today's Asian and Latino groups. The main difference was that back then nobody believed that the government should celebrate and keep alive the native cultures [of arriving immigrants].[5]

As do other assimilation advocates, Fukuyama distinguishes between multiculturalism as a fact and as an ideology. Multiculturalism is a fact because of the surge of immigrants coming mostly from non-European nations. The word *multiculturalism* is also used as an ideology that is rooted in the notion of cultural relativism; as such it insists on the equality of all cultures. Proponents of multiculturalism ideology take the principle of equality, historically applied to individuals, and apply that principle to the cultures represented by America's new immigrants. In their view, American and western civilization must not be viewed as having contributed more, or anything better, than any other nation or civilization. America's educational and political institutions, they say, must be transformed with policies that are in alignnment with this view. Understandably, assimilationists strenuously object.

Because of his conviction that common national identity must be rooted in common national history and that immigrants should learn that history, Fukuyama writes:

George Washington, Thomas Jefferson, and Abraham Lincoln can serve as equally relevant heroes to the children of Asian and Hispanic immigrants today as they did for the children of Italian, Slavic, and Jewish immigrants at the turn of the century. Our goal must be to return our entire society to the values of individual liberty, community spirit, and personal self-reliance that once characterized the American spirit, drawing from the traditions of the Western frontier and Ellis Island.[6]

The Multicultural Model

The most commonly promoted view in current American society is the multicultural model. This perspective seems to facilitate productive interactions in a pluralistic society. The individual in the nondominant group "maintains some degree of cultural integrity while at the same time seeking to participate as an integral part of the larger social network."[7] The larger society benefits from the interactions with and contributions of the various cultural groups in its midst.

The benefits of cultural pluralism are seen to far outweigh the fact that there is no precedent in history of a multiethnic society that has worked. "Heterogeneous empires that lasted, such as the Eastern Roman Empire of Byzantium, which survived until 1453, were generally based on a core ethnic group."[8] In other words, there existed a significant dominant culture group, in this case Greek, which enabled the multiethnic empire to succeed. Peter Brimelow, in his work *Alien Nation*, cites numerous examples of modern societies that split into multiple ethnic components.[9] One example is Czechoslovakia, which was founded in 1918 and split into Czech and Slovak ethnic components in 1993. Another example is the Soviet Union, founded in 1922 and in 1991 split into multiple ethnic nations, some of which are experiencing further ethnic fragmentation. Canada, a multicultural nation, exists in a state of uncertainty as the French culture, dominant in Quebec, continues to push away from the Anglo dominant culture of the rest of the country. Apparently, when a nondominant culture group within the larger culture maintains its separate cultural identity, the possibility of division increases.

Brimelow contends that, in the past, the United States has been relatively successful at bringing together moderately diverse immigrant groups. "But this relative American success did not amount to a Declaration of Independence from history. It depended on time, numbers, degree of difference . . . and, above all, on some very specific policies, like 'Americanization,' which tended to swamp all difference with a common American civic culture."[10] It appears that today in the United States getting diverse cultural groups to live in harmony as one nation is more and more difficult, especially with the substantial abandonment of policies that promoted assimilation and the increasing numbers of immigrants, particularly those from cultures with little similarity to Western culture. If multiculturalism, as defined by the ideology that is rooted in cultural pluralism, has never been seen to work in any society, it is clearly unable to provide the consensus for an American common identity.

Four Personal Strategies for Intercultural Relations

Positive intercultural relations can be most successful—at the individual level—when people from the nondominant group have the freedom to choose and adjust their preference of interaction. To make full use of this freedom, an individual needs to understand the issues that drive the choice of a strategy. Berry maintains that the immigrant must consider two issues: (1) Does he or she value maintaining his or her identity and customs? (2) Does the individual value maintaining relationships with the larger society?[11] How the individual responds to these two issues determines the model of cultural group relations that will be adopted. Different strategies may be employed depending on the domain of location (for example, whether they are at work, with their family, or with their own ethnic group). Berry suggests four strategies that result from the various combinations of responses to the preceding two issues.[12]

Assimilation

In the assimilation strategy, individuals in the nondominant group minimize their cultural identity and desire daily interaction with the dominant culture. Individuals may feel forced to choose this strategy to prosper according to the norms of the larger society. Immigrants who acquire advanced degrees in education or who rise in social status may desire to distance themselves publicly from their ethnic group while privately retaining family ties. This personal tension is epitomized in a young Asian woman pursuing a career in medicine. After completing the requirements of her internship on the East Coast, she struggles with whether to return to where her parents live on the West Coast. Family loyalty pulls her west; career aspirations tell her to settle in the east. West means cultural confinement; east means being free in the land of the free.

Separation

When people use the separation strategy, they value their cultural integrity and choose to avoid interaction with other cultural groups. As in the case of assimilation, separation may be the strategy of choice, but when it is required by the dominant society, it is called segregation.

One of my relatives lived for forty years in one of our states in the northeast. She knew a few words of English but never felt a need to know more because her own ethnic community had the grocery stores, medical doctors, and other services necessary for a good life. When she retired from the factory where she worked, she moved back to her country of origin to live out her retirement years. For her, separation was the strategy of choice. Through it she accomplished her goals while retaining a certain degree of comfort.

Integration

In integration, people are free to pursue both assimilation and separation. Individuals in the nondominant group prefer to retain their own cultural identity while actively participating in the larger society. Many first-generation immigrants, such as my parents, choose this strategy. They fully engage in the uniqueness and benefits of their birth culture as well as in their adopted culture and community.

Marginalization

In marginalization, individuals lack either the opportunity or interest in maintaining their own cultural identity and similarly lack the opportunity for or interest in interacting with the larger culture. Marginalization typically occurs as a result of forced assimilation along with forced exclusion, or segregation. For example, an elementary or junior high student rides the school bus because she has no other option. Kids make fun of her non-American features and clothes. As she grows older, she wants desperately to be accepted by Americans and rejects social contact with her own ethnic group to achieve her goal. She realizes over time, however, that she is accepted by neither group and rejected by both. She joins a gang of similarly culturally rejected people.

A New Model: Mutual Accommodation

Returning to a strict assimilation policy (the mainstream-minority model), as practiced in the past, would probably not be successful in today's environment. On the other hand, multiculturalism does not seem to be viable, primarily because it has proved to be counterproductive in terms of national cohesiveness. Bringing together the necessary elements of assimilation and the benefits of integration could provide a more credible picture of a successful multiethnic society.

The necessary elements of assimilation, described below as the core values of American society, help ensure a national commitment to *e pluribus unum.* Integration potentially benefits everyone in that all parties gain (1) the ability to form and work toward common community values utilizing the strengths of different cultural perspectives, (2) the flexibility of assessing issues and concerns from a variety of viewpoints, and (3) the personal enjoyment of satisfaction of creating a new cultural entity that improves life for all members of the organization. This blending of assimilation and integration can be achieved through mutual accommodation. The concept of mutual accommodation is twofold: Nondominant cultural groups *adopt* the core values of the larger society, while, simultaneously, the dominant group purposes to *adapt* its resources for the well-being of the cultural groups living together in the plural society.[13] The power of mutual accommodation lies in its process. As a diverse community engages in a healthy give-and-take, the negative bias of ethnocentrism is significantly minimized. Breaking down of walls makes way for building relationships.

What are the core values of American society that nondominant cultural groups should adopt? Peter Salins identifies these core values as three precepts to which, historically, all immigrants agreed. "Assimilation, American style, set out a simple contract between the existing settlers and all newcomers. Immigrants would be welcome as full members of the American family if they agreed to abide by three simple precepts."[14] (For Salins, assimilation is synonymous with the mutual accommodation model.)

1. *English as the national language.* Cultural unity was built on the foundation of one primary language. A unified nation was composed of citizens sharing knowledge and understanding in one common language.
2. *Pride in their identity as Americans and a firm belief in the principles of America's liberal democracy and the notion of egalitarianism.* Civic unity and national pride were sustained through faith in the validity and importance of the American democratic system.
3. *Commitment to the Protestant ethic (to be self-reliant, hardworking, and morally upright).* The uniqueness of this work ethic united all Americans, regardless of individual ethnicity, in that each able person contributed to the well-being of the nation.

How does the dominant group adapt its resources for the well-being of all culture groups? The Government Printing Office once printed a

U.S. Department of Labor poster (that I found in an antique store in South Carolina and is now hanging in my office) that described one way in which this aspect of mutual accommodation was accomplished. The poster reads as follows:

> The United States Government and the Public Schools are helping our Foreign-Born Friends who are Applicants for AMERICAN CITIZENSHIP to Learn Our Language and the Principles of Our Government in Preparation for Good Citizenship.
> The Government Furnishes Free Textbooks.
> ENROLL NOW

The poster was signed by James J. Davis, Secretary of Labor, Richard K. Campbell, Commissioner of Naturalization, and Raymond F. Crist, Director of Citizenship.

In all likelihood, the signers of the Department of Labor poster were adapting U.S. resources in the attempt to Americanize immigrants and facilitate the process of assimilation. Mutual accommodation, as a concept, was not in vogue during the 1930s. Nevertheless, the offer made was a legitimate effort to adapt the nation's resources for the benefit of the immigrant population.

Mutual accommodation does not naturally happen between cultures in a civic, political, or religious environment. In these environments, those of the dominant culture may adapt their resources to minority groups, as did the Department of Labor, and minority groups may adopt ways of the dominant culture. Yet these actions may simply reflect the dominant culture's desire to facilitate assimilation and the minority group's desire to thrive in mainstream society. The true spirit of mutual accommodation takes place only when those involved believe that creating a new corporate entity of mixed elements is of higher value than maintaining an entity of a single element. Marriage in the Christian tradition is a form of mutual accommodation. Christian couples understand the biblical statement, "and they will become one," (Gen. 2:24) as not only prescriptive of what God expects of their marriage but as also descriptive of the process in becoming one. Public high schools write policies and implement programs that utilize corporate resources to enable all cultural groups to move toward the goal of oneness. An increasing number of churches, as described in other chapters, have committed themselves to the model of mutual accommodation.

Joel Kotkin adds another dimension to our understanding of how assimilation is possible: Immigrants must adopt the shared values of their new country of citizenship. In citing the successes of Canada and Australia as open, multiracial societies, Joel Kotkin demonstrates how the onus of beginning the process of mutual accommodation rests with those of the dominant culture.

> All these places have been made possible by Anglo-Saxon ideas about the rule of law, fair play, and due process. Without those, you can't have a multiracial society. So no matter who comes or what happens, we have to hold onto this fundamentally Anglo-Saxon culture.[15]

These thoughts reiterate the importance of not allowing these core ideas to be lost through a fragmented-by-ethnicity society.

The dominant culture adapts its values to the immigrant communities by using its power and influence to ensure that these communities are not victimized or used as scapegoats; instead, they are given equal treatment in the rule of law, fair play, and due process of law. Maintaining the dominant culture while ensuring the possibility of integration of immigrants into that culture benefits the entire society. The contact with Anglo-Saxon culture along with individualism and communal responsibility help liberate the potential of all immigrant minorities.[16]

Immigrants need to understand mutual accommodation to become successfully integrated. Though multiculturalism is part of how they see themselves becoming American,[17] and though the dominant culture needs multiculturalism to focus its attention on the important contribution that each cultural group brings to the larger society, the central value of integration cannot be laid aside. For mutual accommodation to take place, the intent must be for all immigrants to integrate into the national and community culture, taking the best of America's culture and blending it with the best of their own.

The Choices Facing the Church in a Culturally Pluralistic Society

The church, a culture of its own within the larger society, struggles as well with its orientation toward society's dominant culture. The church continually strives to maintain its biblical identity as it interacts with the (increasingly hostile) dominant culture. America's increased cultural pluralism has given a new challenge to the church. As an institutional part of the dominant culture, the church must prepare itself to be involved in the process of mutual accommodation. It must begin to adapt its programs and resources to serve the needs of the various cultural groups in its community. The minority groups, in turn, must be open to adopting the practices of the church family, as they attempt to integrate into its culture.

Ethnic newcomers who desire to become part of a local church face the same issues stated previously: To what degree do they prefer maintaining their cultural identity? To what degree do they value relationships with the larger church family? In the same way, the church interacts with these same issues: How important is maintaining church traditions? To what extent are relationships with the various cultural groups valued? How churches respond to these questions determines the model of church fellowship that they choose.

The Dominant-Culture Church

Operating under a strict mainstream-minority model, the dominant-culture church views immigrants as "not really part of us." The dominant-culture church, composed primarily of a traditional American population, believes that the primary method of reaching the nations is by sending to them full-time vocational missionaries. Insofar as reaching the immigrants permanently living in its community, a dominant-culture church unconsciously opts to protect its homogeneity by supporting designated home missionaries who feel called to reach ethnic minorities and start ethnic churches. Dominant-culture churches have little understanding of, or interest in, the function of integration. These churches are oriented toward the separation strategy; they may unknowingly practice segregation by simply doing nothing to welcome the culturally diverse into their church life.

The Multicongregation Church

The multicongregation church is one in which interaction between various ethnic groups varies. Often the multicongregation church begins when an ethnic church makes a request to a dominant-culture church for permission to use its facilities for a meeting place. The dominant-culture church feels obligated to grant permission because of its commitment to the Great Commission. Over time, other ethnically different churches may make similar requests of the same church. Because ownership of the church property is in the possession of the dominant-culture church, it becomes, in effect, a landlord church.[18]

Interdependence between ethnic churches meeting in the same building is normally held at a minimum level; each group is primarily concerned with its own development as a self-governing, self-sustaining, and self-propagating unit. The lack of interaction along with the separation of each cultural group from the larger group has inherent potential for intergroup conflict and resentment.

Another version of a multicongregation church is a blend of the integration and separation strategies. Leaders from the different ethnic congregations see themselves as one church and meet as one staff. Church property is mutually owned. Church policies and programs, decided on by the staff and board, are determined by their mutual benefit to all congregations. Congregations meet separately, except for an occasional mutual celebration event. The First Baptist Church of Flushing, New York, is an example of this version.

The Interethnic Church Celebration

In the interethnic church celebration model, ethnic churches are separate entities that periodically engage in interethnic fellowship experiences. Ethnic churches plan combined services and activities with other ethnic or dominant-culture churches. Fellowship occurs through mutual presentations of music, teachings from God's Word, food, and prayers. In the interethnic celebration model, ethnic churches may or may not have a leasing arrangement with a dominant-culture church.

The Ethnic-Specific Church

Ethnic-specific churches value their cultural integrity and choose to avoid interaction with other cultural groups. These churches can be any group that establishes, nourishes, and multiplies itself in the ethnolinguistic context of the people.[19] The unique nature of each ethnolinguistic church is due to a universal developmental process common to all: Their respective languages have influenced their culture and their culture has influened their language. The common resultant culture of each people group provides a deep sense of belonging. Ethnic-specific churches clearly choose separation as their strategy of orientation toward the dominant culture. Because of the large number of first-generation ethnic populations in the United States, evangelical organizations and denominations are making concerted efforts to establish ethnic-specific churches. Because of the dedication of first-generation immigrants to their own cultural heritage, the best way to reach them is in their own language.

Probably the most widespread ethnic-specific church in our country is the African American church. Unlike many other ethnic-specific churches (such as Hispanic or Korean churches) African American churches worship in English, but, like their ethnic counterparts, they have a culture, history, spiritual heritage, and expression of faith that is uniquely theirs.

The Dominant-Culture Church with a Multicultural Fellowship

A dominant-culture church may begin a multicultural fellowship to meet the needs of a specific group of immigrants. A team of church members leads this ministry. Names used to designate this fellowship may be People of the World Fellowship, Fellowship of All Nations, or, simply, International Bible Fellowship. Churches typically choose one immigrant group (see a sample listing below) on which to focus its ministry.

1. Refugees
2. Foreign graduate students at the local university and/or their spouses
3. Immigrant children in an apartment complex
4. Ethnic entrepreneurs: owners of small businesses, such as cleaners, restaurants, taxicab companies, computer sales
5. Immigrant professionals, including doctors, lawyers, professors, information system analysts, software developers
6. Migrant workers: short-term laborers for harvest seasons or construction projects
7. Short-term specialists: personnel working with international organizations such as the World Bank or hired by the U.S. government for highly specialized jobs or military or embassy employees
8. A specific ethnic group, such as Laotians, Mexicans, Brazilians, or Iranians
9. Non-Americans who do not speak English well, or not at all, and who need ESL training
10. Practitioners of world religions, such as Muslims, Buddhists, Hindus

The era of cross-cultural ministry professionals as the primary means of reaching nontraditional Americans is giving way to another reality. A grassroots movement is spreading in which lay Christians are mobilizing to spread the gospel among the many categories of ethnic groups in our nation. One couple has been active among an extremely unfamiliar group—Buddhist monks.

You probably cannot name a missionary who is reaching Buddhist monks in the Thai temples found throughout the United States. Because the Buddhist monastic world is such an intimidating unknown, most Christians would socially distance themselves from it. I still remember the shock I felt at seeing Buddhist monks strolling along at Andrews Air Force Base. The combination of saffron robes, shaved heads, and sandals just seemed out of place in a military setting. Indeed, the world monks live in seems worlds apart from the rest of American society.

Judy and Brent are not professional full-time Christian workers. She is a flight attendant, and he works for the National Park Service. But for the past five years they have ministered to Thai Buddhist monks who live in their community. Monks are now reading the Scripture and learning the Christian faith. How did such an outreach come about through lay believers? Judy's journey, as she records it below, is a model and an encouragement to follow God's unique path for each of us as we engage in intercultural evangelism.

"Like Thomas in John 20, I have always been a doubter. Not that I doubted that God existed, rather, that God is good. I have had an ever-present fear that maybe God was not the loving Father I longed him to be. I continually looked for indicators, if you will, that God was good and pursues people in love. Yet, when I would stumble on evidence, I immediately devised rationales as to why it could not be so.

"It is ironic that God would use Thai monks to teach me that he is good. It is not their exotic customs or the Buddhist worldview that show me this. Instead, it is that I see God disclosing himself to monks in undeniable ways. Their entire worldview adamantly teaches that God does not exist. Yet many of them are seeking God, though they have never been predisposed to thinking that there even is a God. In fact many wrestle with the worldview they have been taught. For me, this is an indicator that God is real.

"When I listen to the questions that God places in the heart of a monk or observe how God will strategically place his people in a monk's path, I can no longer deny that God discloses himself to people. In fact, as I watch the monks, I see that God enters their world. He woos them. He calls them out of bondage and into light. At times, when I go to the temple, the thought comes to me like a flashing neon sign, *Look, Judy, I am working to seek and save the lost; yes, even here in a Buddhist temple!* When I see the hand of a sovereign God working so specifically, my doubt is replaced with confidence that God is good and he loves people. Here is my story.

"In 1996 I was a volunteer ESL teacher at my church. Three Thai Buddhist monks in their saffron robes came to our program. I remember well that they seemed misplaced. I wanted them to feel welcome so I eagerly approached them and shook their hands, never once noticing that they were backing away from me. (Only later did I learn that touching monks was forbidden for women. They would teach me many things in the coming years. They still laugh about the teacher who didn't know the rules!) They were placed in my class. I was so excited. I knew nothing about their world. I couldn't wait to discover who they were.

"That semester the ESL director and I visited the temple as a goodwill gesture from the church and the community. The gracious welcome we received overwhelmed me. I was stunned. They wanted us there. In fact they wondered why in thirteen years no one from the local church had come to visit. I was ashamed for I had no answer. That night I could not get out of my mind that no Christians had attempted to befriend monks at that temple. Why? How many Thai temples existed in the United States? It seemed so wrong that Christians were not reaching out to them. I determined that I would go back! I wanted to be a part of their world and I wanted them to be a part of mine.

"My husband and I began drinking tea with the monks, having them in our home for butter pecan ice cream, and visiting the temple. The monks liked visiting local sights and learning about American culture. Before I knew it, a friendship had grown. Suddenly I found myself celebrating their birthdays, sending them cards, having them in for the holidays. I would go in the evenings and pray as they chanted. I kept asking that God would open the eyes of their hearts.

"After praying for them every day for two years, on January 27, 1998, they came to my home for a Bible study. Before that we only on occasion talked about the things of God. The Bible study lasted only one month with them coming every week to learn about Christianity and I going once a week to the temple for instruction in Buddhism. I do not know why they decided to come for that window of time, but I do know that they came because of prayer. I have since had many discussions about Jesus Christ with them through my ESL classes in the temple.

"In 1999, a pivotal year for me, I enrolled in a Capital Bible Seminary class taught by Dr. Joe Henriques. That course, 'Intercultural Relations in a Multicultural Society,' took my fascination for a people group to another level. Before the class, I never knew how to intentionally organize fellow believers to reach out to the ninety-two Thai temples in the United States. Dr. Henriques taught me how to mobilize Christians to go into the temples. My husband and I established Befriending Buddhists, a ministry that links Christians with local temples. Suddenly I saw that others could have the pleasure I was experiencing as I shared my love for Christ with the monks.

"God opened the door for me to teach English at the largest of the three Thai temples in my area. This was an answer to prayer. God was beginning to move me into new places and spheres of influence. My research revealed that there are fifteen hundred Buddhist (not just Thai) temples nationwide. The opportunities to influence others for this ministry were increased through workshops that I presented at the Overseas

Missionary Fellowship National Conference in San Francisco. The conference placed me in contact with people much like myself who are eager to share the Lord Jesus with those Buddhist monks, and other Buddhists, that God has brought here. Now it seems as if new opportunities are opening. I am excited about all of the possibilities presenting themselves.

"So this five-year journey has increased my faith. I am certain that I can trust God with my life because he is the author of it all. I have no more fears that his character is anything less than perfect goodness. Psalm 139:15–16 declares, 'My frame was not hidden from you when I was made in the secret place. When I was woven together in the depths of the earth, your eyes saw my unformed body. All the days ordained for me were written in your book before one of them came to be.' God in eternity past knew that I would come into this world. He knew I would be enchanted with the monks and that he would use me in the temple. He knew that I would so desperately want to live for him and yet would feel so inadequate; therefore, I am so encouraged that he has promised that he will never leave me nor forsake me and that he will use me for his purposes."

Traditionally, the notion of being separate from the world is defined, in part, as avoiding situations of potential spiritual contamination. For some Christians, such situations would include entering into a mosque, temple, or any other non-Christian environment or worship. In addition, it is considered unwise, if not unthinkable, to be taught the precepts of another religion, from a teacher of that religion in the very place of its practice. Judy's exuberance for her experience of having done so would not be shared by many in the church. Yet her concern is that if the Lord's people do not enter into the Buddhist's world, they will rarely influence Buddhist monks with the gospel of Jesus Christ.

Can the tension between these two views be resolved? Perhaps. Christians could agree to disagree and suspend judgment indefinitely for those of the opposite view. Or Christians could recognize, encourage, and applaud the calling and gifting of those who are divinely appointed to enter the worlds of the non-Christian. Either position grants freedom for those who are called to this ministry to participate fully in their calling. As Peter was called to the Jews, Paul to the Gentiles, so—we would conclude—Judy is called to the Buddhists, Samuel to the Muslims, and Sarah to the Hindus.

The Multicultural Church

The leadership of a multicultural church is committed to intentional heterogeneity at all levels of the church. This commitment is clearly described in its philosophy of ministry, values, mission, vision, goals, objectives, and strategic plan, which have been developed by a diverse leadership team. Integration of cultures is made possible through emphasis on the common identity all members have in Christ.

It is not uncommon for a church to mistakenly consider itself multicultural because, as I have been told not a few times, "a few internationals are attending our services." Yet a church must meet qualitative and quantitative measures to qualify as multicultural. In terms of the *quantitative* measure, a church must have a significant percentage of its membership composed of various ethnic groups.[20] A church with two races or cultures—such as black and white—would be simply that, biracial or bicultural, and would not by definition be considered multicultural. Manuel Ortiz cites the International Bible Church in Los Angeles as an example of one that meets the quantitative measure as it is composed of "Anglos, American Indians, Asian Indians, Blacks, Chinese, Guatemalans, Filipinos, Koreans, Mexicans, Salvadorans, Russians, Taiwanese, Thais and Ukrainians."[21] The *qualitative* measure of a multicultural church includes the equal distribution of majority and minority leadership throughout the church and the ethnic diversity of its music programs, its teaching styles, and its application of Scripture.

The importance of developing multicultural churches or fellowships in America's current cultural milieu cannot be overstated. Present-day examples of thriving heterogeneous churches are described throughout the book, and one key model is presented in chapter 9.

A multicultural church can be developed in at least three ways:

1. Starting a church with the intention that its membership reflect both the dominant culture and the ethnic groups of its community. Church members would speak English and would desire and be adept at integrating within a multicultural community of believers.
2. Establishing a multicultural fellowship within the context of a dominant-culture church. The assumption is that the intercultural interactions that will naturally occur will gradually influence the church at large to adopt a multicultural philosophy of ministry.
3. Transitioning from a dominant-culture church or an ethnic-specific church into a multicultural one. To achieve their goal, both churches would need to subscribe to two values: (1) English as the community language and (2) commitment to the process of becoming a multicultural church.

Admittedly, many church leaders doubt that their church could transition from a homogeneous to a multicultural, or heterogeneous, entity for two primary reasons: It is neither desirable nor doable. A quick response would be that it is God who works in us both to give us the willingness to do and the ability to do his good purpose (Phil. 2:13). If God's purpose for a church is to become multicultural, it is then possible for that church to do so.

A more complete response to leaders who doubt the advisability of becoming multicultural is addressed in the account below of how a national leader is leading his organization through the transitioning process.

It is interesting to note that while the church agonizes over, or ignores, the issue of becoming multicultural, other institutions and organizations in the United States do not have the same luxury of noncommitment. Can we imagine a public school or the military not dealing with the issues and concerns of integration of a diverse population?

As a chaplain and officer (Lt. Col.) in the United States Air Force/Air National Guard (ANG), I have witnessed firsthand how a national, basically homogeneous organization is able to achieve ethnic diversity in its membership. Maj. Gen. Paul Weaver (current ANG director) has exercised effective leadership in promoting organizational diversity as the right thing to do and the smart thing to do.

Weaver believes it is wrong to exclude any American—regardless of color or culture—from full participation in one of America's most vital military components. Diversity is the smart thing, Weaver points out, in that it is not wise to remain predominantly Caucasian-led while U.S. demographics clearly reveal the trend toward a minority-majority population, meaning that the majority of the population will be comprised of minority groups. The present dominant group will eventually become one of the many minorities.

General Weaver rejects nurturing the status quo in the Air National Guard. Why? Because he sees the emerging new America. He firmly believes that for the ANG to be a viable, strong, and thriving organization in twenty years, it is imperative to educate its members now in cultural differences. He has created a sense of urgency for ANG units to begin recruiting, retaining, and preparing personnel from all ethnic groups for leadership positions throughout the organization.

From its very inception, I have been involved as a facilitator and instructor in the ANG Workforce Diversity Initiative. Many times I have thought how the Lord's people, especially church and organizational leaders, could have benefited from the exciting vision and effective educational process as promoted in the several conferences I have attended.

The ANG has a strategic plan by which each unit can develop an organizational culture of diversity. The plan has eight focus areas and a total of fourteen goals. I have rephrased that plan in terminology that applies to the church. A basic overview of the plan is shown below. The complete version, with accompanying objectives for each goal, is found in the appendix.

Dr. Samuel Betances, a key figure in the ANG educational process, powerfully points out in his lectures that recruiters recruit but organizational culture retains. What is true for the ANG is also true for the church. A church may reach out to the ethnically diverse, but when those people enter the church, will they find a welcoming, hospitable, and inclusive environment? The ANG strategic plan can be a useful tool toward this end.

Focus Areas, Goals, and Objectives for the Local Church to Reach and Reflect the Diverse Population of Its Community

Accountability and Responsibility

Goal 1: Pastors and staff will be held accountable for creating an environment that fosters diversity, acceptance of all cultural, racial, or ethnic groups.

Goal 2: All members will be responsible for understanding and promoting diversity.

Education and Training

Goal 3: Everyone in the church will be provided appropriate training in diversity.

Goal 4: Church members will participate in community outreach programs to reach and prepare the culturally diverse for church membership.

Path of Christian Ministry

Goal 5: The pastor will ensure that every church member, regardless of ethnicity, has access to training and mentoring for Christian ministry in a multicultural environment.

Leadership Policy

Goal 6: The church will review and update church policies to ensure that a culture of diversity is being practiced in every aspect of church life.

Goal 7: The issues of diversity will be reviewed and emphasized when planning and conducting conferences and other special meetings within the church.

Community

Goal 8: Enhanced community relations and media advertising will be used to increase positive perception of the church's commitment to diversity.

Goal 9: Church members will actively participate in local events, youth activities, youth mentoring, and other outreach programs among whites, minorities, and all ethnic groups in the community to establish and enhance community relationships and partnerships.

Outreach and Discipleship

Goal 10: The church will establish a five-year marketing and communication plan that addresses the church's openness to racially, culturally, and ethnically diverse people.

Goal 11: The church members involved in outreach and discipleship programs will reflect the diversity of the minorities and ethnic groups in the community.

Goal 12: The church will establish a highly visible outreach and service presence in minority and ethnic communities.

Measurement

Goal 13: The church will develop, deploy, and periodically review an effective system to measure and communicate progress on the goals of diversity.

Funding

Goal 14: The church will provide sufficient funding in support of the programs and efforts of diversity throughout the church.

Summary

In his book *Finding God in Unexpected Places,* Phillip Yancey retells John S. Dunne's story of early Spanish sailors who reach the continent of South America after a long, hard voyage:

The caravan sailed into the headwaters of the Amazon, an expanse of water so wide, the sailors presumed it to be a continuation of the Atlantic Ocean. It never occurred to them to drink the water, since they expected it to be saline, and as a result, some of the sailors died of thirst. In their case, they were actually seeing what they were looking for. They failed to connect with that water.[22]

This tragic scene is but a metaphor describing churches that are looking for ways to have better missions conferences in the hopes of fulfilling the Great Commission; yet they have no intention of connecting with the ethnically diverse people who actually live in their communities.

The church that desires both growth through service and evangelism in a multicultural society and honor as a relevant institution must plunge into the world of nations that God has brought to our communities. Such determination is in keeping with Paul's prayer that "the message of the Lord may spread rapidly and be honored" (2 Thess. 3:1).

Discussion Starters

1. With your group, identify the strategy of involvement you as individuals have practiced in relation to people from other ethnic groups. Have each person explain why this strategy was chosen.
2. Now consider your church's strategy of involvement with your ethnically diverse community. Why was this strategy chosen? Is it effective in that it fully utilizes your resources and makes the most of your opportunities?
3. Review the last section, on focus areas, goals, and objectives. Could such an approach to becoming multicultural work in your church? What would it take for this kind of plan to be fully implemented?

7

Conversing about Christ

Joseph Henriques

He opened their minds so they could understand the Scriptures.

Luke 24:45

Those with the clearest view of the future are often most free to do their best work. They work with singularity of purpose, like the horse heading back to the barn after a hard day's ride, undeterred by streams to cross or mountains to climb. To obtain such a view, some people even go to the last chapter first when reading a book. From the vantage point of knowing the end result, they claim they are at liberty to enjoy the book, deal with any suspense, and objectively analyze the development of the plot. Francis Schaeffer said that ancient Chinese theater operated in a similar fashion. The audience watched the development of the play on two levels. On the upper-level stage actors performed the play from the middle to the conclusion of the story. On the lower level the play progressed from the beginning to the middle. Fully engaged in the unfolding drama, spectators would call out to the actors on the lower level, telling them what to say and what to decide based on the future they saw developing on the upper level.

By allowing the apostle John to record his vision of the people who would some day contribute to the glory and grandeur of heaven, God gave us a powerful "upper-level" picture to stimulate our best work in evangelism.

> There before me was a great multitude that no one could count, from every nation, tribe, people and language, standing before the throne and in front of the Lamb [saying], "Salvation belongs to our God, who sits on the throne, and to the Lamb" (Rev. 7:9–10).

> The nations will walk by [the Lord's] light, and the kings of the earth will bring their splendor into [the city]. . . . The glory and honor of the nations will be brought into it (Rev. 21:24, 26).

This picture enables us to have a high, futuristic view of our quest to bring the message of God's love in Christ to our immigrant population. The higher we climb, the more clearly we see. The focus shifts away from our inadequacies and anxieties toward a vision of every immigrant in America as a potential member of God's future world. We picture our Russian and African neighbors singing praises to God and contributing to the splendor and glory of heaven. Even while conversing with our Iranian schoolmates or Indian coworkers, we value them as people that God loves, we imagine them welcomed by Jesus himself into the beauty of his eternal kingdom. Keeping our eyes at this level enables us to endure all the challenges of any multicultural endeavor, enduring, like Paul, everything for the sake of the elect. Bringing joy to God's heart by leading people to heaven was all Paul lived for. He lived on the lower level of his sufferings, but his focus was on the highest level possible, combining every act of evangelism with eternal worship. Insofar as his ministry of proclaiming the gospel of God was concerned, he believed that the Gentiles who came to Christ were his "offering acceptable to God" (Rom. 15:16). In the same verse we read that Paul equated his role of an evangelist with that of a priest, calling himself a *leitourgos* (from which we get our English word *liturgy*), whose primary role was to serve God through worship. For Paul, evangelism *was* worship. It was worship that inspired Paul to assume personal responsibility that God's throne would never lack for a multinational congregation of worshipers.

Three Dimensions of Conversing with Others about Christ

Many Christians will concede the wide gap between their desire to see people of every color and culture represented in God's kingdom and their active effort in guiding people to the kingdom gates. Something as basic as conversation can be an important part of the solution in closing that gap. I am not referring to pointless small talk or to mere pleasantries in conversation but rather to dialogue.

Dialoguing with others has the clear purposes of *penetration* and *permeation*. For penetration we use the skill of inquiry to understand another's thoughts about God. Permeation speaks to our firm intention to fill another's mind with the knowledge of God. We engage in each aspect of dialogue with great care: meting out the right measure of information at the right time, in the right place, in the right way. Knowing how to dialogue with others in this fashion is a skill that we can use to help many non-Christians understand and believe the good news of Jesus Christ.

Dialogue—literally meaning to talk things through, to reason with another—is introduced in this chapter with three dimensions: conversational, informational, and rational. In the next chapter I will explain in detail how these three dimensions of dialogue can be used to win people to Christ. Greater attention will be devoted to conversational and informational dialogue because they are new techniques, unique to this book. Conversational dialogue is a method of conversing about Christ to determine what a person knows about him. Informational dialogue is a simple-to-master outline for explaining God to a non-Christian. Rational dialogue receives a brief treatment, as it is already a well-defined discipline with many available resources. Each dimension intellectually and emotionally stimulates non-Christians to receive truths about God that are yet unknown to them or have not been satisfactorily explained.

Conversational Dialogue

The first dimension, conversational dialogue, does not require that you be an expert in another person's religious beliefs. Through inquiry, you discover what a person truly believes, not necessarily what his religion tells him to believe. Every person has a public stage presentation designed to keep others from taking a peek backstage. The skillful use of conversational dialogue enables you to know the answer to, What's going on behind the scenes?

At the outset, I must explain that I am not advocating ecumenical dialogue. While speaking at a church, I mentioned the excellent opportunity that my Survey of World Religions class had in going to a Buddhist temple to learn about the symbols and objects of their worship, observe their chanting, and dialogue with them about faith. After the service, the pastor said to me, "When I heard you say that you were dialoguing faith with Buddhists, I thought to myself, *Oh, Joe, what are you getting into now?*"

It is not unusual for the word *dialogue,* when used in the context of faith groups, to stimulate mental images of Jewish rabbis, Buddhist monks, Hindu priests, Catholic cardinals, and Protestant clergy in their robes and regalia gathering to create common understanding, minimize differences, and promulgate a new religious agreement that would facilitate collaboration for the common good of humankind. Evangelicals view much of ecumenical dialogue as a futile exercise in which important issues are set aside as irrelevant. Nevertheless, there is general agreement that interreligious dialogue can be helpful when societal matters of common interest are clarified and, perhaps, otherwise unlikely allies join forces on issues of mutual concern.

Informational Dialogue

Informational dialogue, the second dimension of our conversation about Christ, flows naturally out of successful conversational dialogue. At an unexpected moment you are given the opportunity, that is, someone specifically asks you to state what you believe about God and the gospel of Christ. In the process of doing so, you state your beliefs in such a way that you are indirectly refuting what you now know your friend believes. This particular schematic for presenting God is modeled after Paul's discourse in Acts 17:22–31. As you talk about your faith, you are hoping to give enough reason for it that others will be persuaded to believe. Conversational dialogue is meant to open a person to reveal his true feelings and thoughts; informational dialogue stands in line to supply, on request, straightforward statements of personal belief. The anticipation is that the way has been prepared for the third dimension, rational dialogue.

Rational Dialogue

Rational dialogue is apologetics. Apologetics defends faith. Coming from the Greek word, *apologia,* it means giving a reason in the sense of giving a defense. "Always be prepared," Peter instructs, "to give an answer to everyone who asks you to give the reason for the hope that you have" (1 Peter 3:15). Peter makes it clear that apologetics is a natural extension of Christ being Lord of our lives. Norman Geisler, in the *Baker Encyclopedia of Christian Apologetics,* comments, "If he is really Lord, then we should be obedient to him as 'we demolish arguments and every pretension that sets itself up against the knowledge of God, and we take captive every thought to make it obedient to Christ' (2 Cor. 10:5). This means we should confront issues in our own minds and in the expressed thoughts of others that prevent us and them from knowing God. That is what apologetics is all about."[1]

Within the development of a friendship relationship, dialogue would normally follow the progression of conversational to informational to rational. However, to think that this approach to dialogue is as predictable as following the path from first, second, and third base is to strike out when the bases are loaded! The person with whom you are in dialogue is like the pitcher who varies his pitching style, sometimes a fast ball over the plate, at other times a curve ball. You must respond accordingly. In real-world conversations, dialogue is actually more like an atom encased in a swirling, three-part hemisphere.

Attitudes That Convey Validity of Truth

Of equal importance to the process of dialoguing faith is the attitude we convey while doing it. The spirit of gentleness, respect, kindness, and patience reveals Christ as much as the message.

> But in your hearts set apart Christ as Lord. Always be prepared to give an answer to everyone who asks you to give the reason for the hope that you have. But do this with gentleness and respect, keeping a clear conscience, so that those who speak maliciously against your good behavior in Christ may be ashamed of their slander (1 Peter 3:15, 16).

> Don't have anything to do with foolish and stupid arguments, because you know they produce quarrels. And the Lord's servant must not quarrel; instead, he must be kind to everyone, able to teach, not resentful. Those who oppose him he must gently instruct, in the hope that God will grant them repentance leading them to a knowledge of the truth, and that they will come to their senses and escape from the trap of the devil, who has taken them captive to do his will (2 Tim. 2:23–26).

In these instructions we can sense the spirit of Christ, the master teacher, who was also a master of dialogue. His two-way conversation with the disciples on the Emmaus road after the resurrection is a masterpiece of dialogue (Luke 24:13–32). Their own reaction to this opportunity to converse with Christ was, "Were not our hearts burning within us while he talked with us on the road?" Conversational dialogue was a key characteristic in the New Testament—there's ample reason to use it today.

Worldviews that are as far apart as the East is from the West do not dictate the same distance between adherents. Dialogue can draw people together who would otherwise remain in their separate worlds. The gentle and respectful spirit of dialogue enabled the students from my class and the Buddhist monks to engage in intense and honest interaction. Was the dialogue successful? Both parties extended a mutual invitation for a future visit. One monk said at the end of our dialogue, "I have never before learned so much about the Christian faith." Surely this encounter further opened him to the knowledge of the truth. Students acclaimed the benefit of speaking personally with a Buddhist monk for the first time; they now view monks as fellow members of humanity made in God's image who are seeking truth.

Dialogue in One Nation with Many Gods

The skill of dialogue is especially critical in light of the fact that Christianity is no longer the only featured entrée on America's religious menu. Christians had it easy, so to speak, when members of society quickly related to stories, terms, and concepts of the biblical record. We must now cope with the worldview, notions, and vocabulary of a wide range of foreign deities.

When Rachel ran away from her homeland to Jacob's native land, she took her father's household gods as a surety of blessing (Gen. 31:17–35). Immigrants, likewise, when they journey to the United States pack their gods to ensure flourishing in the land of the free. So the United States is one nation with many gods. In his book *Alien Gods on American Turf,* Terry Muck claims there are approximately fifteen hundred distinct religious groups in the United States. Of these, nine hundred have Christian roots and six hundred do not.[2] (Is it too much to think that Congress will vote some day to rephrase the pledge of allegiance to say, "one nation under gods"?) Estimates of the number of adherents to other world religions in America are as high as four million Muslims, another 1.5 million Buddhists, and one million Hindus. Mosques and a wide variety of temples have sprouted throughout America's landscape to house the spiritual diversity of her new citizenry. America can explain its past—but neither its present nor its future—in the context of the Judeo-Christian religion. The God of the European Pilgrims who arrived on the Mayflower has marked American history and culture for two centuries. Christianity now competes with the many gods that have arrived by air with modern-day pilgrims. Religious pluralism—the belief that all religious ideologies are equal—obscures the unspoken reality that the ambition of all gods is to conquer.

Yet few Americans seem to attach great concern to the growing number of practitioners of other world religions in our country. Muck cites several perspectives that may contribute to this laissez-faire attitude: (1) Religious diversity is considered an urban phenomenon; (2) practitioners of world religions lack corporate influence; (3) Americans have an enlightened ethos. Americans are committed to tolerance and therefore do not mind other religions living among them; (4) world religions are viewed the same as cults. Christians are tempted to relegate Hinduism, Buddhism, and Islam to the same dustbin as faddish cults that will someday disappear.[3]

The fact is that the faith communities of world religions have no intention of disappearing. They are missionary minded and are increasing in their number of faithful practitioners. As an example, it is estimated that at least twenty-five thousand American Hispanics are looking beyond Rome to Mecca for spiritual direction. In his article "Islam Luring More Latinos," Chris Jenkins provides a glimpse into the lives of Hispanic families illustrating why a growing number of Latino women are replacing their Catholic head veils with Islamic head coverings, and why Latino men are taking their sons to the mosque for prayers and teachings:

At dusk, Aminah Martinez prepares dinner in her small Fairfax kitchen. Corn tortillas for enchiladas, grated cheese and beef for tacos, maybe an avocado for guacamole—all staples of her youth. But dusk is also time for prayer. So every evening, with her husband and two children, she places her hands together and kneels to the east. It is Maghrib, Muslims' fourth prayer of the day, and she begins whispering in Arabic as the subtle aromas of Mexico mix with sounds often associated with the Middle East. Martinez is one of the thousands of Latinos nationwide who have converted to Islam. It is an amalgam of two seemingly disparate communities. But in growing numbers, Hispanics, the country's fastest-growing ethnic group, are finding new faith in Islam, the nation's fastest-growing religion. Moved by what many say is a close-knit religious environment and a faith that provides a more concrete, intimate connection with God, they are replacing Mass with mosques. "Islam has given me a sense of religious community and well-being that I was starting to miss in my life," said Martinez, 26, who converted from Catholicism in 1993. "It's helped give me a sense of completion." The steadily increasing number of Latino Muslims illustrates how deeply rooted Islam has become in the national landscape—even spreading to communities not normally associated with the faith, religious scholars say.[4]

A Forbes.com article "Om Rooms" discusses the strong appeal of Buddhist meditation techniques to overworked and overstressed CEOs:

> Ginny Sharpe used to be a hard-charging corporate attorney in Manhattan, working 100-hour weeks and wired as tightly as a grand piano. Today, she is the definition of calm. What happened? In 1994 she quit the law firm and converted her dining room into a meditation room. Sharpe is just one example of the many people these days that are creating meditation rooms in their homes. From her converted dining room in Westchester County, she looks out over a Zen tableau of rock garden with stream, Japanese maples and a statue of Buddha. "In dealing with stress, meditation is a way to constantly 'come home,'" says Sharpe, who now leads meditation training through New York Insight, a meditation center she co-founded in 1996. "There's peace of mind, and with that, one is able to act from a kind and loving rather than guilty and vindictive place." No wonder the chronically stressed-out—media moguls, celebrities and CEOs—are creating spaces in their homes exclusively for the pursuit of inner peace. Among the celebrities who have added meditation rooms to their homes are Madonna, Courtney Love and hip-hop impresario Russell Simmons.[5]

Hundreds of westerners—among them many Americans and Hollywood celebrities—made a pilgrimage to India to attend the forty-two-day Kumbh Mela festival, Hinduism's biggest event. Among the seventy million pilgrims that competed for a space along the banks of the Ganges River were western converts waiting for the right time to take their chilly, wintry dip in the holy waters to wash away their sins and purify their souls. (For those who preferred a virtual dip, all it took was a credit card on web sites where prayers were offered from the riverbanks!)

Insofar as America's population is concerned, Muslims can no longer be identified as just Arabs, Buddhists as just Asians, or Hindus as just Indians. A visit to the web sites of any of these religions reveals bold, unapologetic initiatives to convert every person possible to their belief system and to become a political force in the process.[6]

New Techniques for a New Era

The increase in the number of people involved in non-Christian religions heightens the need for knowing others through dialogue. And dialoguing about religion is a good way to get to know how others think and feel:

1. Religion is what the heart is feeling. "Love the Lord your God with all your heart" is a principle that applies to all religions in that people feel deeply about what they believe. Opening a person's heart (emotions) is critical. Closed emotions close the mind.
2. Religion is what the mind is seeing. Ask a person, "When I say 'religion,' what do you see?" He will release images that clearly picture how he sees his god and what his god requires of him. How can you speak to him intelligently about God if the two of you are simultaneously seeing two different images?
3. Religion defines the meaning of a person's life. Philosopher and professor Winfried Corduan defines religion as "a system of beliefs and practices that provides values to give life meaning and coherence by directing a person toward transcendence."[7] Through a conversational exchange of ideas, we gain insight as to why a person has embraced a certain system of thought to cope successfully with the issues of life.

Historically, certain popular evangelistic tools were especially useful for sharing one's faith among a population conversant in Christian thought; such tools included the Four Spiritual Laws, Evangelism Explosion, or the Romans Road. Successful evangelistic techniques included encouraging others to make a decision for Christ by raising a hand, walking an aisle (introduced by Charles G. Finney in the nineteenth century), or signing a card. As useful as these tools and techniques have been, we should remember that they were culturally, not biblically, driven and may not achieve the same success with those of non-Western cultures or a non-Christian background.

Tom Steffen notes that, "the 'Four Spiritual Laws' model requires listeners to assume that God exists, life is orderly and planned, individuals make decisions, and the number 'four' is positive."[8] These notions may be comforting for those having the same worldview while potentially nonsensical to those who do not. Steffen points out that *four* is a symbol for wholeness to Native Americans and a signal of death for some Asians.[9] Presenting the gospel to America's multireligious population calls for a careful study of how Jesus and the apostles used tools and techniques to communicate to those outside of the mainstream Jewish society and faith. For reaching the people of our society, dialogue can become an effective technique.

George Hunter identifies an "adoption process," as listed below, a delineation of six stages that people experience in adopting any system of thought.[10] These same stages apply to people coming to accept Christian truth, practice, or lifestyle. Conversational and informational dialogue seem especially needed to "kick start" the process of the first two stages. Rational dialogue, or apologetics, is necessary for stages three and four. Discipleship, leading others in the truth and qualities of Christ, would seem to be the best method for accomplishing the final two stages.

1. *Awareness:* People become aware of Christianity, not as an abstraction but as a particular movement, group of people, church, or truth claim.
2. *Relevance:* People perceive the relevance of that perceived form of Christianity for some unmet felt need or driving motive in their lives, their group, or their society.
3. *Interest:* People respond with active interest, in that they ask questions, read a book, attend a seminar, or visit a church's worship service.
4. *Trial:* People enter a trial stage, in which they consider the possibility, imagine what life would be like if they adopted, and perhaps engage in conversations as if they were already Christians; they are "trying it on for size."
5. *Adoption:* People consciously adopt the faith and are publicly baptized and/or received into church membership at a particular time and place.
6. *Reinforcement:* People typically experience a period of uncertainty or ambiguity about what has happened to them, during which they seek experiences that reinforce their decision and confirm their experience.

Summary

It is often amazing to discover that the simplest solutions can often resolve complex issues. For example, to maintain a high level of health, experts may promote a wide range of easy-to-do daily activities, such as drinking six glasses of water, sleeping eight hours, eating fruits and vegetables, or minimizing negative effects of stress by walking for twenty minutes. Steps that are simple to take seem to have a mind of their own in bringing about a favorable and desirable end.

This chapter is suggesting that simple steps can have extraordinary results in bringing a non-Christian to faith in Christ. These steps include a motivating mental picture of a multicultural multitude worshiping Christ, a demonstrable attitude of goodwill toward non-Christians, and a willingness to lead a normal conversation to the subject of Christ and suspending judgment while doing so (that is, allowing another to freely discuss issues of faith without interrupting to interject our opinion of their thoughts or our own personal beliefs). In other words, a sincere, friendly inquiry regarding another's faith in God can often lead to an invitation for sharing the rationale of the gospel story.

Discussion Starters

1. Review George Hunter's "adoption process."
2. Describe how your own experience of believing on Christ followed this process.
3. Discuss how others used the principles in this chapter to help you in your own adoption process.

8

Using Dialogue
to Win People to Christ

Joseph Henriques

We went a little way outside the city to a riverbank . . . and we sat down
to speak with some women who had come together. One of them was
Lydia from Thyatira, a merchant. . . . As she listened to us, the Lord opened
her heart, and she accepted what Paul was saying.

Acts 16:13–14

The three dimensions of dialogue—conversational, informational, and
rational—are powerful agents for stimulating interest, creating desire,
and encouraging commitment in seekers to fully follow Christ. In this
chapter we will consider in more detail how we can use dialogue to win
people from different cultures to Christ.

Conversational Dialogue

At the heart of conversational dialogue is a sincere interest in the life
of a fellow human being. Friendliness or friendships are not considered

as "setups" for evangelism but a natural outgrowth of being a Christian. People were attracted to Jesus, the quintessential friend of sinners, so authentic and unmistakable was his love for them. His critics attacked him, not because of his insincerity in loving others, or loving them too little, but for loving them too much. Yet, ever true to himself, he never denied who he was or the message he brought. As we identify with the humanity of others and befriend them, interwoven in our conversational dialogue will be the natural expression of what we believe. In this regard, John Stott identifies how true dialogue is possible:

1. True dialogue is a mark of *authenticity*. When we take time to be with people, a relationship is developed. Both parties drop their masks; they respect each other's convictions and understand each other's sufferings. Dialogue puts evangelism into an authentically human context.
2. True dialogue is a mark of *humility*. Distance between people diminishes as we recall that we all have our faults and we realize that we cannot sweep away all our friend's cherished convictions with a brash, unfeeling stroke. When we humbly realize that some of the other person's misconceptions could be our fault, any lingering sense of superiority dissolves. We no longer desire to score points or win a victory. We love the person too much to boost our ego at his or her expense.
3. True dialogue is a mark of *integrity*. As we listen to our friend's real beliefs and problems, we divest our minds of the false images we may have harbored, and we are determined also to be real. We cannot ask him or her to make an unconditional commitment to Christ if we ourselves have not done so.
4. True dialogue is a mark of *sensitivity*. Christian evangelism falls into disrepute when it degenerates into stereotypes. It is impossible to evangelize by fixed formulae. To force a conversation along predetermined lines to reach a predetermined destination is to show that we are grievously lacking in sensitivity both to the actual needs of our friend and to the guidance of the Holy Spirit.[1]

Stott is telling us that people do not normally trust someone they do not know. Trusting in Christ is facilitated as we allow people to know us as fellow, fallen human beings who have been transformed by Christ. If we cross-examine others like a prosecutor, or if we try to sell our wares like a vendor in the market, we increase the probability of closed hearts and minds. Moreover, we may create in people a distrust of the God we claim to know. Other believers who come at a later time with the gospel message will wonder why this person is so resistant to their witness. If we look to Christ to continue his style of proclamation through us, we will naturally strive for the authenticity, humility, integrity, and sensitivity that marked his witness among the people of his day.

The following story illustrates that Christ continues his ministry by speaking directly to people about himself. A student refugee from Iran attended our Christian school to complete his senior year. As a Muslim, he was understandably upset with the Bible's portrayal of Jesus as God, a point of serious blasphemy according to the Koran. One day, during an intense discussion about Christ, we had this conversation:

"Keramat,[2] are you a Muslim?" I asked.

"Of course I am," he answered with pride, noticeably indignant that I would ask such a question.

"Do you ever read the Koran?" I inquired.

Caught off guard, he replied, "Well, no, I don't. At least, not that much."

"Isn't that something," I said. "You claim to be a Muslim and yet you don't even read the Koran to find out about Allah or who Mohammed was. Here is what I would like for you to do. Read one chapter out of the Koran every day. At the same time read one chapter out of the Gospel of John. Before you start your readings, pray and ask God to show you his truth. When you find out what the truth is, come and let me know."

The school staff and church remained in prayer for Keramat as we waited for his answer. At one point he said to me, "Okay, I believe in Jesus but I won't worship him!" Of course, this became my prayer, that he would know and worship Jesus. A few weeks later, Keramat approached me at school and said, "Mr. Henriques, I have believed on the Christ."

"I thank God for that," I said with great joy. "What brought you to that decision?"

"As I read the Gospel of John and thought about what kind of person Jesus was, how he loved people, the claims he made for himself, I knew that he was of God. When I read the Koran and saw the kind of person Mohammed was, I knew that he could not have come from God. I believed on Jesus."

Keramat's answer demonstrates the power of conversational dialogue in another dimension. As Keramat read about Jesus, the Holy Spirit was conversing with him, asking him questions, waiting for an answer, offering replies to his questions.

Principles of Dialogue

How do we interact intelligently within the maze of another person's belief system? Just the thought of it causes some Christians to suffer witness-paralysis. Some important principles of dialogue must be kept in mind and can encourage us:

1. We do not know what a person is thinking. "For who among men knows the thoughts of a man except the man's spirit within him?" (1 Cor. 2:11). There may be a wide divide between what a person truly feels about God and what his or her religion teaches. As Winfried Corduan states, "It is crucial to recognize that there can be a vast difference between the theoretical-historical side of a religion and its counterpart in the lives of its common adherents."[3]
2. We do know what God is saying to people. Based on the Word of God, we know the thoughts that God brings up with people on a regular basis. "We have . . . received . . . the Spirit who is from God, that we may understand what God has freely given us" (1 Cor. 2:12). God has freely given us understanding of what he communicates to people who do not know him. He convinces people of his existence, reveals his standard of righteousness, and convinces people of their accountability to him. With the knowledge and understanding of what God is saying, any Christian can fully engage in a discussion, having a high degree of certainty that he or she is addressing issues already on the mind of the person to whom he or she is speaking. Our primary task in dialogue is to bring up God's thoughts in conversation.
3. As we approach dialogue from the vantage point of what God is saying, it is up to the one with whom we are speaking to interpret his or her beliefs. Our work is to help people clarify what they truly do believe about what God has been telling them. This clarification leads to an opportunity to explain God and his gospel.

God Is Speaking

Conversational dialogue is based on the assumption that God is speaking to people and that he invites us to join him in that conversation.[4] This leads us to ask, What *is* God saying? How and when *do* we engage in conversation?

God Convinces People of His Existence

Although no one has the benefit of personal conversations with God in a pristine garden, every person has sufficient evidence in creation of God's existence.

> What may be known about God is plain to them, because God has made it plain to them. For since the creation of the world God's invisible qualities—his eternal power and divine nature—have been clearly seen, being understood from what has been made, so that men are without excuse.
>
> Romans 1:19–20

Common grace gives people the ability to perceive God through what he has made. While speaking to a young man on a beach in Florida, I sensed that it was time to explain to him how he could know God by believing on Christ. When I paused for a response, he said to me, "I was walking on the beach last night, looking up toward the stars, and praying, 'God, if you are there, I want to know the way to know you. Please show me the way.' I feel that what you have told me is the answer to my prayer."

God Reveals His Standard of Righteousness

People know intuitively God's moral perfections because these laws are written in their hearts. Even people with no scruples and no regrets, as Hitler, reveal their awareness of God's law when they accuse others of wrongdoing. Deep in every heart is the awareness that, not only are they without excuse for doing wrong, but "they not only continue to do these very things but also approve of those who practice them" (Rom. 1:32).

> All who sin apart from the law will also perish apart from the law, and all who sin under the law will be judged by the law. For it is not those who hear the law who are righteous in God's sight, but it is those who obey the law who will be declared righteous. (Indeed, when Gentiles, who do not have the law, do by nature things required by the law, they are a law for themselves, even though they do not have the law, since they show that the requirements of the law are written on their hearts, their consciences also bearing witness, and their thoughts now accusing, now even defending them.)
>
> Romans 2:12–15

To varying degrees, people experience feelings of guilt as a result of their words, thoughts, or actions violating their inner sense of right and wrong.

God Convinces People of Their Accountability to Him

When he comes, he will convict the world of guilt in regard to sin and righteousness and judgment: in regard to sin, because men do not believe in me; in regard to righteousness, because I am going to the Father, where you can see me no longer; and in regard to judgment, because the prince of this world now stands condemned.

John 16:8–11

The great evangelist, the Holy Spirit, is our coworker in the joint venture of bringing others to Christ. Because of the Holy Spirit's faithful witness, people know that:

1. They have done what they know to be wrong (sin). Today's society may attach a higher value on the counseling office or the self-realization seminar than the confessional booth; sins may be considered as bad traits acquired from one's environment or weaknesses to overcome. But even in such an age of excuses and permissiveness, most people will still acknowledge for some situation in their lives, "I shouldn't have done that."
2. They have failed to achieve a high moral standard (righteousness) that they intuitively know exists. Whenever someone acknowledges failure by comparing himself or herself to another, he or she may say, "I am not as bad as he is." The person is thus acknowledging three standards: his or her own, that of the other person, and a higher standard that he or she is unconsciously using as the standard of evaluation. Stating that he or she is not as bad as another person also admitting to not attaining to the higher standard he or she is using for comparison.
3. They will someday be held accountable for this failure (they will be judged). Even those who do not believe in a future judgment will argue for criminals being brought to justice for wrongs they have committed; they believe such people should be in court to receive their appointment for judgment. In this admission we see God's truth casting its shadow over their soul, namely, "man is destined to die once, and after that to face judgment" (Heb. 9:27). To underscore every person's culpability for his sins, Paul claims that even the worst offenders "know God's righteous decree that those who do such things deserve death" (Rom. 1:32).

A Model for Our Interactions

God's interaction with Adam and Eve in the garden (Genesis 3) can be a model of how we are to interact with people today.

Choosing the Setting and Time

Choose the appropriate setting and time when a person is most open to God's speaking. The sound of the Lord walking was heard by Adam and Eve in the cool of the day, a time when their ability to listen was evidently enhanced. God is the master of choosing the perfect ethos (environment) for communicating his logos (message) that is appropriate for the pathos (feeling) of the one to whom he is speaking.

> Then the man and his wife heard the sound of the LORD God as he was walking in the garden in the cool of the day, and they hid from the LORD God among the trees of the garden. . . . He answered, "I heard you in the garden, and I was afraid because I was naked; so I hid."
>
> Genesis 3:8, 10

As we consider the best environment in which to interact with others about Christ, we must keep in mind the issue of "noise" in communication: mental, emotional, physical, or sensory hindrances to mutual understanding. A benefit of the friendship context of conversational dialogue is that people enjoy spending time together. Low- or no-noise settings, when others are most susceptible to hearing God's truths, are readily available. My sons have dialogued their faith with others while playing video games, discussing in English class expressions of faith in literature, sipping lattes in the coffee shop, or rappelling. Others have used cooking a meal, hiking on the trail, and traveling in the van to Disney World as their setting for dialogue. As these examples clearly show, the definition of noise is a highly subjective matter! God chose the Garden of Eden as his divinely appointed place for conversing with Adam and Eve; so you will likewise choose the setting and time that fits those with whom you are conversing about God.

Using Questions

Use questions to initiate an interactive dialogue with non-Christians in reference to those topics you know God is already making known to them, namely, his existence, his moral law, and their accountability to him. To Adam and Eve God asked specific questions intended to elicit specific responses: "'Where are you?' . . . And he said, 'Who told you that you were naked? Have you eaten from the tree that I commanded you not to eat from?' . . . Then the LORD God said to the woman, 'What is this you have done?'" (Gen. 3:9, 11, 13).

The kind of questions we use with friends to initiate an interactive dialogue must match our right to ask them. Some factors that determine that right are the level of trust others have in us, the depth of personal knowledge others have allowed us, and our shared experiences. These kinds of factors determine the freedom we have and the level at which we are able to ask bold, penetrating questions. If we know our non-Christian friend well, we can ask questions similar to those God asked Adam and Eve: "Where are you in your relationship with God?" "How did you know that these things you did were wrong to do?" "Did you deliberately commit this wrong, knowing full well that you would offend God and bring harmful consequences to yourself and others?"

Discovering God-given mechanisms to draw out information from another is an exercise in which few engage. Those impatient with the slow process of questions and answers too often resort to a quick data dump of salvation truth or they use questions that seem too aggressive, such as "Are you saved?" to present the gospel. Such efforts are sincere but largely ineffective. A priceless insight for interaction is found in God's instruction in Proverbs 20:5: "Counsel in the heart of man is like deep water, but a man of understanding will draw it out" (NKJV). The writer is telling us that "the depths of the heart of man are not easily fathomed."[5] Contained in the depths of the heart are the secrets of the heart that cover the spectrum of human experience, whether it is subtle evil, deep wounds, confusion, or enlightened thoughts. What is the importance of drawing out that counsel? It is like deep water. When the writer penned the words *deep water,* he had the image of a well in mind. Of what significance was a well? It was so significant, that if a well of water could not be found, a city would not be built. If the well dried, the city would perish. Deep water was a precious substance that sustained life. The counsel within every human heart is what sustains that person's life. Focusing only on surface discussions may miss the counsel under the surface that is critical in leading another person to life in Christ.

Moving beyond surface issues requires being a person of understanding. "Natural sagacity of intellect is deepened and enlarged by spiritual light."[6] Jesus knew the hearts of men because his piercing insight had been honed by God's truth. His disciplined observation of human behavior led him to conclude, "Out of the overflow of the heart the mouth speaks" (Matt. 12:34). Mechanisms that God has provided for us to become people of understanding include careful listening, open-ended or close-ended questions, the Socratic method,[7] appeal of inquiry, reflective statements, pause, and empathic words.

Let us say that Raj, a doctoral student from Pakistan attending the local university, and I have known each other for about six months. At the appropriate time in our conversation, I may make use of:

An appeal of inquiry: "Help me to understand what the Vedas (early sacred writings) mean to a Hindu."

A close-ended question: "When Hindus say 'God,' what do they mean?"

An open-ended question: "Why are humans interested in the afterlife?"

A reflective statement: "So, you don't think there is any life after death."

A pause: "Oh." Follow with silence.

Empathy: "I think I felt the same way when I went overseas for the first time."

The use of these mechanisms helps us open the heart and mind of another to know how he or she is responding to God.

Connecting with People

God connects us with people to participate in his conversation. God's Spirit leads his children to those who need to understand what he is saying (Rom. 8:14).

Now an angel of the Lord said to Philip, "Go south to the road—the desert road—that goes down from Jerusalem to Gaza." So he started out, and on his way he met an Ethiopian eunuch, an important official in charge of all the treasury of Candace, queen of the Ethiopians. This man had gone to Jerusalem to worship, and on his way home was sitting in his chariot reading the book of Isaiah the prophet. The Spirit told Philip, "Go to that chariot and stay near it."

Then Philip ran up to the chariot and heard the man reading Isaiah the prophet. "Do you understand what you are reading?" Philip asked. "How can I," he said, "unless someone explains it to me?" So he invited Philip to come up and sit with him.

The eunuch was reading this passage of Scripture: "He was led like a sheep to the slaughter, and as a lamb before the shearer is silent, so he did not open his mouth. In his humiliation he was deprived of justice. Who can speak of his descendants? For his life was taken from the earth."

The eunuch asked Philip, "Tell me, please, who is the prophet talking about, himself or someone else?" Then Philip began with that very passage of Scripture and told him the good news about Jesus.

Acts 8:26–35

Divine-human encounters may not always be as spectacular as this one, but each one is unique. Every story of God's leading his people to truth seekers is a divine drama.

Uncovering Hidden Thoughts about God

What do you say when God directs you to an encounter with another person? The following are ways to enable a person to reveal his or her views of God, feelings about personal sinfulness, and thoughts about judgment after death.

God as Creator

Uncover a friend's thoughts regarding God as the powerful, eternal Creator (Rom. 1:20–21).

If you are riding with an unsaved friend in a car and you see a beautiful sunset, an ominous thunderstorm on the horizon, or trees laden with freshly fallen snow, this is the moment during the conversation to ask, "Nature is so beautiful, so powerful, so amazingly intricate. What does your religion say is the cause of nature?" Once the person has given a response, be sure to ask a follow-up question, "Is that what you think, as well, or do you have other thoughts that come to your mind?" Do not assume that a response is always necessary. Just your question alone may stimulate further reflection. If your friend then asks you, "What do you think?" You can answer, "I believe that God made nature and that he has given us all the beauty and power of nature to tell us that he exists and that he is powerful. Have you ever had those thoughts?"

See where the stream of conversation takes you. If you see it leads you to a river flowing with thoughtful interaction, step in carefully. If you see your conversation is becoming a dry riverbed, turn to other topics of discussion. Be assured that God has other moments planned.

Personal Sinfulness

Uncover a friend's thoughts concerning his or her sins and sense of failing to achieve a higher standard of righteousness (Rom. 2:15–16; John 16:8–11).

Let us say that you and your friend are listening to the evening news together. A report is given regarding war or some other kind of interpersonal or international conflict. Certain questions can lead into a conversation about the issue of sin. For example, you might say, "It is so awful that people don't treat each other with respect and, as a result, these terrible things happen. Why do you think people act that way?

Every nation seems to have natural enemies. Do your own people have conflicts with other countries? What are the causes of these conflicts?" Wait for the response. You may have an opportunity to say, "Well, it seems to me that even the nicest people all have something in them that does what is wrong." Interact according to the answer you receive, paraphrasing Scripture or, if the conversation naturally calls for this, mention a Scripture as support for what you believe about sin in human nature and God's standard of righteousness.

Judgment after Death

Uncover a friend's thoughts about judgment after death (John 16:8–9; Heb. 9:27).

If a news report tells of an evil ruler dying or of innocent people dying, begin talking about details of the event itself. At an appropriate time, you may then ask questions like, "Where do you think this person/these people are right now? Is there a judgment after death? What do you think happens after death?" After hearing the response, you might say something along these lines: "I am intrigued by how many religious systems have ideas about life after death. It seems there is a universal idea about certain places people go when they die. Good people go to a good place that has rewards for a good life; bad people go to a bad place with some kind of punishment for a bad life." Pause to hear the response. Again, see where the river of conversation takes you.

Speaking with Silence

Punctuate your conversations with silence. There are times when the person to whom you are speaking has nothing in particular to say or is not ready to say anything. With no silence on your part, dialogue risks becoming a monologue. Your silence may be God's opportunity to speak, the person's opportunity to reflect, or your opportunity to evaluate what is being said.

Cultural norms of silence need to be recognized. As Americans, we seem to be addicted to noise. When we get in the car or settle in the office, we turn on the radio. In some households the television stays on all day. Social chitchat doesn't stop; a lull in conversation is considered uncomfortable. Illustrative of our intolerance for silence is the tiny fifteen- to thirty-second "moment of silence" that is given at a public meeting to remember those who died for their country.

As we have seen, people from other cultures may not have the same view of silence. The Japanese feel that a pause before replying shows respect to the person who just asked a very important question. (One American businessman made an offer to sell his product for a certain price to a Japanese businessman who, in turn, said nothing. The silence was interpreted to mean the offer was not good enough. To the amazement of the Japanese businessman, the American kept lowering the price to a level far below what the Japanese was already willing to pay!) Fear may cause a Ugandan to pause before he replies to a question; in his war-torn country people have learned to think carefully before answering.

Deliberately allowing moments of silence in our conversation can assist a person unfamiliar with the Christian faith to internalize one biblical concept before continuing to another. When I told an Asian international graduate student that God answers prayer, she thought for a moment before asking, "How can God listen to so many people at once?" Now it was I who pondered. My reply was slow and deliberate, "Because God . . . is God." It was a couple of minutes before she said, "Oh, I see." Obviously not all conversations about God need to be so often punctuated with silence. But silence is a technique that should be employed more often in dialogue. In the case of this international student, silence provided her the time needed to fully comprehend God's truths; she is now an active member of his family.

Letting Questions Work for You

It is important to reemphasize that in conversational dialogue we are not interacting with people about their religion, whether Buddhism, Hinduism, Islam, Santeria, or any other religion. Rather, we are interacting with a Buddhist, atheist, Muslim, or Hindu regarding the specific issues about which God has been speaking to him or her. Effectively interacting with someone about these issues does not require in-depth knowledge of his or her belief system. It does mean that we have to develop skill and patience in at least knowing which questions to ask. The purpose for conversational dialogue is to bring to the surface the individual's thoughts about what God has been saying.

This method of sharing the good news takes time, requiring several conversations within the context of a developing friendship. From my observations of the normal witnessing pattern of many of my fellow Christians, adjusting to this method would be uncomfortable. We have been taught that real skill in witnessing is getting from point A (meeting the person) to point B (fully sharing every aspect of the gospel that we feel is important) in the shortest time possible. Closing the deal, pressing for an immediate decision, is of high value. To do otherwise is to feel that we have not been fully faithful. While this approach may indeed have its place in certain situations, it should not be considered the norm. It is beneficial to remember how many of us came to believe on Christ. It was the result of numerous conversations by faithful Christians who invested many hours to bring us to that point of decision.

That God is actively involved in speaking to people and that he invites us to join him in that conversation is illustrated by the experience I had with a medical doctor on a five-hour flight. The Asian man and I engaged in a nonstop conversation. His fascinating story—of escaping from his Communist homeland and living as an outsider in America's mainstream culture and achieving a medical degree—captivated my attention and piqued my curiosity. As he responded to a range of inquiries, our conversation drifted to the meaning of life, Jesus, and God.

When I suggested that it was because of the endless heartaches of life that people seek God, he looked at me and said, "I believe that God is seeking us, we don't seek him."

"Why?" I asked. "What happened that caused you to believe that?"

He described the time he was performing a delicate operation that required slipping a closed, surgical knife down a patient's throat. He then opened the knife, made the necessary incisions, and proceeded to withdraw the instrument. To his horror, the knife would not close. "I was sweating," he confessed. "I asked the nurses, 'What should I do?' They answered, 'We don't know; you're the doctor!'"

"So, what did you do?" I asked.

"I'm a Buddhist," he replied, "but I prayed and asked God to help me. The knife closed." Knowing that he had admitted to being one of many Buddhists who do not believe in the notion of a personal deity that hears and answers prayers, I understood the significance of this event for him. He continued, "That happened to me on one other occasion, which makes me believe that God is seeking me. I wasn't looking for God." Buddhists may not talk to God, but God talks to Buddhists anyway.

At the end of our flight, he said, "I never talk about spiritual things to anyone. But I really benefited from our conversation. Thank you."

It took several hours of conversation for this doctor to reveal his belief that God speaks personally to people. To my knowledge, I am the first person who knows of his experience of God talking to him and of his response in return. I knew that seeds were planted, someone else would water, and God would give the increase.

Informational Dialogue

As conversational inquiry is at the heart of the first dimension of dialogue, so clarity of presentation is the focus of the second dimension.

"What made you decide to believe the way you do?" When the lieutenant colonel asked the question, I knew that my time had come. It was my moment of opportunity to fully share the truth about the gospel. I had worked with this person over a couple of years on several joint projects; we had had brief conversations along the way about faith. The fullness of time had come.

Informational dialogue is concerned with what to say when the moment arises for us to present our faith. The plan we follow was modeled for us in Paul's presentation to the educators and philosophers at Athens. Luke records that from the beginning of his arrival in the city Paul had engaged in extensive conversations about the gospel with many people in the synagogue and in the marketplace. Evidently he had stirred their imagination into thinking that he was preaching some good news about worshiping two gods they had never before considered (Jesus *and* the resurrection). It was not long before Paul was escorted to the meeting of the Areopagus, the Athenian council that considered itself "the custodians of teachings that introduced new religions and foreign gods."[8] "May we know what this new teaching is that you are presenting?" they inquired. "You are bringing some strange ideas to our ears, and we want to know what they mean" (Acts 17:19–20). In so many words, those with whom we faithfully engage in conversational dialogue will ask us to explain the full meaning of what it is we believe.

A request to know about our faith does not necessarily imply a heart hungry to know truth or respect for us or for our message. Paul's audience considered him a "seed picker," a small, insignificant bird that mindlessly picked up seeds from here and there (Acts 17:18). In their estimation Paul was nothing more than an amateur philosopher, his shallow thinking merely an ad hoc mixture of unrelated thoughts tossed forth without first having been digested. Even with this dim view of Paul, the philosophers were nevertheless inclined to listen because of their quest to always hear some new thing.

It is important to note that when Paul gave his presentation, it was not because he was following the progression of dialogue as presented in this chapter—from conversational, to informational, to rational. When he spoke his message, it was from his divinely appointed role as "a herald and an apostle and a teacher" of the gospel (2 Tim. 1:11). In all probability, when Paul visited a town, he did not invest time in conversational dialogue. He went immediately to the synagogues, marketplaces, or individuals with the intention of proclaiming the gospel and per-suading people to believe on Christ. Using Paul as their model of evan-gelistic style, some Christians debunk the notion of friendship evange-lism altogether. We must keep in mind that Paul was in a class by himself; no one else had his calling, roles, and responsibilities. To whom else did God say, "This man is my chosen instrument to carry my name before the Gentiles and their kings and before the people of Israel"? (Acts 9:15). The gospel that others received from witnesses, Paul received by direct revelation (Gal. 1:12). Paul's ultimate goal was to establish churches in areas that had no gospel witness. He insisted that, "It has always been my ambition to preach the gospel where Christ was not known" (Rom. 15:20). His itinerant lifestyle was so consumed with dis-seminating the gospel of Jesus that he called it "my gospel." While striv-ing to emulate Paul's devotedness to the gospel, we will probably find that, in most instances, the dialogue-of-progression approach is more conducive to our daily witness with neighbors, coworkers, and school colleagues.

Regardless of the context surrounding Paul's presentation in Acts 17, the fact that he accomplished it successfully gives us confidence and a model to follow. Paul spoke forth his personal beliefs about God with the full intention of demonstrating to the Athenian educators and philosophers the superiority of Christ to any of their gods. We have our own modern-day counterparts with whom we must speak. To enhance the effectiveness of our dialogue, we will extrapolate the fundamental concepts delivered by Paul, his strategy, and his progression of thought.[9] These elements have stood the test of time and are appropriate for use with any audience, regardless of their religious or ideological persua-sions or of their cultural heritage.

Acknowledging Beliefs

When the door opens, begin by acknowledging your friend's beliefs. You might say, *"You are a religious person"* or *"You are a person with firm beliefs."* Following Paul's pattern, you will want to touch on four areas:

1. *Recognition of their religiosity.* Paul's opening comment was a recognition of the Athenians' identity, "Men of Athens," followed by a basic acknowledgement of the display of their spirituality, "I see that in every way you are very religious" (Acts 17:22). Paul did not think it necessary to attack what they believed, thereby incur-ring their anger, or to discuss what they believed, thereby incur-

ring their disrespect if he was found to know very little. He simply acknowledged that they were a religious people.

2. *Observations of their religious devotion.* It was important to let the Athenians know that he had taken time to make his own personal observations about their belief system. He said to them, "For . . . I walked around and looked carefully at your objects of worship" (v. 23).

3. *Your impression that they desire to worship God.* Taking the opportunity to transition from the beliefs of his audience to his own, Paul said, "I even found an altar with this inscription, TO AN UNKNOWN GOD" (v. 23). Perhaps this altar pointed to the Athenians' belief in a supernatural being that was beyond their ability to understand. Or it may have been their way to ensure that they had not somehow overlooked a god.

4. *Your intention to explain to them what you know about God.* The place comes in every dialogue when you are able to say, "What therefore you worship in ignorance, I proclaim to you." Note that Paul chose the point where they had the least knowledge to launch his presentation.

Talking about God

At this point in the conversation you might say, *"I would like to tell you about the God I worship."* As you share specific thoughts about God, your audience will unconsciously compare their religious experience with those thoughts.

1. *As far as the universe and world are concerned, God is:*
   - the Creator of the world and all it contains (Acts 17:24). The Epicureans believed that matter was eternal and therefore there was no creator.
   - Sovereign over the entire universe (v. 24).
   - self-sufficient, in need of no one or nothing to sustain him (vv. 24–25).
   - the one who gives life (v. 25). The Epicurean and Stoic philosophers in the audience were materialists who believed God existed yet was removed from involvement with people. They did not believe that life continued after death, but rather that the body and soul disintegrated.
   - the one who provides for all life (v. 25).
2. *As far as we humans are concerned, God is:*

- the originator of every group of people in the human race (v. 26). Paul was saying in essence that all the world's people were different but equal. The notion that everyone came "from one blood" was probably not well received. The Greeks had an elitist view of themselves. They were a superior race; the rest of the world were barbarians, people who were not conversant with Greek culture or language. The Greek name for barbarians was *barbaros,* perhaps because their speech to the Greek ear sounded like br-br-br-br, unintelligible and unintelligent chatter.
- the one who determines at what point in time and in which culture on earth every person will live (v. 26). God is in control of everything from the rise and fall of empires to the very culture and race into which a person is born.
- very desirous that every person experience seeking him and finding him (v. 27). God is deeply concerned for every person in the world and intends for people to personally know him.
- completely accessible to everyone (v. 27).
- the source of our life, the cause of our movement, and the reason for living (vv. 28–29). Paul quoted Aratus, a poet from Paul's home region of Cilicia, "We are God's offspring," to promote the idea that this God could not have been made if he is himself the Maker.

3. *My God wants every person to know that:*
   - he expects every person to turn from what he or she knows to be wrong and turn to him (v. 30).
   - a day of judgment is awaiting those who do not do so (v. 31).
   - Jesus Christ will preside at the judgment (v. 31).

4. *God did something to prove to us that everything he has said is true:* He raised Jesus Christ from the dead (vv. 31–32). As stated earlier, Greek thought did not accept the resurrection of the body, as they held that the body and soul disintegrated at death.

We may assume that Paul, in the midst of the interaction that occurred in verse 32, attempted to persuade his listening audience to believe on the resurrected Christ. The last verse of chapter 17 (v. 34) indicates that some of his listeners believed his message.

Your statements about your faith will not necessarily flow in the order delivered by Paul, and they may include more or less than Paul included. Nevertheless, all true informational dialogue will include truths about the nature of God, God's relationship to humankind, and God's planned purpose for humankind through Jesus Christ.

Rational Dialogue

Although God does speak to individuals, this does not mean ipso facto that people are willing to acknowledge the issue God is trying to bring to their attention.

"The man said, 'The woman you put here with me—she gave me some fruit from the tree, and I ate it.' Then the LORD God said to the woman, 'What is this you have done?' The woman said, 'The serpent deceived me, and I ate'" (Gen. 3:12–13). These two statements show how Adam and Eve engaged in blatant blaming instead of confessing their guilt. Of all people, Adam and Eve should have conceded the naked truth of their transgression. They knew it was God's voice that asked for an explanation of their actions; there was no question that the command they had broken was God's command. Evidence so saturated their environment that faith and reason were as one. It's amazing that, having had no previous experience with sin, they still sinned.

When sin entered the world, matters were made worse for Adam and Eve's descendants. We were programmed with a propensity to intuitively follow the steps of humankind's first parents. Without the same sensory evidence of God, with sin permeating the soul, faith and reason eventually drifted apart. Spiritual sight went blind, our hearing became dull, and our conscience became scarred. Sin propelled a deteriorated imagination toward the exact opposite direction of what God intended. The Bible describes this downward historical trend in terms of an attitude refusing to glorify God, not giving him the gratitude due him, and not worshiping him as the Creator. The result? "Their foolish hearts were darkened. Although they claimed to be wise, they became fools" (Rom. 1:21–22).

Motivation for Rational Dialogue

It would seem that with God already speaking through creation, through his word written in our hearts, and through the witness of his people, there would be no need for further reasoning. Yet God commands us to offer reason for our faith to those who ask. He calls us to blend Scripture and sound reasoning in serious dialogue in the effort to convince people that he is and that he has graciously revealed the way to know him. It seems that rational dialogue (apologetics) is but one more measure of grace God pours on people. Apparently God wants to make it hard for people not to believe, so strong is his desire that no one should perish but that all would come to repentance. In the next world, "every knee [will] bow, . . . and every tongue confess that Jesus Christ is Lord, to the glory of God the Father" (Phil. 2:10–11). God desires for that confession to be made in this world where grace abounds for those who believe rather than for it to wait for the time when judgment awaits those who do not.

God's grace and his love for people become our motivation for apologetics. We build our case to offer a credible explanation for why we have chosen the God of our salvation. We offer our explanation to others with intensity so that they too will believe in God. Geisler packages together several insights as to the motivation for apologetics, two of which reinforce this discussion: God commands it and reason demands it.[10]

God Commands It

Peter's teaching that we should be always ready to offer a reason for our faith (1 Peter 3:15) is affirmed by Paul in claiming "I am put here for the defense of the gospel" (Phil. 1:16). If we are to follow Paul as he followed Christ, apologetics becomes an essential part of our strategy. Indeed, God himself calls on us to use reason (Isa. 1:18) with him, to discern truth from error (1 John 4:6), and to skillfully slice through a situation to bring to light the right from wrong (Heb. 5:14).

Reason Demands It

Being made in God's image means that human beings are not only able to reason, they were made to reason, and they have a need to reason. This is not to say that we must be able to reason every point of our belief system with the non-Christian. At the minimum, we must demonstrate that our faith is plausible; then, that it is possible and probable. At the highest levels, we give evidence that our faith is solidly predictable, valid, and reliable, worthy of being trusted once and for all.

This is not to say that all non-Christians feel compelled to examine the evidence for the truth of the gospel. All the evidence many need is the gospel story itself. They hear a presentation—perhaps several times over—of the life, death, burial, and resurrection of Christ and his free offer of salvation. Before long they believe on Christ and become children of God. In either case, whether easy or hard to persuade, Paul said that he was not ashamed of the gospel because of its inherent power to save anyone who believes.

Rationale for Dialogue

The most fashionable dogma in America's new spiritual marketplace is that each person must be about finding a spirituality that works *for him or her*. As one fills a plate at a church potluck supper—sampling a little of what everyone brings to the table—so it is expected that one would mix and match creed and ritual according to personal taste. For many, the expectation is that churches, synagogues, temples, and mosques will be repositories of dogma for loyal followers but, ideally, should double as warehouses of spirituality in which patrons can pick and choose and come and go as they fancy.

In this context, it is easy to see why biblical apologetics can rouse negative emotions: The intention of rational dialogue is to convince others that Jesus Christ and the Bible are superior, without equal, to any other religious personage or belief system. The formidable apologist Cornelius Van Til posited, "Christianity must be presented to men as the objective truth, and provably so. It is not only a moral lapse, but also an unjustifiable intellectual error to reject the message of God's revealed word."[11] Yet, even when the Christian faith is presented with sound arguments and Christlike civility, the mere implication of one winner and the rest losers is socially fatal. Our religiously syncretistic society values varieties, not verities, of faith.

If it were not for our conviction that all truth is not equal and that, like currency, counterfeits abound, we would encounter little, if any, opposition. But we live in a politically correct society that awards those who believe in equality of ideas and punishes those who do not. The Scripture promotes the view that all people, not all ideas, are equal in their standing before God. The apostle John's admonition is as current for us as for the believers of the first century: "Dear friends, do not believe every spirit, but test the spirits to see whether they are from God, because many false prophets have gone out into the world" (1 John 4:1).

It's ironic that evangelical Christians, who are frequently accused of narrowmindedness, are the ones who demonstrate the broadmindedness of true liberal thought: (1) We validate the right of others to claim their dogma as the absolute truth and to insist that all people accept it as such, and (2) we defend their right to do so in a responsible manner without penalty. It is in this posture that we satisfy specific scriptural criteria for being an effective witness: "Live such good lives among the pagans that, though they accuse you of doing wrong, they may see your good deeds and glorify God on the day he visits us," and "by doing good you should silence the ignorant talk of foolish men" (1 Peter 2:12, 15). The following context of Peter's admonitions is noteworthy: "Live as free men, but do not use your freedom as a cover-up for evil; live as servants of God. Show proper respect to everyone" (1 Peter 2:16–17). Could it be made more clear that every Christian should hold tenaciously to the value of showing respect to others who express themselves, especially in a democratic society that highly values freedom of thought?

Apologetics Made Easier

Apologetics is made easy because, at the broadest level, there exist only two basic worldviews. Briefly stated, one worldview sees life as intelligible and meaningful without reference to God as he is presented in the Scripture. All nonbiblical belief systems hold this view in some form. They differ in many other respects. The biblical worldview believes life is intelligible and meaningful only in full relationship with God in whom we all live, move, and have our being; with Christ who alone reconciles people to God; and with the Holy Spirit who enables us to live as Christ lived on earth.

Friendship is the context for dialogue. Between these two opposing worldviews that are clearly at war with each other, there can exist a demilitarized zone. Those who have built cultivated friendships through conversational and informational dialogue enjoy a noncombat zone in which both sides, with freedom, express, discuss, debate, and attempt to persuade others to their views.

A wide range of resources is available. The bibliography lists several excellent resources in apologetics that contain links to still many other sources of information. Organizations offer conferences, seminars, and workshops on thinking logically and making sound arguments for the Christian faith. With such a massive arsenal of gospel weaponry in apologetics, a Christian in America may feel ill-prepared but should never be ill-equipped for making his or her defense of the faith.

We have the advantage of Scripture as a powerful ally. Paul's dialogue experience in the synagogue at Thessalonica (Acts 17:1–3) demonstrates the indispensable use of a powerful ally, the Scripture, in conversing about Christ with a biblically illiterate society. Use of the Scripture gives us home court advantage as we employ Paul's two-step technique of explaining and proving truth. Explaining simply means to open the Scripture and clarify its meaning. Proving is laying side by side a selection of passages that further amplify the points being made. Once released into the mind, the Scripture engages in guerrilla warfare, guided by the Spirit of God in penetrating "even to dividing soul and spirit, joints and marrow; [judging] the thoughts and attitudes of the heart" (Heb. 4:12). The entrance of God's Word will give light to an otherwise darkened inner world.

Summary

The three aspects of dialogue presented in this chapter—conversational, informational, and rational—have but one view of the future in

mind: for non-Christians to know God through Jesus Christ and to glorify him by worshiping him forever. There is no greater incentive to
become involved in dialogue that opens the mind.

The philosopher Unamuno contended that, "those who deny God
deny Him because of their despair at not finding him."[12] May that despair
never be traced to our inability or, worse, our unwillingness to present
or defend the faith that was once delivered and entrusted to us for the
benefit of the people of the world.

Discussion Starters

You have just read an action plan, not a theory, on conversing about
Christ. Choose a timetable appropriate for accomplishing the steps listed
below with a non-Christian friend with whom you feel comfortable. The
sooner you begin the better.

1. Ask and discuss the questions posed in the section on conversational dialogue.
2. Memorize the outline for presenting God, as described in the informational dialogue section. Either wait for your friend to ask what
   you believe about God, or ask if he or she would be willing to listen to what you have to say.
3. Inquire as to whether there are questions about God for which he
   or she would like an answer. Research, prepare, and share what
   you discover. Remember: Do not data dump! Allow plenty of time
   for reflection, silence, and inquiry.
4. If you feel you need a "before-game warm-up," practice these steps
   with a Christian. Ask for a critique and for prayer support as you
   converse with non-Christians about Christ.

9

A Captivating Model
of the Multicultural Church
Michael Pocock

> This mystery is that through the gospel the Gentiles are heirs together with Israel, members together of one body, and sharers together in the promise in Christ Jesus.
>
> Ephesians 3:6

Multicultural ministry is a noble idea. St. Paul made it clear that in Christ believers from different cultures are fused into one body. Why, then, do we still think it is such a mystery? Are there actually multicultural churches in North America today that are effectively reaching their culturally diverse communities? Absolutely! In the opening chapter of this book we cited several examples. We really hope readers will want their own church to reflect the community in which it is located. There are many levels and varieties of response to a culturally diverse community.

179

We have tried to show what these ministries look like and how they are accomplished.

Homogeneous ethnic churches are very legitimate for distinct cultural groups in a community, especially where language is still a factor. God has blessed departments or congregations of distinct ethnic groups meeting in the same facilities. Homogeneous ethnic churches have been started by churches as cross-cultural missions in their own cities, but one of the most vibrant multicultural ministries we have seen and offer as a model to follow is New Life Community Church in Chicago, Illinois.

A model church in a multicultural community is one that authentically represents what God calls for in the New Testament, one he makes possible through his Spirit. It is a community in which people of any background, ethnicity, or station in life experience the regenerating power of God to break down walls of hostility, overcome personal limitation and sin, and unite people in love and respect for each other. A model church does not keep its "secret recipe" to itself, but shares it, the liberating Good News of the Lord Jesus Christ. In a church like this, leaders mirror the diversity found in the community. They guide, edify, and release the members to become effective agents of outreach and a healing presence in their city. New Life Community Church, by the grace of God and gifting of its leaders, is this kind of fellowship. Let's take a closer look at this exciting church.

The Development of New Life Community Church

New Life is a great example of the promise of the Lord Jesus, "I will build my church, and the gates of Hades will not overcome it" (Matt. 16:18). Moody Bible Institute staff and students began a ministry in the Back of the Yards area of Chicago in 1948. It came to be known as Berean Memorial Bible Mission. Over the years students from Moody taught Sunday school classes in the storefront on South Ashland Avenue. Adult staff from the Institute and others joined to give this fledgling ministry some continuity.

I came to know Berean while a student at Trinity Evangelical Divinity School, located on the north side of Chicago. Having assisted in worship in a church in Maryland and preaching almost every weekend in prisons before becoming a student at Trinity, I found it hard to simply sit still on Sundays. Seeing a notice that a small church on the south side needed a pastor, my new bride and I decided to inquire and soon found ourselves involved at Berean Mission.

In those days the Back of the Yards was just that. It was an area adjacent to the world's largest stockyard. It had an aroma that actually smelled like the gates of Hades but which I was finally able to manage by isolating what I thought was the smell of boiled ham! Immigrants from all over the world labored in the meatpacking business. Berean had Polish families and American Appalachians sitting beside each other, along with a growing presence of Mexicans and some African Americans from the deep South.

Those were great days! Only about thirty-five people were gathering on Sunday mornings and evenings, but even at that stage, Berean was a multicultural mirror of the community. My wife and I already knew that God had a place for us in Latin America, so we soaked up the hospitality of Mexican families. We came to know their food and customs and, to some extent, their way of thinking.

As second-generation children of immigrants, Berean's members were getting assimilated into the American scene. English was our medium of communication, and even though the ethnic backgrounds were different, they were a relatively homogeneous socioeconomic group of people who lived and worked in the community. While we were there, the group grew, and sometimes as many as sixty people crowded the store-front premises.

A nearby Russian Orthodox church decided that their congregation should move to the suburbs, and we began to negotiate the purchase of their property. After my wife and I left to teach at Toccoa Falls College and later in Venezuela, Berean purchased the Russian Orthodox church. Berean was one of the few evangelical congregations to have a church building with an onion dome for a spire! The size of the membership prevented Berean from acquiring a full-time pastor, but various part-time pastors came and went. Despite various ups and downs, the congregation stubbornly refused to die, and, even though their numbers were limited, there was always someone coming to Christ. Still today there are families who were there in the sixties and are a part of what has become New Life Community Church. One daughter, Donna, is on staff at New Life. Another daughter of one of those original families, whom I remember as a bright little nine-year-old, was Deedee Marquez. She is now the wife of the pastor, Mark Jobe.

Pastor Mark Jobe

Mark became a part of Berean while a student at Moody. He had been brought up by missionary parents in Spain and was attracted to the predominantly Hispanic community surrounding the church. He loved to preach, and when he did, he was passionate. People's lives were being changed. He had a fearlessness about living and working in the com-

munity that attracted others to him and to the ministry. The church was
at a low point when he arrived—only some eighteen people remained—
but it was not to be that way for long![1]

One day in 1986 I was visiting the church, which always made us welcome when we were in the area. Mark had taken a survey of the people
in the neighborhood. He wanted to find out what they knew or thought
about Berean Memorial Bible Church. "Berean?" they asked. "What's
that? Memorial? Sounds like a funeral home!" Obviously the old name
had little appeal, so they changed it to what they hoped it would
become—New Life Community Church. That's when their era of growth
began.

Fifteen years later, when it meets with all its satellites, New Life Community is a church of more than seventeen hundred people. They no
longer fit in their old Russian Orthodox church. New Life Central meets
at the Illinois Institute of Technology. The old facilities have simply
become their offices, training space, and storage area. New Life Central
conducts its ministries in English with a congregation that is about 60
percent Hispanic and 35 percent Anglo. There is a scattering of other
ethnic groups, including African Americans, among them. Everyone
seems happy with what they have in common. They are urban people
with a vital relationship to Jesus Christ and lives committed to change.

New Life Community Church manages the distinct needs of urban
ethnic people by creating multiple ministry sites for what is really a single church. They have ninety-five home groups in which individual needs
can be met. Each satellite uses the language appropriate to the people
in its neighborhood, and the ministry of each satellite has outreaches
that fit local needs. Where English is the preferred medium, the congregations are nevertheless multicultural. This is the case for New Life
Central, the largest and "mother" of the five other congregations.

The pastors and leaders of all satellites are part of a unified New Life
staff. The staff meets weekly, and all the congregations get together several times a year for united events like Taste of New Life, a takeoff of
the highly popular local event Taste of Chicago. The united meetings
are bilingual, involving the worship teams of all the satellites, and followed by a lengthy meal and time of fellowship. More than seventeen
hundred gathered for the spring 2001 Taste of New Life.

Satellite Congregations

The congregations of New Life are scattered around Chicago. Nueva
Vida de la Villita is Spanish speaking. It is located in the south-side community known as The Village. New Life South is an English-speaking

satellite to the southwest, Nueva Vida Sur is Spanish speaking, as is Nueva Vida Norte on the near north side of Chicago.

New Life North is an English-speaking, multicultural congregation formed from Galilee Baptist Church. During the hundred years since the founding of Galilee Baptist, there had been several transitions in ethnic makeup and even in denominational affiliation. Church members at Galilee decided they were unable to reach the community with their traditional approach and they asked New Life to assume their ministries and church and do what was needed to reach the community. Over a period of time, Galilee had shrunk to about fifty older people, but they were open to whatever changes might be necessary. Mark Jobe and his staff emphasized that worship, music, preaching style, and church life would all change, but the true gospel would be preached and authentic worship practiced.

With these assurances the transition from Galilee Baptist to New Life North was accomplished with dignity. The older members believe the change has resulted in effective outreach. For many of these older people, the transition was a stretch, but they have been gracious and have in turn been treated with respect and appreciation. After becoming New Life North, the congregation has grown to 250 in a little over a year. The newcomers are young, urban Anglo and Hispanic professionals, living in what has become a gentrified, upscale urban area. Though ethnically mixed, the church orientation is mainstream American. This example of an established but diminishing congregation opting for radical change led by an effective outside ministry is worth consideration by other struggling urban churches.

New Life continues to spin off satellite congregations. The latest in 2001, New Life Logan Square, is a predominantly Puerto Rican group using English as their language of choice. In the majority of satellites, leadership reflects the community, generally Hispanic and Anglo, though pastor Tony Wasso of New Life South is a Gypsy and this has attracted a number of the Gypsy culture to the church.

Not every venture or merger of New Life works out. New Creation, or, corporately, La Villita Christian Development Corporation, managed an after-school program for children, a day camp, a youth mentoring program, the Peace Intervention Project to protect school children, and the Naomi Center for abused women and their families. Lawndale Christian Health Center was also a part of this enterprise. All these ministries were designed to bring about community transformation.[2] Now this constellation of community development outreaches continues under other management. New Life anticipates forming a separate nonprofit development corporation.

The Leader Makes the Difference

Throughout this book, the authors have maintained that intentional leadership is the key to multicultural ministry. No church will initiate the changes necessary to incorporate effective ministry in a diverse community without strong leadership. Others have repeatedly made this clear.[3] Godly, effective leaders usually deflect any praise for themselves, insisting that God is the one who made their success possible. I constantly praise my wife, Penny, for building a complete Christian elementary school from a little school with a kindergarten and two grades in six years. But she will always point upward and give God the glory.[4] That would be the same with Mark Jobe of New Life Community Church. Nevertheless, it has been through him that God has so significantly blessed this congregation, which could be described as a multicultural urban church movement. Let's look at the factors that make Mark so effective.

A Good Fit

His background fits. Mark was raised in northern Spain until he was seventeen years old. He is fluent in Spanish. Although New Life Central ministers in English, it is not unusual for Mark to switch briefly to Spanish to make a point. All of the Hispanic people sense his understanding and solidarity with them. He can easily converse in Spanish with the many Hispanic newcomers to Chicago. As a bilingual pastor, he represents a model that both Roman Catholic and some Protestant seminaries now feel is necessary for ministry. The Washington Theological Union and the Chicago Divinity School both aim to have their graduates bilingual by commencement. Graduates may know Greek and Hebrew, but they also learn languages that are currently used in the culturally diverse communities where they will minister.[5]

His formation fits. Having met Mark's mother and father and listened to his father preach, it's clear that Mark has inherited his father's straightforward, unambiguous, passionate approach to preaching and indeed to life itself. I believe that while this is needed in any church, it is especially so among working-class, urban people. Finely nuanced, tentative, or hesitant statements about sin, salvation, relationships, and character don't work among people who struggle daily to live in the city. Urban people of every ethnicity face struggles with gangs, drugs, sex, unemployment, and a variety of injustices. These combine to produce a hard exterior. While desperately needy, they respond only to authentic love and truth offered on a continuing basis. There is a godly confidence that springs from a home life marked by mutual love and respect between the parents, Christ-centeredness, and the opportunity to observe and do ministry from a young age. This has been the inheritance of Mark Jobe.

His family fits. Mark's marriage to a godly Hispanic woman who knows what it is to grow up and live in an urban setting only enhances his effectiveness. Dee Jobe is not simply Mrs. Jobe. She has a distinctly pastoral role among the women. She helps Mark understand the significant Hispanic sector of the community. She is at home in the city. Her presence in the congregation from childhood when her mother and father modeled hospitality to young pastors, like me and my wife, helps her make a home that is open to others, a key ingredient in any pastor's ministry.

Passionate Spirituality

He is a man of passionate spirituality. While I have been teaching and writing about multicultural ministry, many have told me that you cannot expect people of different ethnic groups to get along in the same church. You have to operate according to the homogeneous principle, which in simple terms means birds of a feather flock together. This principle holds true partly because we are all conditioned to feel at home in our particular cultures. This is not all bad. People should be happy about the culture in which they grew up, but there is a carnal aspect to this as well. We tend to excuse our prejudices as simply cultural dynamics. We can only overcome the walls of hostility between cultures in the power of the Spirit. In other words, it takes a miracle.

Sociological and personal miracles are exactly what Mark Jobe believes in. He passionately contends that God changes people who give themselves to him, but he knows he must depend on God to an unusual degree to see change and growth among people in a culturally diverse community. Mark testifies to this in his own explanation of New Life Community Church.[6] He also lives it out in days, nights, and even weeks of fasting, which have become characteristic of Mark's ministry, with many church members following his example. I had an opportunity to meet with six young men of the church, who, under mentorship and monitoring from a responsible leader, Dwayne Eslick, were engaged in a forty-day, juice-only fast. During that time these young men were active in community ministry, studying the Word, and living together. They hoped to experience personal spiritual change and get a vision for what God wanted in their lives. They were asking God for a thousand Chicago teens to be saved through their ministry.[7]

Vision and Gifts

He is a man of vision. We'll look at the vision statement of New Life in just a moment, but visions come to visionary people. They are not invented by people but given by God. Mark sees his work affecting the whole Chicagoland area. He is not simply building a local church, but a regenerative, multicultural church movement across the area. Vision is not simply a "clear mental picture of a preferable future."[8] It is a picture of the future given by God in response to the openness, availability, and commitment of a person to what God communicates. I believe Mark sees not only a rapidly multiplying church movement but, based on his experience of watching God change lives under difficult circumstances, he can see anyone he is talking to as a possible follower of the Lord Jesus. It is in this sense that he is a man of vision.

His gifting fits. Compared to all those who have ministered at Berean before it became New Life, Mark is an unusual person. Others may have been gifted, and did in fact accomplish some things in the life of the people, but God's work through Mark is unusual. There were never more than one hundred people involved in the church at any one time in the four decades prior to his ministry. As he acknowledges in his own case study of New Life, he was challenged point blank by a veteran Chicago pastor not to use his opportunity in the urban community with New Life as a stepping stone to some other ministry.[9] The other pastor challenged him to do a long-term job. At thirteen years, he has been at the church longer than any pastor before him.

Longevity is certainly a key, but besides that, in Jobe there is gifting. The Chicago multicultural community requires the gift of faith to believe that God can do something. When the gift of faith is added to that of evangelism, teaching, and administration, it really begins to add up!

Examine the tapes of messages available after each service. Check the teaching guides. Observe the division of work between a multitude of well-discipled leaders and a network of over ninety-five home groups. Notice the set-up and take-down teams moving chairs and electronic equipment from site to site, and you begin to see the multiple gifting of the man who helped make this happen. He represents what Paul talks about in Ephesians 4:11–13, not just a person who *has* gifts but who *is* a gift to the church for the building up of the saints.

Being Realistic

He understands himself. A person like Mark Jobe, with God's enabling, achieves significant results, but that also means he can be rapidly overwhelmed. To his credit, he is realistic about his own capacities and lim-

itations. Like Jethro with Moses when Moses was overwhelmed in leading Israel, Mark's experienced missionary father counseled him to divide
up his work and release it to responsible individuals whom he developed for ministry.[10]

It is significant that the other leaders and pastors at New Life also
mirror the communities in which they live. Hispanic, Anglo, and Asian
leaders are all entrusted with significant responsibilities. It was a pleasure to meet with some of the satellite pastors like Al Leyva, Tony Wasso,
and Mike Berry and watch them interact with Mark about the details of
their ministry. The capacities and limitations of each worker are carefully taken into account. Since the entire New Life structure, including
its satellites, is considered one church, the staff meets weekly for encouragement, accountability, direction, and prayer.

Could anyone else achieve the remarkable results in an urban multicultural ministry that Mark Jobe has achieved? The answer is yes! Other
outstanding ministries in Chicagoland come readily to mind: The hugely
successful Willow Creek, led by Bill Hybels, actually reaches the whole
Chicagoland area. The Lawndale ministry of Wayne Gordon and the
ministry of Ray Bakke have significant impact. Any of these leaders
could be called a uniquely gifted person, but men and women like them
exist in many urban areas. The fact is that particular gifting and calling
is needed. The church that hopes for significant progress in multicultural ministry needs the right leader. This calls for fervent prayer and
great discernment. The impact of each person's ministry will vary, but
a look at New Life's lead pastor gives an idea of who's needed for successful multicultural ministry.

The Vision of New Life Community Church

Throughout this book, you have read about the impact of vision on
the life and development of the church. Anyone who understands how
to enhance church vitality and growth will emphasize the importance
of vision.[11] New Life Community understands the need for vision. The
point for us to grasp is that for any ministry to become multiculturally
effective, it must intentionally focus on doing so. The leadership must
focus on what it expects to produce. It has to bring the people in the
congregation to where they embrace and act on a vision that is kept constantly before them. Consider this vision, this visual map of the future,
that guides New Life Community Church:

It is our aim to cooperate with God in building a church that is great
enough to impact Chicagoland and focused enough to make genuine dis-

ciples. This picture includes a growing church reaching one percent of Chicago (30,000 people). New Life will gather to worship weekly in auditoriums across Chicagoland called satellite churches. These satellites will come together regularly for city-wide celebrations. Black, White, Hispanic, Asian, street people and CEO's, young professionals and teens, suburban and inner city; each individual will be involved in a small group of about ten people that meets nearby and seeks to keep people connected to each other, God and those in need of God. Prayer and fasting will permeate every aspect of ministry. A twenty-four hour prayer chain will be functioning seven days a week along with a Prayer Center that will help network, train and coordinate people for prayer in Chicago. A Training Center will help equip, educate and empower believers for ministry throughout the year. An equipping track will be in place to form and launch pastors and missionaries into ministry. A Compassion ministry will help the church meet the needs of needy communities. A Networking Center will seek to build, bless, partner and share with other life giving churches and ministries in an effort to reach Chicago and other parts of the world. We will seek to do this, to the glory of God, by the grace of Christ and in the power of the Spirit.[12]

You could be excused for feeling winded after reading this breathtaking vision statement, but it represents what is actually happening! It is not completely realized, but it paints the picture of the coming reality God has impressed on the hearts of leaders and people at New Life Community Church. The 1,100 members of New Life in late 1999 became 1,700 by early 2001. Notice that the vision comprehends the totality of what the church hopes to be and do, not simply its culturally diverse makeup, but it clearly includes the distinct social and ethnic groups it intends to reach and enfold. A multicultural church will never simply happen! It must be the intention of the leaders.

The Structures of New Life Community

A Strong Center with Multiple Satellites

Today there are several fully functioning satellites, but New Life Central began first and the satellites were added as needs became apparent and leaders became available. It is understood that New Life Central is the core of the movement; nevertheless, its leadership does not control the life of the satellites. All satellite pastors are a part of the total congregation and are considered to be part of the leadership as a whole.

In a large urban zone like Chicago, there are many advantages to having fellowships in diverse locations. No one has to travel a great distance in heavy traffic to be a part of New Life. Even those who are willing to travel a long distance to be a part of New Life will probably become a part of, or start, a home group in their neighborhood, which may in turn become a satellite church.

The existence of a vibrant center creates a model and inspiration for the satellites. Resources, equipment, and personnel are available to the satellites to enhance their services. Moving equipment around is not a chore for these satellites, several of which, like New Life Central, rent the facilities they use. Even relatively new believers, if they are faithful, can get involved with the moving crew or help with a host of other tasks.

Several times each year, as I mentioned earlier, the entire church meets for their Taste of New Life celebrations. These combined fellowships, which include lively, extended bilingual worship, encouraging reports, and an extended time of fellowship over food that represents the varied cultures of the members, help keep the culturally diverse believers of all the satellites "on the same page."

Leadership Teams

Each satellite of New Life has its own pastor. The large New Life Central has associate pastors as well. It's interesting that the members of the leadership teams for each satellite are not called elders or deacons. The pastors are considered elders, the rest of the leadership team in each congregation are either elder or deacon qualified, that is to say, they meet the criteria for elders and deacons given in 1 Timothy 3 and Titus 2, but they are simply known as the leadership team. All satellite pastors gather for a weekly staff meeting and there are regular joint meetings of the leadership teams for prayer, development, and planning.

Small-Group Structures

Everyone who becomes a part of New Life is encouraged to become a part of a small group. There are seventy-five groups at the time of this writing.[13] Some are general in purpose, and some relate to special situations or needs. There are women's and men's groups, support and recovery groups, youth groups, groups for those with marriage and family problems, and any of these may also be a Spanish or an English language group. Group leaders are well trained, and all are equipped with a home group resource manual. Leaders also meet with one another regularly for prayer, instruction, and coordination. Before new believers join a group, they are led through *First Steps*, a three-part New

Life–produced study series on the basic elements of the Christian life. All the church's printed materials are available in Spanish and in English.

In addition to the small groups, each believer is encouraged to find a "growth partner." These partnerships are for mutual encouragement, accountability to the Word of God, and witness.

Special Youth Outreach

For several years New Life rented a warehouse where hundreds of young people met on Saturday nights for a program called Soul Purpose. This was a high-energy Christian "rave party." It served two purposes: It gathered and challenged Christian teens to more committed Christian living and, when designated as an outreach event, it gave Christian teens a highly attractive venue for inviting friends who were not believers. It was also a tremendous alternative to the many negative and destructive activities on the streets of Chicago.

Many ethnic congregations are concerned that their second and third generations are leaving the church, no longer interested or able to speak the language of their parents. New Life attracts the younger generation that is assimilating into the American mainstream. At New Life programs, ethnic youth are welcome as they are, no questions asked. It's an opportunity not simply to be a part of the mainstream, but the *right* stream with other urban Christian youth.

More recently, the united Soul Purpose has been discontinued in favor of decentralized, weekly youth programs, which overcome the transportation problems of a single central event. A Hispanic young man or woman would feel at ease in any New Life program, and so would any other urban youth. This could probably not be said of many predominantly Anglo programs, in spite of the good will of the people there.[14] An aggressive mentoring program for all the New Life youth is developing responsible young adult Christians who can face the challenges of modern urban life.

Summary

In observing churches that have become multicultural or multiethnic, I am often tempted to think that it could never happen through the transformation of any existing single-culture church. Indeed, it may be difficult. Churches that are multicultural frequently started that way. Others have been born out of desperation. Urban churches that were large and thriving in the '50s and '60s shrank in size as their people moved out to other areas. People of other ethnicities took their place in the community. Finally, like Galilee Baptist Church, as a remnant of fewer than fifty people, they decided to do something. They reconnected with the changing community, embraced the need for change in the way they did things, and became an effective multicultural church.

In the case of New Life, they were never a large church until the past ten years, but they were always multicultural. In the providence of God, a gifted individual sensed a call to trust God to do a truly great work from a very small body of people. He committed himself on a long-term basis. The people of Berean Bible Mission were flexible enough and open enough to welcome change. As a result, New Life Community Church was born and it lives as evidence that God still delights in making something out of practically nothing.

I am struck by the apostle Paul's questions and comments to the Corinthians (1 Cor. 1:20–31). Do we miss the fact that he is talking about the desire and ability of God to build a multicultural body, the church, out of very disparate people? Do we understand that he is not simply talking about the universal church, but a specific local church at Corinth? Paul talks about God's power to save Jews and Greeks, wise and foolish by the world's standards, rich and poor. By doing this, God demonstrates that he is not the God of the *usual*, but of the seemingly *impossible!* It must break God's heart to watch us constantly settling for the conventional wisdom that people will gather only in homogeneous settings. He wants to unite us in faith communities that literally *shout* his power to save from any and every background and condition. Here's how Paul puts it:

> Where is the wise man? Where is the scholar? Where is the philosopher of this age? Has not God made foolish the wisdom of the world? . . . God was pleased through the foolishness of what was preached to save those who believe. . . . but we preach Christ crucified: a stumbling block to Jews and foolishness to Gentiles, but to those whom God has called, both Jews and Greeks, Christ, the power of God and the wisdom of God. . . .
>
> Brothers, think of what you were when you were called. Not many of you were wise by human standards; not many were influential; not many were of noble birth. But God chose the foolish things of the world to shame the wise; God chose the weak things of the world to shame the strong. . . . so that no one may boast before him. It is because of him that you are in Christ Jesus, who has become for us wisdom from God. . . . Therefore, as it is written: "Let him who boasts boast in the Lord."
>
> 1 Corinthians 1:20–21, 23–24, 26–27, 29–31

New Life Community Church represents the way God works. It's a kaleidoscope! People from different ethnic backgrounds, most not very rich or educated, many struggling with serious problems, are discovering they can get along and grow as redeemed people in the family of God. That's why New Life Community is the captivating model of a multicultural church we want to recommend to our readers.

Discussion Starters

1. Discuss the similarities and differences between your church's community and that of New Life Community Church.
2. We have emphasized the crucial nature of leadership in forming multicultural churches. If you are the pastor of a church considering new, more multicultural directions, what do you represent in disposition, calling, gifting, or experience that would make you the leader needed? If you do not have all the necessary gifts, what kind of staff might you need to assist you?
3. New Life asked Galilee Baptist Church to accept changes if they wished to be effective in their changing urban multicultural situation. What changes might be necessary in your church for people of other cultures and the new generation to feel at home?
4. Could your church become a "network" church with various satellites meeting particular needs, such as separate languages and transportation challenges? Have you considered using home groups to help meet these needs?
5. Would your church ever consider becoming part of an existing multicultural ministry? Are you aware of any dynamic church ministries in your city with which you could either network or which could serve as a model for your church?

10

A Call for Commitment

Michael Pocock

> Once to every man and nation comes the moment to decide,
> In the strife of Truth with Falsehood, for
> The good or evil side . . .
> Then to side with truth is noble,
> When we share her wretched crust,
> Ere her cause bring fame and profit,
> And 'tis prosperous to be just.
>
> James R. Lowell, "The Present Crisis"

Decision time! Associating with those who are ethnically and culturally distinct has never been popular. Many of us learned as children to associate with people like us, but should Christians and churches live by what is simply a convention of humanity in the flesh? What shall we do personally or as a church in the light of what we have discussed? By now several points should be clear:

1. America continually changes. Transitions are inevitable.
2. Ethnic diversity has characteristically enhanced our country.
3. The presence here of peoples from around the world is for us a divine opportunity.
4. In Christ, through his Holy Spirit, diverse peoples *can* thrive together.
5. Existing multicultural churches prove that diversity in church life *is* possible.
6. Doing multicultural outreach and becoming a multicultural church don't just happen. They require a deliberate decision.

In this chapter we will first think about what we as individuals can do to engage those of other cultures, then we'll discuss how our churches should respond to the kaleidoscopic changes around us.

Intercultural Friendships

Left to ourselves, most of us associate with people like ourselves. This is as true for those who are preparing for ministry as for laypeople. As a professor of intercultural studies, I assign students each semester in Introduction to World Missions to befriend an international student off campus. Many students get in touch with this person on their own at work or in their community. Others are paired with foreign students through the ministry of International Students Incorporated who have workers around the country and cooperate with us in this endeavor.[1]

The students' first response to this assignment is usually that it will be a strange and uncomfortable experience. It's amazing what students report by the close of the semester! Though initially unsure of themselves, they discover another world of experience through the friendships they form. Many of these associations continue on beyond the time of the assignment. They eat with each other, talk on the phone, e-mail one another, attend ball games together, and often the international student is invited home for a weekend.

Sometimes it's the other way around. The American student is invited to the international student's home. Imagine the thrill of sitting down to a wonderful meal prepared by Kuwaiti Arabs or being in a Chinese home and learning about the challenges of life and education in China. Students learn new customs. They learn to take their shoes off on entering a Japanese home or dorm room and appreciate the effort it takes to master complex course work in English. Many discover that the student they befriend is more eager to discuss spiritual issues than are most

North Americans. Christians are able to share their faith as well as learn firsthand about Islam, Buddhism, Hinduism, or Marxism.

This is the kind of thing individuals can easily do, as was described more fully in earlier chapters, but it will not happen without a decision to do so or without encouragement and facilitation by leaders who serve as resource people. If we live in a community where those of other cultures have also come to live, it is not too difficult simply to greet those we meet while out walking the dog or tending to the garden. My wife and I usually take cookies and simple gifts around to all our neighbors at Christmas. This has been a very natural way to discover who lives around us. If we already know the nationality, culture, or religion of a neighbor, we can take food or gifts at their special seasons. Muslims, for example, fast all day during the month of Ramadan, the ninth month of the Muslim year. But they do eat at night, and a three-day celebration and feast mark the end of the month. This is a great time to get together. Asians, particularly ethnic Chinese, celebrate a different New Year than westerners. This, like the Western celebration, is a time of rejoicing and calls for visiting one another. Latin Americans frequently visit house to house in their communities on Christmas eve. They also celebrate the sixth of January, the Day of Kings. For some, that is the day for the exchange of presents rather than on Christmas day.

There are many opportunities to get to know those of other cultures in a personal way. Even if we have lived near people for quite some time without getting to know them, we can begin now! How hard is it to say something like the following to your neighbor? "Ahmed, Carlos, or Mariko, it's amazing that we've lived so close and have never gotten to know each other. My wife and I would love to sit down with you for a cup of coffee and a piece of pie. When could we do that?" Most of us need to get definite about taking first steps. Like jumping off a diving board, it may look high at first, but the water's softer than you think.

Education is valued highly by many families coming to North America. Although they may be initially bewildered about navigating the system, they may be happy to get involved with parent-teacher organizations at the local schools. They will appreciate your efforts to show them how to connect. The American Field Service facilitates an exchange program for high school students from abroad. American students can be placed with families overseas for a semester or a school year.[2] About twenty-five hundred students were placed with American families in the year 2000.[3] Once a family or two in the church are doing this, ask them or the students they are hosting to share their experiences with the church family, explaining how it works. These are ways to broaden the experience and education of our families by sharing our lives with those from other countries.

Following the attack on the World Trade Center in September 2001, a number of Anglo American women began to accompany Middle Eastern Muslim women when they went shopping, so the Muslims would feel safe. It was heartening to discover when I visited a nearby Pakistani family to reassure them during the critical aftermath of the WTC attack that many other Christians had visited them, bringing pies, gifts, and flowers.

When it comes to change in a community or church, the enlightened attitudes and actions of individuals will precede communal initiatives, especially in Western cultures. Somebody has to be first. Until there are a number of church members personally interested, involved, and enjoying intercultural friendships, it is unlikely that the church as a body will take steps to engage the culturally diverse people in the neighborhood. Once several individuals or families have had a taste of intercultural friendships, they will more likely become supporters of a wider program through the church. Encouraging individual or family "pilot" initiatives would be a strategic move by leaders who hope their church will get more involved in multicultural ministry.

People who feel impatient with their church about adopting bigger initiatives in intercultural ministry can always get involved on their own and encourage others to do the same. The satisfaction that individuals experience can be contagious. It will grow as people pray and wait for momentum to build. *Anticipation* rather than *agitation* will win the day.

The Church Decision on Multicultural Ministry

In previous chapters, we have suggested various levels of church response to a multicultural community. These have varied from tentative, easy steps all the way to profound change where the church becomes substantially multiethnic. The Southern Baptists distinguish six levels of local church involvement in a multicultural community.[4] All of these can be found among their churches. Although the majority of the Southern Baptist churches are white, reflecting various levels of response to those of other cultures in their community, they also have more than four thousand churches in the United States where 110 other languages are used. The six levels of multicultural involvement evident among Southern Baptists are these:

1. Churches with ethnic departments
2. Separate ethnic congregations on the same premises
3. Churches assisting exterior ethnic congregations
4. Churches with ethnic outreach ministries

5. Churches sharing catalytic workers with ethnic churches
6. Multicultural churches

Clearly, local churches can decide on several distinct types of ministry in multicultural communities. Churches may progress from one level to the next, but the decision to engage at one level does not mean the church *must* move on to a deeper level of involvement. Satisfactory experience with one configuration of multicultural ministry does, however, lay the groundwork for deeper involvement. First Baptist Church has started or encouraged the start of fifty-five churches during its one hundred years in Dallas. Many of these are now ethnic churches enjoying their own facilities in other parts of the Dallas and Fort Worth area, and two are multiethnic in makeup.

Lanny Elmore, the leader for ethnic ministries at First Baptist, says the church itself did not initiate all these ministries. They simply made their facilities available to small ethnic groups that requested a place to meet.[5] In a sense, this needed no decision by the church apart from allowing its facilities to be used. Although there does not appear to be a great deal of integration of ethnic groups within the generally Anglo congregation, there is a lot happening under the same roof. And churches of many cultures have been spread throughout the metropolitan area to the glory of God. At one point or another, five out of the six Southern Baptist levels of multicultural ministry involvement have been in evidence at First Baptist.

Many churches located in changing communities fail to initiate outreach to newly arriving ethnics, until "white flight" has reduced the churches to less than viable size. George Barna shows that when this happens, it is almost impossible to turn the church around. "Once a church loses its momentum, the most probable outcome is either death or stabilization at a much smaller size."[6] Fortunately First Baptist has been facilitating ethnic outreach during most of its existence. At the same time, it has retained its overall strength and continues as a strong city-center church. Its decision to become involved with multicultural ministry did not arise from desperation about diminishing size but from a desire to respond to opportunities in the community.

Many churches, however, consider a multicultural ministry because they are losing members and the community around them is changing. Barna admits his suggestions for turning churches around are better understood as proactive steps for churches that are still strong yet understand they must act in the present to avoid loss in the future. Although the odds are against recovery for a declining church, Barna's *Turnaround Churches* references thirty churches that did face their crisis, took the appropriate steps, and recovered their momentum. *Turnaround*

Churches is well worth study in conjunction with this book, simply because churches considering multicultural ministry are frequently doing so because they have reached the point where there is no alternative in their present situation.

When we suggest that churches consider new patterns of outreach, it is with the assumption that leadership is attending to the basics, and this process is going on in an atmosphere of prayer and in accordance with the Word of God. What about worship, prayer, preaching, and teaching? How about fellowship, evangelism, and service? None of these can be forgotten when thinking about new initiatives. Airplane pilots are taught that when facing a crisis in the air, they should always remember to *fly the plane!* Good advice! A pilot cannot walk about the aircraft checking for problems and still keep it flying. The apostles understood this principle when in Acts 6 they faced the problem about inequitable distribution of food to needy widows—and that was a multicultural issue. The apostles paid attention to their principal ministry, teaching the Word of God and prayer. They made sure other wise and spiritual persons were involved in planning a response to the needs that had arisen.

A simplified process for determining the church's response to its changing community involves five steps:

1. Recognition of reality
2. Assessment of needs and resources
3. Recasting the church's vision
4. Implementing the vision
5. Evaluation

A Scenario for Adopting New Directions for Multicultural Ministry

After a brief synopsis of the steps that will help a church engage a culturally changing community, we'll go into greater detail concerning the five steps of the process.

Step One: Reality Recognition

An individual leader, possibly the pastor, realizes the community is changing and believes that a response is necessary. He calls for prayer and study of the situation to determine the best approach. A task force of selected leaders and church members undertakes a study and reports its findings to the congregation.

Step Two: Assessing the Situation

First, the leadership group, then the congregation, evaluates the facts gained in the previous step, interpreting the significance for the church.

Meanwhile, the leadership appoints a task force to study what resources the church currently enjoys in terms of spiritually gifted people, skills, expertise, experience, and facilities. A report back to the congregation shows how these could be used in the developing situation in the community.

Step Three: Recasting the Vision of the Church

Next, the congregation meets to pray and reflect in an attempt to discover the relationship between the data and assessment gathered in steps one and two, the relevant biblical teaching, and the resources they represent as a congregation. This may require a series of meetings over a period of time. The congregation thinks about its purpose, mission, values, strategy, people, and location. A group may be assigned to each of these six points. They will suggest a selection of responses similar to those that have been illustrated in earlier chapters.

One person, who enjoys the confidence of the group and is passionate about the new direction, is assigned to construct a unified statement of the vision he believes the congregation is ready to grasp and adopt. This task calls for some creative imagery in word crafting as well as clarity and specificity.

The congregation meets again to question and clarify their understanding of the proposed vision statement. The leadership honestly states the implications of each point for the life and ministry of the church. People are given more time to reflect and pray about adopting the new vision statement.

Step Four: Implementing the Vision

Generally beginning with small steps or "pilot programs," the church puts the vision into practice. Every step must intentionally flesh out a part of the vision. It's been said that what is everybody's business is nobody's business, so it's important that individuals and couples take responsibility for each new activity. If part of our vision is that those of different ethnicities will feel welcome at our church, then certain people must be given or take the responsibility to see that it happens.

Step Five: Evaluation

Any initiative needs ongoing refinement. There will be some mistakes, some unforeseen outcomes. Periodic evaluations at stated intervals give opportunities to identify difficulties and plan to overcome them. It's also reassuring to a congregation to know that a new initiative will be evaluated or reviewed and that leadership is open to modifying the plan.

Now let's look at these steps in more detail.

Recognition of Reality

From the very beginning, the Anglo congregation of Faith Lutheran Church in British Columbia wanted to be a church that served the whole community. They could see that as their community grew, its businesses, housing, and schools all reflected the diversity found in Vancouver and other major cities across Canada. Faith Lutheran faced the reality that they were in a multicultural community and decided to become a missionary church in obedience to Christ's Great Commission.[7]

Some churches exist in stable monocultural communities for many years before cultural diversification becomes evident. This was true of East Grand Avenue Baptist Church in Dallas. They grew from their founding in 1916 to a size of 2,574 in the 1960s. The construction of an interstate highway nearby did away with the homes of many in the congregation and set the stage for the arrival of new minorities. These events were the wake-up call for the church, as it recognized a new community reality. In their case, a longtime member, who was Hispanic, became the catalyst in forming a new Hispanic congregation on the same premises. A Spanish-speaking associate pastor was called in 1974.

Vietnamese began to arrive in the community following the Vietnam War. The nearby Buckner Baptist Children's Home received and resettled many families. In 1979 East Grand called a Vietnamese assistant pastor and a second ethnic congregation was formed.

The Hispanic and Vietnamese pastors and their congregations maintained considerable interrelationships with the Anglo majority congregation. All pastors were considered to be on the same staff. Joint communion services and other celebrations were held regularly and the second-generation (English-speaking) young people were involved in joint activities. Hundreds of diverse young people headed for camp programs each summer. These days were recalled by veteran staffer Sylvia Green as the best in the church's history.[8] We'll come back to East Grand Baptist's story later in the chapter.

Understanding a Changing Community

How can you really understand your community? Never underestimate the value of getting out of your car and walking through a community to discover what is actually there. I often send students out on a walking tour of the shops, restaurants, housing, and municipal facilities of our community. This has usually been an eye-opener for them, even though they drive through these communities every day on the way to classes. There is much that eludes us when we're in our cars. By going through the community on foot, students discover just how diverse it is. They see Laotians, Vietnamese, Cambodians, Middle Easterners, Hispanics, and African Americans, as well as both wealthy and poverty-stricken Anglos. The experience has an impact on students as they see that this is the real America to which they will be ministering, and it desperately needs the gospel.

Newspapers are a great source for studying the community. A very good book on the multicultural makeup of the Dallas area could be compiled simply from the carefully researched and thoughtful articles published by the *Dallas Morning News*. These articles describe the life, aspirations, and challenges facing all the various ethnic groups in the area. Characteristics of the spirituality of the groups are also described, giving helpful material to any individual or church attempting to understand the community. In this modern electronic age, newspapers frequently have the full text of their articles online, and it is possible to target categories of articles published over a period of years through their web sites.

For example, when it was reported that the Hispanic Catholic parishioners in Dallas had increased from 99,929 in 1992 to 401,652 in 2001—a 400 percent increase in eight years—it should have been a reality check for both the Catholic Diocese of Dallas and everyone concerned about ministry to such a rapidly growing minority.[9] This has precipitated a need for more priests and other ministry workers and more ample physical facilities. It is my belief that the Catholic Church faces and deals with the reality of ethnic change more rapidly than many Protestant and evangelical churches. Part of the explanation is the Catholic parish system. Each parish deals with the parishioners who live there, so even if one ethnic group moves away and another enters, the Catholic Church continues to minister to its people. This means they have to adapt to different cultures. As I mentioned earlier, the Washington Theological Union, a consortium of Catholic seminaries, proposed some years ago that all priests in training be bilingual before graduation—not in Hebrew and Greek but in languages spoken in the communities of America.[10] The Chicago Theological Seminary made a similar commitment in 1994.

Using newspapers, real estate offices, chambers of commerce, the public library, the municipal office of city planning, and data gleaned from sources on the Internet, such as the U.S. Bureau of the Census, any church can form an accurate picture of its community, past, present, and future. Church associations or denominations research communities across the continent. They can furnish expert assistance, as can seminaries whose job is to prepare ministers for the future, the very future now presenting itself to local churches.

Feeling Helpless

This book has attempted to establish the continent-wide reality of increased ethnic and cultural diversification. Most readers would not be holding this book if they did not already have some sense of this fact and its implications for modern ministry. But an intuitive grasp of America's multicultural reality may not be sufficient to compel churches to adopt new initiatives. They may need hard data. The information from this book, coupled with information gleaned from the sources just mentioned, should help readers make a case for change in their churches.

Recognizing new realities, even if it seems overwhelming at first, is the key to developing a ministry response. The helplessness felt in such a situation may be exactly what God needs to move the church toward dependence on him.

Massive urban migration to Lima, Peru, in the late 1960s led one city congregation to ask God for wisdom about how to respond. Well-known Christian businessman R. G. LeTourneau teamed up with the Christian and Missionary Alliance to form an initiative called Lima Encounters Christ.[11] It resulted, over the years, in growth from a single congregation of 185 members to more than 40 churches with 35,000 believers today. Many of the congregations are healthy community churches with about 500 members each. A few are super churches in highly visible and accessible locations around the city. Asked what he thought was the key to this growth, Alfredo Smith, the Argentinian pastor around whom much of the early growth took place, responded: "The original congregation was willing to say, 'We don't know what to do, but we are willing to learn.'" That is a good response to feeling overwhelmed by new realities. It is the kind of receptive spirit God uses.

Jehoshaphat expressed this attitude in 2 Chronicles 20:12. After realizing his troops were faced with overwhelming numbers of Moabites and Ammonites, the king prayed, "We do not know what to do, but our eyes are upon you."

Assessment of Needs and Resources

Assessment moves beyond the gathering of facts to weighing their significance for decision making. Studying a community is something like studying the Bible. Oletta Wald popularized a three-step approach to biblical interpretation. The steps are observation, interpretation, and application. If "recognition of reality" corresponds to the "observation" step in biblical interpretation, "assessment" corresponds to "interpretation." What do the facts mean? What is their significance for the congregation and its future? One helpful way to categorize the information gained through observing the community is to group the data according to the *transitions* they indicate. Manuel Ortiz, following James Westgate—both with extensive backgrounds in urban and ethnic ministries—notes six transitions that typically occur in our communities:[12]

1. Generational transitions: The younger replace the older.
2. Economic transitions: The money of businesses and families moves.
3. Geographical transitions: The inhabitants move, new ones replace them.
4. Cultural transitions: New people bring new cultures. This is the single biggest factor affecting churches.[13]
5. Racial transitions: Attitudes and prejudices become evident.
6. Spiritual transitions: Churches lose spiritual vibrancy, orthodoxy. New religions arrive.

Distinguishing these transitions and grouping observations according to them give a multidimensional understanding of the data gathered. This process helps prevent oversimplification by encouraging the church to account for changes in each category. For example, a church in the community may be losing members and may attribute it to the fact that new ethnicities are arriving. In reality it may be that the spiritual vitality of the church has diminished. It no longer communicates the message that had been vital to its growth. I once had the opportunity to preach in a dwindling church. My message was about salvation and the need to share the gospel with others. As one member greeted me at the door she said, "My, that was an inspiring message. We haven't heard anything like that for years!" Unfortunately, pastors in some churches simply stop preaching on certain themes, without telling anyone that they no longer believe in them. Churchgoers assume the pastor believes as the church always has, but in reality he has changed.

What Transitions Mean

Transitions in the community are indicators of changes the church must make if it hopes to have a relevant ministry. Let's return to the story of East Grand Baptist Church. East Grand Baptist recognized and responded to changing ethnic realities in a timely way; nevertheless, the base of their Anglo membership continued to migrate to the suburbs. The size of their properties was such that even though their ethnic con-

204 Cultural Change and Your Church

gregations were of viable size, they could not hope to either buy or fully utilize the facilities. Both the Hispanic and Vietnamese congregations obtained other facilities that were convenient and affordable for them.

Eventually, the church had to face the decision of whether to move or stay. The number of Anglos in both the church and community was diminishing. The recent history of other churches in the community or in similar communities helped East Grand Baptist assess their situation.

They studied eight Baptist churches in similar circumstances.[14] Without referencing the exact six transitions noted above, East Grand Baptist's study actually touched on most of them. They were able to graph a thirty-four-year decline in membership and resources. This happened in spite of vibrant, Bible-centered ministry and the initiation of ethnic ministries, which evidenced a considerable amount of integration in spite of major linguistic differences. Their study showed that all the churches in similar circumstances relocated and grew significantly, although the changed location only gave a new *opportunity* rather than a *guarantee* of growth. They found other factors were needed, such as dynamic outreach, relevant ministry, dedication, and exciting worship. Several of the churches studied continued ministry to ethnic minorities in their old communities after they had relocated.

When churches do decide to move from a community, they should lay the groundwork for continued ministry to the people who remain behind. In the case of East Grand, now Grand View Baptist Church, their old facilities were sold to a church with similar spiritual and doctrinal commitments, in spite of offers by the school district and by congregations with radically different agendas. But some churches, desperate for funds to build new facilities, have sold their old buildings to whoever would buy them. In doing so, they advanced the growth of groups they earlier sought to win for Christ. One such church invested heavily in sending people and money for missions to other lands, but failed to reach out seriously to people from those countries when they moved to its own backyard!

Understanding People

Assessing or interpreting the community involves more than the quantification of data. We need to understand the diverse groups of people in the community if we are to become a church that attracts them. Hispanics may appear to non-Hispanics like a relatively homogenous group of Spanish-speaking people with roots in Latin America, but in reality they come from twenty-two countries on the continents of North and South America and from Central America and the Caribbean. They identify themselves in terms of their country of origin, unless they have been in the United States or Canada for more than two generations. There is more to being Hispanic than speaking Spanish and having roots to the south. Millions of second-generation Hispanics and other minorities speak English but still cherish their cultural roots. Asian Indians could be from any one of more than three hundred groups with distinct languages. Many Indians are Hindu, but others are Sikhs, Muslims, or Christian. Chinese come not only from the People's Republic of China but from Taiwan, Singapore, or Chinese communities scattered all over the world.

The apparent complexity of other cultures is not a cause for exasperation. It's actually fascinating. But it calls for study and interaction leading to better understanding. I personally enjoy fishing. It's possible to catch fish with a cane pole and a worm. Many different species like worms, but what makes fishing enjoyable to me is finding out more about the different fish, what they eat, their habitat, and so on. What there is to know about fish and fishing is practically inexhaustible, but that does not discourage me. The more I learn, the more rewarding are my efforts. (Well, most of the time!)

Ministry to, for, or with various ethnic groups requires us to understand their special characteristics, allegiances, and preferences. We can learn about these groups by reading books like those distributed by the American Intercultural Press.[15] The mission of A.I.P. is precisely to help Americans who work with those of other cultures and vice versa.

An even better way to learn about various ethnic groups is directly from those of other cultures. This can be done by interaction in homes and businesses and by inviting ethnic minorities to your church to explain their culture.

The best way to understand others is by learning with them. To do this we must accept each other on the same level, as colearners. There are issues in every community that challenge its people. Getting together to learn about solving community problems, like drugs, the environment, employment, or health issues, is a way to understand not only the issue at hand but the ways people think about it.

Local churches need to connect with the community around them. When they don't, they become ingrown. One predominantly African American evangelical church jointly sponsors health fairs with a Muslim mosque across the street from them. The Muslims are Middle Eastern in origin. The interaction has brought goodwill and improved understanding between the two groups, and both openly share their spiritual commitments with each other during these times.

At the assessment stage, we learn what matters to the community around us and what should matter to the church. Needs, interests, and aspirations become clearer. Trends are identified and weighed. We begin to sense a possible range of responses. The next step is to envision a new reality for the church that reflects the changes in the community. We should then be in a position to adjust the church's mission and prioritize the needs and possibilities of ministry.

Recasting the Church's Vision

What churches will look like in the future will always be connected and grow out of the past, but they may not look much like the old model. The house church movement in England looks very different from the classical Anglican picture captured in quaint village churches and gothic cathedrals. Even a small rural American church looks completely unlike second-century Christian churches that met as burial societies in the catacombs of Rome. New contexts bring forth new paradigms even as the church seeks to remain a fellowship of redeemed people, worshiping the Lord Jesus, guided by the Word of God, and encouraging each other in personal spiritual growth and witness. As communities change, churches must continually reenvision what and how they must be while remaining true to the core values of Christ.

We have been discussing cultural and ethnic change in North America. These changes present many challenges and opportunities, but as we sort these out, other changes may add to the range of possibilities laid out before the churches. Recently the Bush administration noted the success of many faith-based community programs. The government proposed to make grant monies available to ministries meeting community needs. Help in the past has been in the form of tax exemption for charitable organizations and tax deductions for gifts made to them. The availability of additional funds may tempt many churches to add programs they previously could not have afforded. Among immigrant communities, English programs, legal assistance, and housing for refugees are just a few of the needs that churches may be called on to meet. They may be offered government help to do this. Some evangelicals have objected, showing that religious organizations and churches do not always do the best job or show the best accountability for funds invested in community programs. Furthermore, there are fears that the separation of church and state may be compromised, and churches may be forced to accept government criteria for the use of funds that clash with church convictions.[16] The very programs mentioned above do represent real needs and opportunities for churches in changing communities, but churches must use caution in regard to sources of funding and must always use funds properly whatever the source.

A Vision Statement

A standard is needed by which churches can decide which ministries they will undertake. For evangelicals, that standard is the Bible, but each church needs a more specific point of reference, based in Scripture but sufficiently narrowed to be useful. A vision statement crystallizes a church's understanding of what it hopes to be and accomplish. A vision statement helps a church decide among the many possibilities for ministry, but it cannot be developed without reference to the context or environment in which it serves.[17] Recognizing the reality of what's happening in the community and assessing its needs and resources will help the church grasp and implement a new vision.

If the church lacks a vision statement, now is the time to think seriously about writing one. Older existing statements may need to be reexamined in the light of community changes. We cannot undertake a full discussion of how to grasp the vision God has for a leader or a church. Others like George Barna, Andy Stanley, and Aubrey Malphurs have very helpful books on developing a vision. These are listed in the resources section of this book. But we must spend some time on the elements of formulating a vision. Discovering, stating, and communicating a vision to the church is indispensable. As the writer of Proverbs put it: "Where there is no vision, the people perish" (Prov. 29:18 KJV).

At the risk of treading familiar ground, let's briefly focus on the nature of vision and its relationship to decision making about multicultural ministry. The word *vision* brings to memory incidents in Scripture where key people came to understand something of God's future for them. In Isaiah 6, the prophet had a startling vision as his call to prophetic ministry. Peter's vision in Acts 10 made him aware of the cross-cultural ministry he would have with Cornelius and the spread of the gospel among Gentiles. Paul's vision in Acts 16 led him out of an existing area of ministry into a new and wider ministry on another continent. Our vision may not be as startling or dramatic as these, but we can and must have a vivid sense or picture of what's needed that comes from prayerful consideration of the way God worked in the past and is working in our present community situation.

George Barna expresses well the idea of vision as it applies to an individual or church today: "A vision for ministry is a clear mental image of a preferable future imparted by God to his chosen servants and is based upon an accurate understanding of God, self and circumstances."[18] Every word of the foregoing statement is significant, but notice the basis for vision: "an accurate understanding of God, self and circumstances." This book has attempted to describe the way God thinks in regard to the diversification and movement of peoples. We have also described the developing multicultural environment in North America as our "circumstances." If your church has described and assessed the reality of your own community, you may lack only an understanding of yourself, that is, how God has put you and your community together and what you or your church can do best as agents of change in your community.

If a *vision* is a mental image of *what* will exist in the future, *mission* explains *how* the vision will be realized. Malphurs distinguishes the two, pointing out that the *vision* has an emotional quality to it; it moves people. Vision comes from the heart and is aimed at the heart. The *mission* finds its source in the mind and is aimed at the minds of those to whom it is communicated.[19] The vision is a picture and the mission is the path to that picture.

Generating a vision is a lot like the process of invention. Imagine the process Thomas Edison went through on his way to inventing the incandescent lightbulb. First came problem recognition: Candles, whale oil lamps, kerosene and gas lights are messy, dangerous, and inconvenient. Wouldn't it be wonderful to have clean, consistent, convenient, and adequate lighting on every street and in every room? Edison already knew a range of possibilities. Electricity was known. Dynamos to make electricity and electric motors to run machines had already been invented. Some others had made attempts to produce light from electricity but with limited success. Edison knew that when electricity passed through a carbonized thread of cotton, it made it glow, but the thread soon burned up. He also knew that fire, rapid oxidation, requires oxygen. After a period of time—what today would be called incubation—he hit on the idea of passing a wire filament through a glass bulb from which all oxygen had been removed. He had the lightbulb! That's a lot like discovering a new vision for the church.

Like Edison, churches and ministry leaders know the basic principles of ministry, and in the case of culturally diverse communities, they can see the challenges and possibilities. They know what some others have tried. But what is the right combination that will work for this church? More important, which of all the possibilities does God want this church to attempt? If the church has an existing vision statement, it may help, but does it really deal with the new realities in the community? These questions mean that leaders must first teach, preach, and study God's perspectives regarding a multicultural environment. As Frank Tillapaugh explains, concerning the preparation of Bear Valley Baptist Church for a multifaceted, highly effective ministry, that imparting a new orientation to a congregation takes time.[20]

Fifty years ago churches may very well have had a mission statement by which they meant to capture their purpose and emphasis. Let's say that the statement read like a slogan: "Reaching the world with the gospel and our community for Christ." That has a certain ring to it. It reflects the Great Commission, it is Christ centered, it mentions the message of the gospel, and it includes the immediate community around the church. Is this the same as a vision statement? Could it be used in a culturally diverse community today? Would it help decide what should be done and what must be left undone today?

There are a number of ways that life in North America, the world, and the church have changed. Notice that the statement above says nothing about *being*—the quality of the church. It seems to assume that the world is a long way off. The founders probably thought of the world as masses of different cultures overseas and the community as a homogeneous group of people like themselves. What has changed in the intervening years? The world has come to North America. We are not just a variety of Europeans as was mostly the case before 1965. Our communities have become very culturally diverse and will become more so. The generations have changed from the familiar Builder generation, that Tom Brokaw called "the Greatest Generation"[21] to the Boomers, born after World War II; to the Busters, sometimes called Generation X.

The media has exposed hypocrisy in persons of authority in government and also in our churches. This has led the current generation to thirst for reality and relationships (many settle, however, for "virtual reality" and brief encounters). Families have fragmented and moved around to such a degree that, for many, meaningful, lasting relationships are only a dream. Increased options for every commodity and increased speed in communication and transport have all made for frenetic lifestyles, even among Christians. Life is too full to accommodate a deep commitment to Christ and the local church. We now have "McWorld," as author Tom Sine has put it.[22]

All these changes call for reenvisioning ministry. Many churches are in the process of doing exactly this. Relatively young churches, like the amazing Willow Creek Community Church in Illinois, just twenty years old in 1996, did a complete review of their vision and ministry. Their pastor, Bill Hybels, told them that at today's rate of change, they could only project for the next five years.[23]

Recheck your vision and mission statements in the light of the reality around you and with your eyes on the God who calls, guides, and empowers you. If your statements are outdated, take time to study them before undertaking any serious initiatives with multicultural ministry, but don't back away from engagement with the America of today just because it calls for changes that may be uncomfortable. Invest the serious time, prayer, and waiting on God that authentic ministry merits.

If the church believes its purpose or mission statement truly represents its intended direction, the question is whether, in the light of current developments, the church has the best strategy and methods for enfolding people of diverse cultures into its fellowship. Aubrey Malphurs suggests that an adequate vision statement may include any or all of six components: the ministry's purpose, mission, values, strategy, people, and location. Each church's vision statement will be unique, depending on its particular makeup and circumstances.[24]

Because others have developed vision statements, it's tempting to simply pick one that seems to fit the church and adopt it. This would be a mistake. People give their hearts and efforts to plans they have had a hand in developing. Therefore every church should develop its own vision. But other vision statements can be instructive, suggesting possibilities that otherwise might not be considered.

Vision statements are meant to be faith stretching, but they can provoke anxiety. When Jesus' own disciples gathered to receive the Great Commission, Matthew records that some "worshiped him; but some doubted" (28:17). Anxious people are helped when they see that others have also had the courage to dream big dreams and take new steps. Look at the multicultural intentionality of the mission statement of the Asian-American Baptist Church (AABC) in Richardson, Texas:

> Our mission (is) to reach the culturally diverse Asian-American community with the Gospel of Jesus Christ, leading the lost to the saving knowledge of Christ and the saved to spiritual maturity through evangelism, worship, prayer, instruction, and fellowship using predominantly English and ministering to all people as God enables.[25]

Many members of Arnold Wong's congregation are second-generation Chinese, Korean, Filipino, Japanese, or Anglo. These are the people they *intended* to enfold. The AABC is solving the dilemma of many second-generation ethnic Americans who are assimilating into the mainstream. They no longer feel fully at home in a single-ethnicity church yet still retain appreciation for their roots and heritage.

Vision statements bring *intentional specificity* to church planning and outreach. A church will never "accidentally" accomplish a goal it never stated—unless that goal was failure.

Adopting the New Vision

When the leadership feels the congregation knows all it needs to know about the new vision and is spiritually ready to move ahead, they lead the group to a vote. The leadership should make clear in advance the size of the majority it expects if the new vision is to be adopted. It would be pointless to proceed without a large majority in favor. The leaders should encourage those who are not in favor to give the church time to see if things work out better than they had envisioned, assuring them that the basic, biblical values always held by the church will be retained and ministry to them will continue even as the church implements needed change.

The congregation should then covenant together to adopt and work toward the realization of the vision.

Implementing the Vision

In earlier chapters we suggested various levels of response to an ethnically changing community. We have seen that there are individual opportunities that do not require a group decision, and there are a number of possibilities for the church that will require group decisions. Some steps are easier than other steps; the former will usually precede the latter.

Since the congregation has at this point adopted a fresh vision, we can presume that there are people willing to get involved with implementation. Clearly the strongest allies in the formation and adoption of the vision are the most likely to take direct action. These are the people to whom the Holy Spirit has given a burden for ministry. Frank Tillapaugh writes:

> How does the pastor persuade people . . . to carry on a four-year work with refugees? The pastor doesn't; the Holy Spirit does. This ministry goes on without committees or fanfare . . . because of a desire to be obedient to God's call. We are confident that God will give our people the deep desire to do whatever ministry He wants them to do.[26]

This attitude of expectancy and dependence on the Holy Spirit led to the establishment of more than fifty ministry outreaches at Tillapaugh's church, Bear Valley Baptist in Colorado, all of them initiated and led by laypeople. Tillie Burgin, leader of the well-known Mission Arlington at the First Baptist Church of Arlington, in Texas, takes a similar approach to that of Tillapaugh in Denver. The way she recruits the workers she needs for outreach to needy apartment dwellers in the area works like this: She carries around a set of three-by-five cards with a separate task on each one. When a person asks her if he or she can help, Tillie simply gives him or her one card and tells the person to call her when the job is done. If the volunteer does it, she gives the person another job. If the job is not completed, she doesn't pursue the person for further involvement.

Mission Arlington has more than thirty house churches located in at-risk apartment complexes around the city. These are all cared for by lay workers, some of whom receive an apartment free of charge if they will live in and serve the residents of the complex. The residents of these apartment complexes are generally ethnic minorities who are also poor. Every Sunday about as many people are gathered in the apartment house churches as meet at the main church facilities.[27]

What are the lessons for implementing a vision for multicultural ministry? The pastor must be the "standard bearer," committed to seeing the vision realized. When people express their God-given concern, the pastor entrusts them with ministry initiatives. Continued responsibility is given to those who prove themselves faithful.

How can people do what they were never trained to do? We can be thankful that God places gifted people in every local body of believers. Spiritual gifting provides a basic resource for ministry. Scripture mentions gifts like hospitality, administration, mercy, leadership, and contributing to the needs of others (Rom. 12:6–8). These gifts are more than a predisposition to exercise a particular skill. They ensure that what's done is a channel of spiritual blessing to those who are the beneficiaries.

There are also resource groups to train laypeople in the context of the very ministry they hope to do. Does the church want to amplify its outreach to international students at a local university or community college? International Students Incorporated will take volunteers with them and introduce them to students who would like to meet with American families.

How about meeting housing needs for ethnic families on limited incomes? Habitat for Humanity specializes in building new homes and reconditioning older ones for families that qualify. Your people don't need to be construction specialists, although the expertise of many of your members could become a ministry in connection with Habitat for Humanity. Habitat will take groups from your church, show them what to do, and supervise them. In the process, your people will be working alongside the very family that will occupy the house. What better way to bond with people in the community or around the world? It won't be long before your church can spearhead manageable housing projects in a way that harnesses the ministry aspirations of the laypeople and connects the church with needy people from the ethnically diversifying community.

Do families want to host an exchange student from abroad but don't know how to arrange it? The American Field Service can help. Local high school counselors can help. There are faith-based programs like the International Christian Youth Exchange. Check the resources in this book for these and other groups that can help you implement your vision for outreach to your kaleidoscopic community.

Evaluation

Everyone in the congregation will be reassured to know that there will be periodic checkups to evaluate the important steps that have been taken to implement the vision. These checkups help ensure that the church's objectives are being met, and they reaffirm the significance of each initiative. Evaluation underlines the significance of a particular program to the overall ministry.

Set regular times for evaluation, then the anxiety about being evaluated is reduced. The people in outreach ministries are usually volunteers, but keeping their goodwill is as important as it is with paid staff.

Multicultural Ministry: Let's Hear from the People!

What do ordinary people feel about a church that becomes more multicultural? What are the benefits for those who get involved with outreach to those of other cultures? Here are comments from those who have done it.

Hosting an Exchange Student

Harold and Thelma Reynolds hosted two exchange students while their own children were in high school. One was from Ethiopia, the other from Indonesia. The students fit in well with the children in their own family. "It was a concrete experience with people from around the world. We discovered their needs and aspirations were very much like our own." Thelma reflected on the delight she felt simply hot-combing the hair of the beautiful Ethiopian girl. She had never really known what people of other races do for their own beauty care. Both the students took an active and appreciative part in the family's church life, and they have stayed in touch as much as possible after the girls went home. "We'd do it again," said Harold and Thelma, "and we recommend it to others."[28]

Friendships with International Students

Heather Turner wondered what it would be like to befriend an international student on a nearby university campus. Fortunately the student had already indicated she wanted to meet an American. "I was very nervous to be one-on-one with a Chinese student, because my impression was that Chinese girls were very timid and guarded. How wrong I was! At our very first meeting, Yue was very open and talkative. Instead of making small talk about families and culture, she asked me directly if I believed in God and was a Christian."[29]

Apparently the Chinese student was hoping for an opportunity to talk about Christianity because she had already met several Christians who had been very kind to her. Heather continued to meet with Yue and exchanged many e-mails. Only a month and a half into their friendship, Yue indicated she would like to become a Christian. She spent Thanksgiving with some Christian Chinese friends she had met. That's when she came to Christ. "Her [e-mail] writing spilled over with the happiness in her heart and the excitement she had about her decision." Heather and Yue attended a Christmas concert together where Yue expressed her desire that all her family would know the gift of Jesus. Heather's original reluctance to meet foreign students has been replaced with the joy of discovering a precious friendship.

Belonging to a Multicultural Church

Earlier we referred to the Asian-American Baptist Church in Richardson, Texas. This is a congregation intentionally founded to enfold second- and third-generation Asians and others of diverse ethnicity. Poul Prip, a son of Danish immigrants, who himself found Christ in a Chinese church in California, now fellowships and teaches at AABC in Texas. He and others feel comfortable in an ethnically neutral place enjoying an international flavor. There is room for individual ethnic styles, but no single one predominates. Mixed couples feel comfortable there, and the worship style is more contemporary than in single-ethnicity churches that have a more conservative outlook.[30]

An Ethnic Congregation under an Anglo Roof

As we conclude this chapter of the book, another chapter is just beginning in the life of the Ethiopian Evangelical Baptist Church. Today they are on the front page of the *Dallas Morning News*, joyously celebrating their "coming of age" as an independent church in their own facilities.[31]

I stopped by the church to congratulate the staff and chat with a graduate of Dallas Theological Seminary, Aweke Mugeta, who is now on the church staff. They had had a wonderful weekend celebration. Eighteen years ago a handful of Ethiopian believers had gathered at a picnic and began Bible study and prayer together. Under the guidance of an Ethiopian Airlines pilot, who had become the group's pastor, they approached Highland Baptist Church in 1983 and asked if they could meet in their facilities. Pastor Aubrey Patterson said he'd be thrilled for them to meet there. He'd been asking the Lord how their church could be used to help newcomers in the area, and here was the answer!

EEBC grew at Highland until there was not enough room for them and the growing Anglo congregation, so Lakeside Baptist Church became their second home. The Anglo congregations had encouraged the Ethiopians by helping with their pastor's salary, but before long the Ethiopian congregation accepted the challenge of being solely responsible for their group's expenses.

Even though they had some lean times, excellent Ethiopian pastoral leaders, like Pastor Zeleke Alemu, were the key to further growth and better organization. Later Pastor Seifu Kebede led the way to purchasing the church building they now own. Kebede's assistant, Bedilu Yirga, became pastor and under him the church is now completely on its own, but dependent on the Lord. As more than three hundred members rejoiced, a Lakeside Anglo leader recalled appreciatively the partnership with the Ethiopians. "We have enjoyed having them over at our church," said Robert Bleakley. "We wanted to be a part of this (celebration) today!"

Pastor Yirga added, "We were a mission fellowship. We were not by ourselves. We are in a place now where we can help others; we can send out missionaries and evangelists."

"We appreciated the help given us over the years by Highland Baptist and Lakeside. They encouraged us financially until we could manage things ourselves, but the biggest thing is that they gave the 'green light' to meet in their facilities," said Aweke Mugeta.

Summary

It's up to you, and your Lord will help you do it! What will your first steps be? Whether you read this book as an individual searching for the right response to the kaleidoscope of your community or as part of a group considering a church response, it's time to move into action! None of the churches and people you have met in this chapter and book would go back to a monocultural, monochromatic existence. Faced with the vibrant new face of North America, they want to *experience* it rather than retreat from it.

We have used the kaleidoscope as our metaphor for what America is becoming. That's because every turn of the kaleidoscope brings a fresh and beautiful new arrangement into view. As you see your community changing, why not move with it? Appreciate the new depth that diverse friendships can bring to your life. Participate in the new life that people from other cultures breathe into your own. Celebrate the beauty of worship, the satisfaction of service, and the warmth of relationships when you experience the *reality* of a Scripture promise: "God was reconciling the *world* to himself in Christ" (2 Cor. 5:19).

A multicultural personal and church life gives you an opportunity to experience now some of the glory of what will one day be an even larger reality, a reality that God himself will bring to pass, when people of "every nation, tribe, people and language," gather around the throne of the Lamb exclaiming:

> Salvation belongs to our God,
> who sits on the throne,
> and to the Lamb. . . .
> Praise and glory
> and wisdom and thanks and honor
> and power and strength
> be to our God for ever and ever.
> Amen!

Revelation 7:9, 10, 12

Discussion Starters

1. This chapter dealt with personal and church decision making leading to involvement with those of other cultures. At the personal level, what have you or other group members decided to do? Can you name a person or family of another culture in your community with whom you plan to initiate a friendship? Who is it?
2. What activities will you do together with the person or family you selected?
3. Does your church have a vision and mission statement? Study them to see if they include specific reference to reaching and shepherding families of the various ethnicities in your community.
4. Do you or the leadership of your church believe this is the time to modify the church's vision statement to include reference to other cultures in the community?
5. Discuss the steps you believe the church should take to initiate ministries among those of other cultures in the community. What resource people, settings, and methods could be used to encourage the church to adopt the initiatives necessary for truly multicultural ministry and church life?
6. What changes are necessary in the life, ministry, and fellowship of your church for it to reflect the diversity of its immediate community?

Appendix

Goals and Objectives
for Local Church Diversity

*Guidelines Adopted by Joseph Henriques
from the Air National Guard's Objectives
for Managing Diversity*

Accountability and Responsibility

Goal 1: Pastors and staff will be held accountable for creating an environment that fosters diversity, acceptance of all cultural, racial, or ethnic groups.

Objective 1: Create a culture where diversity is adhered to as the church's way of life and is viewed, therefore, as an investment in the future.

Objective 2: Apply an evaluation system that includes levels of expectations of behavior and attitudes among its members and clear feedback, along with an understanding of the rewards of diversity and consequences of favoritism toward one group while neglecting others.

Objective 3: Implement written, leadership-developed plans that will include objectives for achieving a culture of diversity.

Goal 2: All members will be responsible for understanding and promoting diversity.

Objective 1: Survey church members periodically on the effectiveness and implementation of the impartiality initiative and provide feedback on survey results.

Education and Training

Goal 3: Everyone in the church will be provided appropriate training in diversity.

Objective 1: To achieve the desired ethnically diverse church culture, incorporate diversity into existing programs (Sunday school, newcomers class, worship service, visitation, etc.) to include initial and ongoing training, using materials provided by Christian ministries, publishing houses, and other educational sources.

Objective 2: Empower and train a staff and/or church member to advise and oversee training of all church members in diversity.

Goal 4: Church members will participate in community outreach programs to reach and prepare the culturally diverse for church membership.

Objective 1: Design plans and implement programs that will enable the church's members to reach out to all cultural, racial, and ethnic groups in their communities and to prepare them for church membership.

Objective 2: Provide resources and time away from church programs to enable church members to participate in a diverse array of community outreach programs to specific ethnic people.

Path of Christian Ministry

Goal 5: The pastor will ensure that every church member, regardless of ethnicity, has access to training and mentoring for Christian ministry in a multicultural environment.

Objective 1: Expand existing training programs to include a diversity of church members.

Objective 2: Establish a discipleship program that trains all church members regarding diversity.

Leadership Policy

Goal 6: The church will review and update church policies to ensure that a culture of diversity is being practiced in every aspect of church life.

Objective 1: Conduct a timely review of church programs and policies to ensure a diversity mind-set among current and potential church members.

Objective 2: Eliminate barriers that prevent any qualified church member, regardless of ethnicity, to assume positions of leadership in the church.

Goal 7: The issues of impartiality will be reviewed and emphasized when planning and conducting conferences and other special meetings within the church.

Objective 1: Establish guidelines that will enable those leading the meetings to include all ethnic groups.

Objective 2: Integrate diversity concerns in the agendas of conferences and special meetings, including recognition of achievements of the church's diverse membership.

Community

Goal 8: Enhanced community relations and media advertising will be used to increase positive perception of the church's commitment to diversity.

Objective 1: Provide adequate finances from the church to support community outreach that will communicate the church's activities and accomplishments among the church's diverse communities.

Goal 9: Church members will actively participate in local events, youth activities, youth mentoring, and other outreach programs among whites, minorities, and all ethnic groups in the community to establish and enhance community relationships and partnerships.

Objective 1: Establish clear guidelines for individuals to participate in community cultural activities.

Objective 2: Help support the efforts of church volunteers in a community missions programs among ethnic people.

Objective 3: Maximize use of church resources to enhance involvement in youth and community programs among ethnic groups in the community.

Objective 4: (Non-youth activities objective) Increase the visibility of church members in community organizations dedicated to diversity.

Objective 5: Establish a partnership with local educators to build a community relationship that fosters the church's involvement in the education and well-being of minority and ethnic families in the community.

Outreach and Discipleship

Goal 10: The church will establish a five-year marketing and communication plan that addresses the church's openness to racially, culturally, and ethnically diverse people.

Objective 1: Incorporate and coordinate diversity issues and themes within the church's strategic, outreach, and membership plans and budgeting process.

Goal 11: The church members involved in outreach and discipleship programs will reflect the diversity of the minorities and ethnic groups in the community.

Objective 1: Ensure all church members have an equal opportunity for involvement in the multicultural outreach and discipleship ministries of the church.

Objective 2: Employ interns, as necessary, to create a diverse outreach and discipleship force for the church.

Goal 12: The church will establish a highly visible outreach and service presence in minority and ethnic communities.

Objective 1: Identify the most strategic target area(s) and establish a church presence in coordination with community leaders.

Measurement

Goal 13: The church will develop, deploy, and periodically review an effective system to measure and communicate progress on the goals of diversity.

Objective 1: Ensure that the church's leadership are involved in the assessment process.

Objective 2: Identify and track key variables that measure progress in impartiality.

Objective 3: Gather data that clearly reflect the growth and recognition of minorities and ethnic members in the church through their involvement in leadership positions, Sunday school teaching, youth team, choir, church membership, other church functions, and their reasons for leaving the church.

Objective 4: Develop a way to measure diversity and include it as a key result area in the church's self-assessment.

Funding

Goal 14: The church will provide sufficient funding in support of the programs and efforts of diversity throughout the church.

Objective 1: Identify requirements and sources of funding for minority and ethnic programs and make it part of the annual church budget.

Notes

Chapter 1: Kaleidoscope America

1. John F. Kennedy, *A Nation of Immigrants* (New York: Anti-Defamation League of B'nai B'rith, 1958).

2. "American Indians," in *Encyclopaedia Britannica*, vol. 1 (Chicago: The Encyclopaedia Britannica, 1993), 329–32.

3. Stephen A. Rhodes, *Where Nations Meet: The Church in a Multicultural World* (Downers Grove, Ill.: InterVarsity Press, 1998), 15.

4. Rhodes states: "From 1980–1990, the United States experienced the largest amount of immigration since the turn of the century, as well as the most racially and ethnically diverse ever" (*Where Nations Meet*, 15). He cites Ruben Rumbout who gives a detailed analysis of the composition of this immigrant wave in, "The Crucible Within: Ethnic Identity, Self Esteem and Segmented Assimilation among Children of Immigrants," in *The Second Generation*, ed. Alejandro Portes (New York: Russell Sage Foundation, 1996), 121.

5. Peter D. Salins, *Assimilation, American Style: An Impassioned Defense of Immigration and Assimilation as the Foundation of American Greatness and the American Dream* (New York: Basic Books, 1997), 39. Salins disputes the "current hand-wringing" about the apparent nonassimilation of newer immigrants. He admits that there have always been "con-flicts between immigrants and natives and between blacks and whites [but says that these] could be resolved peaceably because America's first principles could not, in the end, be denied." These first principles will be explained later on, but they are found in Salins, 37–38.

6. Michael Novak, *The Rise of the Unmeltable Ethnics* (New York: Macmillan, 1972).

7. Scofield Memorial Church, Dallas, Texas, partners with SIM Inc., formerly the Sudan Interior Mission. The latter now focuses on North America as well as their historic operations in Africa. Dr. Terrill Nelson guides SIM's Ethnic Focus Ministry in North America. Contact SIM Inc., P.O. Box 7900, Charlotte, NC 28241-7900.

8. "The Keenest Recruits to the Dream," *The Economist*, 25 April 1998, 1, available at www.economist.com.

9. Ibid., 3.

10. Dianne Solis, "Coming on Strong," *Dallas Morning News* (4 Feb. 2001), 1H.

11. Georgie Anne Guyer, "U.S. Joins Third World," *Dallas Morning News*, 25 May 1993.

12. Roger Hernandez, "English Only Furor Dies from Absurdity," *Dallas Morning News*, 26 May 1998, 13A.

13. Salins, *Assimilation, American Style*, 33.

14. Edward Retta, "The Hispanic Evangelical Agenda" (presentation made

to the ministry at Dallas Theological Seminary, 1996), 4.

15. Mark Jobe, "Rethinking the Church to Reach the City," in *A Heart for the City,* ed. John Fudor (Chicago: Moody, 1999), 204. Interview, 17 April 2001. Jobe said attendance in March 2001 had reached 1,700.

16. Ibid., 205. Jobe cites Charles LeRoux and Ron Grossman, "Chicago's Racial and Ethnic Evolution," *Chicago Tribune,* 10 Feb. 1999, sec. 1, 17.

17. Interview with Mark Jobe, Chicago, 5 Nov. 1999. The author was privileged to spend four days in the Jobe family home, observing the ministries of New Life around the city and worship at the New Life Central congregation. Ministry and visits to this church over a period of thirty-five years have given me a deep appreciation for what it is now doing on a greatly amplified scale.

18. Helen Lee, "Silent Exodus: Can the East Asian Church in America Reverse the Flight of Its Next Generation?" *Christianity Today* (12 Aug. 1996), 50–53. See also Berta Delgado, "A Question of Honor: Asian Christians Struggle to Balance Respect with a Call to Convert Their Parents," *Dallas Morning News,* 1998, sec. G1.

19. This is evident in the three-part series called *First Steps* (Chicago: New Life Community Church [1700 W. 44th St. 60609], 1995).

20. Todd Davis, *Open Doors: Report on International Educational Exchange* (New York: Institute of International Education, 1998–99), 3.

21. Telephone interview with Derrah Jackson, ministry worker in Dallas, Texas, for International Students Inc., P.O. Box C, Colorado Springs, CO 80901, 7 Feb. 2000. Jackson regards 80 percent as a reliable estimate he has heard a number of times and which squares with his experience with international students.

22. Telephone interview update with Barbara Sixsmith, Missions Coordinator for Steve Murray, Missions Pastor, First Baptist, Atlanta, 7 Feb. 2000.

23. See contact information in note 21 above.

24. People of the World, Inc., P.O. Box 1784, Centreville, VA 20122.

25. Telephone update interview with Rev. Huang Soo Kim, Faith Lutheran Church, 17086 124th St., Surrey, B.C., Canada, 26 Jan. 2000.

26. Canadian evangelicals have shown great concern for ministry to their nation, which, like the United States, is experiencing rapidly increasing ethnic diversity. According to Pastor Kim of Faith Lutheran, they did obtain demographic data from the Canadian government on the area of Surrey, but the situation of ethnic diversity was really self-evident. Canadian readers should consult *Transforming Our Nation: Empowering the Canadian Church for a Greater Harvest,* eds. Jacqueline Dugas and James Montgomery et al. (Richmond, B.C.: Church Leadership Library, 1998). Also check the resources section for the works of respected Canadian sociologist of religion Reginald Bibby. Bibby details the changes ethnic diversity has brought to the religious scene in Canada and the implications for the life of the nation.

27. Brian Seim, "Unreached Peoples in Canada," in *Transforming Our Nation,* eds. Dugas and Montgomery, 157.

28. Harry Boer, *Pentecost and Missions* (Grand Rapids: Eerdmans, 1961), 200–201.

29. Bill Deener, "Dallas Little Asia: Refugees Endure Crime, Unfulfilled Dreams," *Dallas Morning News,* 11 May 1986, A18.

30. Nouwen expressed these ideas in many of his works, see particularly his *Road to Daybreak* (New York: Image Books, Doubleday, 1988) and *In the Name of Jesus* (New York: Crossroad, 1996).

31. George Alexander, *New Americans* (Cypress, Fla.: P and P Enterprises, 1997).

32. Ibid., 74–75.

33. Lee Weeks, "SBC to Elect Ethnic President within Five Years Envisions President," *The Baptist Press,* 4 Feb. 2000, 2.

34. Telephone update interview with Lanny Elmore, Dallas, Texas, 26 Jan. 2000.

Chapter 2: Clouds in Our Communities

1. From an *Intercultural Journal* article, submitted by Caroline R. Gorham, a student at Washington Bible College, Lanham, Md., on 10 April 2000.

2. Alexis de Tocqueville, *Democracy in America*, http://xroads.virginia.edu/HYPER/DETOC/home.

3. R. Albert Mohler, "Back to No Future?" *World* (22 April 2000), 9.

4. Paul C. Rosenblatt, Terri A. Karis, and Richard D. Powell, *Multiracial Couples* (Thousand Oaks, Calif.: Sage Publications, 1995), 289.

5. At the time Jesus was born, Hebrews saw the world divided into two types of people—Jews and everyone else. Jews regarded foreigners (Gentiles) as morally unclean and spiritually lost. Jews were God's people. Peter himself declared, "You know how unlawful it is for a Jewish man to keep company with or go to one of another nation" (Acts 10:28 NKJV).

6. This discussion assumes a universal sense of right and good according to two gifts of God: (1) the image of God in every person, and (2) God's common grace given to all people to know basic right (a standard of rightness and wrongness) and good (how we should treat others). All cultural mores are subject to the measurement and definition of truth as defined in Scripture.

7. James and Lillian Breckenridge, *What Color Is Your God?* (Wheaton: Victor Books/SP Publications, 1995), 20.

8. Craig Storti, *Cross Cultural Dialogues* (Yarmouth, Me.: Intercultural Press, 1990), 15–16.

9. An assessment of prejudice as written by Hyang-Hee Beh, a Korean student at Washington Bible College, describing her experiences during her first year in the States and in a high school. Lanham, Md., February 2000.

10. L. Robert Kohls and Herbert L. Brussow, *Training Know-How for Cross Cultural and Diversity Trainers* (Duncanville, Tex.: Adult Learning Systems, 1995), 25.

11. Ok Cha Soh "A Descriptive Analysis of Racial Attitudes Between African-Americans and Korean-Americans Toward Each Other."(Ph.D. diss., Union Institute, 2000). Dr. Soh, professor of multicultural counseling at Washington Bible College, Lanham, Md., has researched extensively on the issues, concerns, and methods of conflict resolution within the African American and Korean American communities.

12. Salins, *Assimilation, American Style*, 19.

13. *This Week with David Brinkley*, 25 July 1993, cited in Peter Brimelow, *Alien Nation* (New York: Random House, 1995), xxi.

14. Linda Chavez and Sally Piper, *Strangers at Our Gates: Immigration in the 1990s* (The Manhattan Institute, 1994), 38.

15. Rhodes, *Where the Nations Meet*, 126.

16. Terry M. Neal, "Candidate Buchanan Vows to 'Clean Up.'" *Washington Post*, 3 March 1999, A1.

17. Brimelow, *Alien Nation*, xvii.

18. Chavez and Piper, *Strangers at Our Gates*, xxi.

19. Ibid., 7.

20. Script from the MGM/UA video version of *Fiddler on the Roof*, Mirisch Productions, Inc., and Cartier Productions, Inc., 1971.

21. "Histories", 5.5, *The Word in Life Study Bible* (Nashville, Tenn.: Thomas Nelson, 1993), 1665.

22. Ibid., 1729.

23. "The Sultanate of Oman," *Washington Times*, 21 Dec. 1999.

Chapter 3: Catching the Idea of Kaleidoscopic Change

1. *Big Blue Marble*, is a television program syndicated in 1974 by Alpha Venture Productions. For further informa-

tion, visit http:/www.yesterdayland .com/ saturday/shows/synopsis.

2. Paul Tillich, "The Effects of Space Exploration on Man's Condition and Stature" in *The Future of Religions,* ed. Jerald C. Brauer (New York: Harper and Row, 1966), 39–51.

3. A. C. Ainger (1841–1919), *Songs of Praise* (London: Oxford University Press, 1931).

4. For an excellent treatment of the migration of peoples worldwide, see Robin Cohen, *The Cambridge Survey of World Migration* (Cambridge, U.K.: Cambridge University Press, 1995). Each population group receives a brief historic overview followed by more recent migration patterns and dynamics.

5. "North America," in *Encyclopaedia Britannica Macropaedia,* vol. 24 (Chicago: Encyclopaedia Britannica, 1998), 997, 1019.

6. Denis Twitchett and John K. Fairbanks, *Cambridge History of China* (New York: Cambridge University Press, 1978), 191. Genghis Khan's empire extended across Asia from the Pacific Ocean to the Caspian Sea. Mongols of the Golden Horde extended farther west to present-day Hungary and Romania.

7. James L. Newman, *The Peopling of Africa: A Geographic Interpretation* (New Haven: Yale University Press, 1995), 140ff. Newman shows that Bantu peoples originated in the present area of Nigeria-Cameroon in 5000 B.C. They were in Uganda by 2000 B.C., lower Congo by 1400 B.C., Zaire-Zambia by A.D. 500, central Zimbabwe by A.D. 1000, and Mozambique and South Africa by 1500.

8. "Celtic Peoples," *Encyclopedia Americana,* vol. 6, 152–54. This gives a chronology of the arrival of the various groups who have populated the British Isles. It dates the possible arrival of Celts in the eighth century B.C., certainly by the third. Britain was invaded by Romans in 55 and 54 B.C. and colonized by A.D. 43. For more in-depth treatment of these movements, including Saxons, Danes, and Normans, see Lloyd and Jennifer

Laing, *The Origins of Britain* (New York: Scribners, 1980), 188–89.

9. "England," *Encyclopedia Americana,* vol. 10, 367.

10. Ellis Cose, *A Nation of Strangers: Prejudice, Politics and the Populating of America* (New York: William Morrow, 1992).

11. Cheryl Russell, *Racial and Ethnic Diversity: Asians, Blacks, Hispanics, Native Americans and Whites* (Ithaca, N.Y.: New Strategist Publications, 1998), 349–50.

12. Paul Lovejoy, "The Volume of the Slave Trade: A Synthesis," in *Slave Trades, 1500–1800: Globalization of Forced Labor in an Expanding World,* ed. Patrick Manning (Aldershot, U.K.: Ashgate Publishing Co., 1996), 37–64. The author takes Philip Curtain's well-researched figure of 9.6 million African slaves imported to the Americas between 1451 and 1870 as a baseline. He compares succeeding critiques of Curtain by others including J. D. Fage and J. E. Inikori, concluding that Curtain's figure should be elevated. "As a rough guide, therefore, an estimate of the slave trade derived from import based data is approximately 10,210,000 slaves" (64).

13. Herbert Klein, *The Middle Passage: Comparative Studies in the Atlantic Slave Trade* (Princeton: Princeton University Press, 1978), 85–86.

14. Marilyn C. Baselar, *Asylum for Mankind: America, 1607–1800* (Ithaca, N.Y.: Cornell University Press, 1998), 119. Baselar's work is excellent, balancing Cose's dark yet realistic view of America's history of legalized prejudice with the fact that for millions, the United States has been a refuge and asylum. She admits we have been inconsistent and recognizes the horror of the slave era.

15. George Barna, *The Index of Leading Spiritual Indicators: A Statistical Report on the State of Religion in America* (Dallas: Word, 1996), 33. This reflects an annual January count of church attendees in the United States. Overall, about 33 percent attend church on any given Sun-

day, but the number is declining. Patrick Johnstone, *Operation World* (Grand Rapids: Zondervan, 1993), cites 11 percent attendance in Great Britain.

16. Baselar, *Asylum for Mankind*, 32.

17. Ibid., 40.

18. Salins, *Assimilation, American Style*, 40.

19. Baselar, *Asylum for Mankind*, 224.

20. Cose, *A Nation of Strangers*, 23.

21. Twitchett and Fairbanks, *Cambridge History of China*, vol. 10, 194–201.

22. Salins, *Assimilation, American Style*, 28.

23. Mary Elizabeth Brown, *The Shapers of the Great Debate on Immigration: A Biographical Dictionary* (Westport, Conn.: Greenwood Press, 1999), 49.

24. *United States Statutes at Large: 47th Congress, 1881–1883*, vol. 22 (Washington: Government Printing Office, 1883), 58ff. See also Brown, *Shapers of the Great Debate on Immigration*, 45.

25. *United States Statutes at Large: 68th Congress, Session One, 1923–24*, vol. 43, chap. 190 (Washington: Government Printing Office, 1925). This Act required identification of all immigrants by birth nation. It froze the ratio of immigrants permitted from every country at the level of their representation within the general population of the country, less blacks and American Indians, in the census of 1890. The maximum number of legal immigrants admitted in 1890 was 150,000. Since the vast majority of Americans born abroad were from Europe, the effect of the ordinance was to keep America primarily European.

26. Cheng-Lin Tien, chancellor of U.C. Berkeley, explains in his introduction to *Who's Who among Asian Americans, 1994–95*, that 110,000 Japanese were interned in the United States during World War II, even though 50,000 Japanese Americans served with distinction with the armed forces in Europe. Amy L. Unterburger, ed., *Who's Who among Asian Americans: 1994–95* (Detroit: Gale Research, 1995).

27. Ibid. See also Helen Zia and Susan B. Gall, eds. *Notable Asian Americans* (New York: Gale Research, 1995).

28. Cose, *A Nation of Strangers*, 106.

29. Ibid., 111.

30. Georgie Anne Geyer, "U.S. Joins Third World," Viewpoints, *Dallas Morning News*, 25 May 1993, 19A.

31. Cose, *A Nation of Strangers*, 109.

32. Ibid., 112.

33. Emma Lazarus, "The New Colossus," cited in "The Statue of Liberty," *World Book Encyclopedia*, vol. 12 (Chicago: Field Enterprises, 1973), 209.

34. Cose, *A Nation of Strangers*, 125.

35. The Church World Service cites the U.S. Committee for Refugees 1999 World Refugee Survey. Actually, 85,006 arrived in 1999. Ecumenical churches assisted 400,000 refugees to resettle in the United States between 1950 and 2000. churchworldservice.org/immigration/FAQ /html.

36. "Asian Refugees," *Stars and Stripes*, 10 Aug. 1996, notes Asian refugees peaked in the years 1981–90, corresponding with passage of the 1980 act. A total of 324,483 arrived in this ten-year period.

37. Exact numbers of Asian refugees resettled by the Christian and Missionary Alliance (C.M.A.) were unavailable, but Bouathong Vangsoulatda of the C.M.A. Laotian District indicated that 200,000 Laotian refugees came to the United States, many of them assisted in resettlement by the C.M.A. (Fax 27 June 2000).

38. Lee, "Silent Exodus," 50–53. Lee states, "There was 500% growth in Chinese churches in America between 1968–90 for a total of 644 congregations." There are now more than 2,000 Korean churches. The point of Lee's article, however, is that this growth would be greater if it were not for the loss of second-generation Asian Christians. This will be dealt with later.

39. George Alexander, *New Americans: The Progress of Asian Indians in America* (Cypress, Calif.: P and P Enterprises, 1997), 21.

40. Ibid., 13.

41. *Annual Report—Legal Immigration 1998* (Washington: U.S. Dept. of Justice, Immigration and Naturalization Service, 1998). See ins.usdoj.gov/graphics/aboutins/statistics/index.html.

42. Alexander, *New Americans*, 75–76, 82.

43. John A Siewert and Edna G. Valdez, eds., *Mission Handbook: U.S. and Canadian Christian Ministries Overseas* (Monrovia, Calif.: MARC, a division of World Vision, 1997), 32.

44. William M. Stark with Raymond H. Swartzback, "A Multicultural Church in a Multicultural Community," in *Center City Churches: The New Urban Frontier* (Nashville: Abingdon Press, 1993), 99–108.

45. Rhodes, *Where Nations Meet*, 103–4. Rhodes both exemplifies intentionality in his approach to multicultural ministry and shows that area superintendents were equally intentional about the direction of Culmore United Methodist Church.

46. Alfredo Corchado and Dianne Solis, "A Force for Change," *Dallas Morning News*, 19 Sept. 1999, 1A.

47. "The Keenest Recruits to the Dream," *The Economist*, 25 April 1998, 3 available at www.economist.com, This article discusses the nature and extent of Latino economic activity, the prevalence of Mexicans as 63 percent of all Hispanics, their (then current) buying power of 348 billion dollars, and their struggle for assimilation in the U.S. culture.

48. Cose, *A Nation of Strangers*, 132.

49. Ibid., 142.

50. Bruce Frankel, "We Try Harder," *USA Today* (20 July 1996).

51. Michael E. Young, "A Crossing to Bear," *Dallas Morning News*, 7 Sept. 1998;, 33A.

52. Solis, "Coming on Strong," 1H.

53. *Statistical Yearbook of the Immigration and Naturalization Service, 1999* (Washington: Department of Justice, 1999), 200–201.

54. Young, "A Crossing to Bear," 33A.

55. Table DP-1, "Profile of General Demographic Characteristics: 2000" in *Profiles of General Demographic Characteristics: 2000,* the 2000 census of population and housing—United States, issued May 2001.

Chapter 4: The Compass for the Journey

1. Robert Service, "Pines," *The Spell of the Yukon* (New York: Barse and Hopkins, 1907), 43.

2. James A. Scherer, "Missiology as a Discipline and What It Includes," in *New Directions in Mission and Evangelization,* vol. 2 of *Theological Foundations,* eds. James A. Scherer and Stephen B. Bevans (Maryknoll, N.Y.: Orbis Books, 1994), 173–87.

3. David J. Hesselgrave, *Scripture and Strategy: The Use of the Bible in Postmodern Church and Mission* (Pasadena: William Carey Library, 1994), 6.

4. Rhodes, *Where Nations Meet*, 19.

5. William Dyrness, *The Earth Is God's: A Theology of American Culture* (Maryknoll, N.Y.: Orbis Books, 1997), 58.

6. Ibid., 25.

7. Roland Allen, *Missionary Methods: St. Paul's or Ours?* (Grand Rapids: Eerdmans, 1962), 4.

8. Laird Harris, *The Inspiration and Canonicity of the Bible* (Grand Rapids: Zondervan, 1969), 154–79.

9. Everett F. Harrison, *Introduction to the New Testament* (Grand Rapids: Eerdmans, 1964), 176, 192.

10. Harris, *The Inspiration and Canonicity of the Bible*, 154.

11. Clinton Arnold, *The Powers of Darkness* (Downers Grove, Ill.: InterVarsity Press, 1992), 48.

12. George Peters, *Biblical Theology of Missions* (Chicago: Moody, 1972); Ralph D. Winters and Stephen C. Hawthorne, *Perspectives on the World Christian Movement*, 3d ed. (Pasadena, Calif.: William Carey Library, 1999).

13. Reginald Bibby, *Unknown Gods: The Ongoing Story of Religion in Canada* (Toronto: Stoddart, 1993), 20–21.

14. Ron Rhodes, *The New Age Movement* (Grand Rapids: Zondervan, 1995), 8–9.

15. Dyrness, *The Earth Is God's*, 58.

16. Paul G. Hiebert, *Anthropological Insights for Missionaries* (Grand Rapids: Baker, 1985), 30.

17. Barbara F. Grimes, ed., *Ethnologue: Languages of the World*, 11th ed. (Dallas: Summer Institute of Linguistics, 1988), 740.

18. Allen P. Ross, *Creation and Blessing: A Guide to the Study and Exposition of Genesis* (Grand Rapids: Baker, 1988), 243.

19. Ibid., 233–48.

20. Walter Elwell, ed., "Judgment," in *Evangelical Dictionary of Biblical Theology* (Grand Rapids: Baker, 1996), 336–37.

21. Leon Morris, "Judgment," in *The New Bible Dictionary*, 2d ed., J. D. Douglas and F. F. Bruce, eds. (Wheaton: Tyndale House, 1992), 640–41.

22. Peters, *Biblical Theology of Missions*, 21.

23. Eugene Merrill, *A Kingdom of Priests* (Grand Rapids: Baker, 1987), 469.

24. Boer, *Pentecost and Missions*, 76.

25. Christolf W. Stenschke, *Luke's Portrait of Gentiles Prior to their Coming to Faith* (Tuingen: Mohr Siebek, 1999), 148–49, 311–13.

26. Mal Couch, gen. ed. *A Biblical Handbook to the Acts of the Apostles* (Grand Rapids: Kregel, 1999), 50.

27. Manuel Ortiz, *One New People* (Downers Grove, Ill.: InterVarsity Press, 1996), 51–52.

Chapter 5: Colliding Cultures

1. Craig Storti, *Figuring Foreigners Out* (Yarmouth, Me.: Intercultural Press, 1999), 15.

2. Thomas Sowell, *Race and Culture* (New York: Basic Books, 1994).

3. Ortiz, *One New People*, 132.

4. Sowell, *Race and Culture*, 28.

5. Marvin K. Mayers, *Christianity Confronts Culture* (Grand Rapids: Zondervan, 1987), xi.

6. Edgar H. Schein, *Organizational Culture and Leadership* (San Francisco: Jossey-Bass, 1992), quoted in the Quality Awareness Seminar by the Air National Guard Quality Center.

7. Donald K. Smith, *Creating Understanding* (Grand Rapids: Zondervan, 1992), 260.

8. Edward T. Hall, *The Silent Language* (New York: Doubleday, 1967), 41.

9. Paul Greenberg, "The Power of Myth in Shaping Destinies," *Washington Times*, 12 Feb. 2001, A15. Greenburg cites Abraham Lincoln's speech in Independence Hall, made at a critical time in our nation's history, as an example of a story that provides to our citizenry an understanding of our purpose as a republic. He cited the words of the Declaration of Independence, issued many years earlier: "We hold these truths to be self-evident, that all men are created equal, that they are endowed by their Creator with certain unalienable Rights."

10. Hall, *The Silent Language*, 37–56.

11. Rhodes, *Where Nations Meet*, 168.

12. Paul G. Hiebert, *Cultural Anthropology* (Grand Rapids: Baker, 1983), 113–14.

13. Ibid., 114.

14. Roger E. Axtell, *Do's and Taboos of Hosting International Visitors* (Toronto: John Wiley and Sons, 1990), 71.

15. Richard Lederer, *Anguished English* (New York: Dell, 1987), 84.

16. Ibid., 84–89.

17. Roger E. Axtell, *Gestures: The Do's and Taboos of Body Language around the World* (Toronto: John Wiley, 1991), 10.

18. Smith, *Creating Understanding*, 260.

19. Joseph A. DeVito, *Interpersonal Communication Book*, 4th ed. (New York: Harper and Row, 1986), 233.

20. Axtell, *Gestures*, 42–43.

21. Ibid., 43.

22. DeVito, *Interpersonal Communication Book*, 268.

23. Hiebert, *Cultural Anthropology*, 34.

24. Some cultures place great importance on the past. Since events are circu-

lar and recurring, the wisdom of yesterday is of utmost importance for today
and tomorrow. An Indian with a Hindu
philosophy would lean toward a *past orientation.* Other cultures have a *present
orientation,* that is, activities of the present are the most important. Time is considered well spent, not for future
rewards, nor for tradition's sake, but
rather for the enjoyment of the moment.
Latinos or Arabs tend to be more present-
focused than others.

A society with a *future orientation*
gives primary attention to the issues of
saving, working, and denying certain
enjoyments and luxuries (hence the
expression, "delayed gratification")
because of preparation for the future.
Americans who feel they control their
destiny and who emphasize objectives,
deadlines, budgets, and quotas are, as a
whole, future-oriented people. A common
expression for their value of time would
be, "the biggest bang for the buck."

Different perspectives on time is one
reason for cultural misunderstanding. For
example, how would a futuristic American view a Native American who follows
the footsteps of his ancestors and bases
his life on the notion that everything
comes to pass in its season? The Native
American would probably be considered
lazy. On the other hand, how would those
with a present orientation consider a
future-oriented person? Probably they
would consider him or her as obsessed
with achievements and unwise for not
making the most of relationships and
enjoyment of the moment.

25. DeVito, *Interpersonal Communication Book,* 255–56.

26. Sowell, *Race and Culture,* v.

27. One had economic connections
and was "gold-fingered." So important
was it for a man of high social status to
have many rings, Rome even had shops
that rented rings! The rich men wore fine
apparel current with the fashions of the
day, brilliant and flashy in color with glit-
tering ornamentation. James's condemnation was not that men wore such clothing

but, rather, that God's people were swept
away by the seductive power of these
transient riches.

Chapter 6: Choices for the Journey

1. John W. Berry, "Individual and
Group Relations in Plural Societies," in
Cross-Cultural Work Groups, eds. Cherlyn
Skromme and Stuart Oskamp (Grand
Rapids: Sage Publications, 1997), 18–19.

2. Ibid., 19.

3. Ron K. Unz, "A Return to Ellis
Island," in *Strangers at Our Gate: Immigration in the 1990s,* ed. John J. Miller
(New York: Manhattan Institute, 1994),
31.

4. Francis Fukuyama, "Immigration,
Assimilation, and Family Values," in
Strangers at Our Gate, 80.

5. Ibid., 81.

6. Unz, "A Return to Ellis Island," 37.

7. Berry, "Individual and Group Relations," 22.

8. Brimelow, *Alien Nation,* 125.

9. Ibid.

10. Ibid., 128.

11. Berry, "Individual and Group Relations," 21–22.

12. Ibid., 22.

13. Ibid., 24.

14. Salins, *Assimilation, American
Style,* 6.

15. Joel Kotkin, "Making Americans,"
in *Strangers at Our Gate,* 96.

16. Reed Ueda, "Asians and the American Idea," in *Strangers at Our Gate,* 66.

17. Peter Skerry, "Deracinated Ethnics," in *Strangers at Our Gate,* 84.

18. Ortiz, *One New People,* 66.

19. Oscar L. Romo, *American Mosaic:
Church Planting in Ethnic America*
(Nashville: Broadman, 1993), 147.

20. Ortiz, *One New People,* 88–89.

21. Ibid., 91.

22. Phillip Yancey, *Finding God in
Unexpected Places,* (Nashville: Moorings,
1995), x.

Chapter 7: Conversing about Christ

1. Norman L. *Geisler, Baker Encyclopedia of Christian Apologetics* (Grand Rapids: Baker, 1999), 37.

2. Terry Muck, *Alien Gods on American Turf* (Wheaton, Ill.: Victor, 1990), 14.

3. Ibid., 14–15.

4. Chris L. Jenkins, "Islam Luring More Latinos," *Washington Post*, 7 Jan. 2001, C1.

5. Angelo Ragaza, "Om Rooms," www.forbes.com, 23 Feb. 2001.

6. Start with www.beliefnet.com and choose "religions" from the menu options, or you can go to any server and type in the name of the religion you wish to explore.

7. Winfried Corduan, *Neighboring Faiths*, (Downers Grove: InterVarsity Press, 1998), 21.

8. Tom A. Steffen, *Reconnecting God's Story to Ministry: Crosscultural Storytelling at Home and Abroad* (La Habra, Calif.: Center for Organizational and Ministry Development, 1996), 69.

9. Ibid.

10. George G. Hunter, *How to Reach Secular People* (Nashville, Tenn.: Abingdon Press, 1992), 76–77.

Chapter 8: Using Dialogue to Win People to Christ

1. John R. Stott, *Christian Mission in the Modern World* (Downers Grove, Ill.: InterVarsity Press, 1975), 71–74.

2. This is not the student's real name.

3. Winfried Corduan, *Neighboring Faiths* (Downers Grove, Ill.: InterVarsity Press, 1998), 37.

4. A Christian may feel that when he or she is witnessing, this may be the first time that anyone has spoken to this person about the Lord. This approach can create a certain anxiety. The truth is that God has already been speaking to that person about himself. Although boldness is still required to faithfully impart the gospel to others, the burden for its success falls on the Lord who initiates and concludes all conversations regarding himself.

5. Charles Bridges, *Proverbs*, Geneva Series of Commentaries (Carlisle, Pa.: The Banner of Truth Trust, 1981), 338.

6. Ibid.

7. The Socratic method is composed of five components: (1) *Wonder* is posing a question such as, "Why do you suppose people do bad things to each other?" As people share their answers put yourself in the posture of a learner. Questions are not to be used as a ploy to draw people into a conversation that you control and for which you think you have all the answers. (2) *Hypothesis* is offering a plausible answer that can be deduced by a hypothetical proposition like, "Perhaps people with good intentions are still capable of doing or thinking bad things because even good people have within them some source of inherent evil. Do you know of anyone like this?" You are offering your ideas. (3) *Testing* is an experiment in which you imagine your hypothesis being cross-examined or refuted. The person you are talking to could say, "Yes, but does that also mean that bad people can do good things? If so, are we saying that . . ." You can then use a case or example, conforming to what you are proposing that clearly fails to exemplify your proposition, or vice versa. Such cases, if successful, are called *counterexamples*. (If a counterexample exists then you return to step 2, otherwise you go on to step 4.) (4) Accept the hypothesis as provisionally true. Return to step 3 if you can conceive any other case that may show the answer to be defective. (5) Act accordingly.

8. NIV Study Bible (Grand Rapids: Zondervan, 1995), note on Acts 17:19.

9. Commentators and scholars package the Mars Hill discourse from different angles. For example, Wilbur Smith highlighted the themes of creation, resurrection, and judgment as the main points of the gospel that Paul meant to promote. R. C. Sproul feels that Paul placed high emphasis on God as *the* Cause in whom we live and move and have our being. In

so doing, Sproul proposes that Paul both raised and gave answer to the major philosophical questions of the day.

10. Geisler, *Baker Encyclopedia of Christian Apologetics*, 37–38.

11. Greg L. Bahnsen, *Van Til's Apologetic: Readings and Analysis* (Phillipsburg, N.J.: Presbyterian and Reformed Publishing Company, 1998), 34.

12. Hunter, *How to Reach Secular People*, 53.

Chapter 9: A Captivating Model of the Multicultural Church

1. Jobe, "Rethinking the Church to Reach the City," 211. This article is a case study of New Life Community Church, focusing primarily on its urban situation. Portions are cited or used by permission of Moody Press. A great deal of the material for this chapter is taken from my personal experience from 1966 to 1968 at Berean, from New Life publications and literature, repeated visits over many years, and a delightful week spent in Chicago with Mark and Dee Jobe in 1999. Subsequent visits and interviews through April 16, 2001, have amplified and updated certain data in Jobe's chapter in *A Heart for the City*.

2. "Welcome to New Life Community Church," orientation material, November 1999.

3. See Ortiz, *One New People*, 107. "Leadership determines the future of multicultural churches."

4. Casa View Baptist School, a ministry of Casa View Baptist Church, Dallas, Texas.

5. Marina Herrera, *A Strategic Plan for Ministers for the Multicultural Church: A Response to the Demographic Changes Facing Our Society in the 1990s and Beyond* (Silver Spring, Md.: Washington Theological Union, 1992), 24, 36; and Toinette M. Eugene, "Multicultural Ministry: Theory, Practice, Theology." *The Chicago Theological Seminary Register* 84, no. 2 (spring 1994), 8.

6. Jobe, "Rethinking the Church," 209.

7. Interview with Dwayne Eslick, Rudy Arroyo, Mitchell Vargas, Roy Obregon, Joshua Holek, Nick Vester, and Eric Marquez at New Life Community Church Administrative Center, 44th and Paulina, Chicago, 4 November 1999. These young men continued to the conclusion of their fast on 20 November 1999. All but one continue to serve in the life of the church and had already seen God move in the hearts of many teenagers they had dealt with during the time of their fast.

8. George Barna, *The Power of Vision: How You Can Capture and Apply God's Vision for Your Church* (Ventura, Calif.: Regal, 1992), 28.

9. Jobe, "Rethinking the Church," 203.

10. Ibid., 211.

11. See Barna, *The Power of Vision*, and Aubrey Malphurs, *Developing a Vision for Ministry in the 21st Century*, 2d ed. (Grand Rapids: Baker, 1999).

12. Jobe, "Rethinking the Church," 209–10. Used with permission of the publisher.

13. Telephone interview with Linda Wasso, 16 April 2001. Linda is a New Life staffer and wife of satellite pastor Tony Wasso.

14. Jobe, "Rethinking the Church," 207.

Chapter 10: A Call for Commitment

1. International Students Incorporated, P.O. Box C, Colorado Springs, CO 80901.

2. American Field Service International at http://usa.afs.org.

3. Patricia Lowell, "Traveling New Paths," *Dallas Morning News*, 7 Feb. 2001.

4. Patti Lane, director of Intercultural Initiatives, Baptist General Convention of Texas in a class presentation in Ministry in Multicultural America, Dallas Theological Seminary, fall term, 1996.

5. Telephone interview with Lanny Elmore, pastor of Missions, First Baptist Church, Dallas, 26 Jan. 2000.

6. George Barna, *Turnaround Churches* (Ventura, Calif.: Regal, 1993), 17.

7. Telephone interview with Huang Soo Kim, Faith Lutheran Church, Surrey, B.C., 26 Jan. 2000.

8. Personal interviews with church member Brannon Claxton, Royce City, Tex., 8 Jan. 2001; and Sylvia Green, Mesquite, Tex., 17 January 2001.

9. Susan Hogan-Albach, "Making Room for the Masses," *Dallas Morning News*, 14 Jan. 2001.

10. Herrera, "A Strategic Plan," and Eugene, "Multicultural Ministry," 1–11.

11. The United States–based organization advancing this ministry to major Latin American and Iberian cities is Church Ministries International, Rockwall, Tex., www.ChurchMinistries.org.

12. Ortiz, *One New People*, 120.

13. Keith Phillips, *Out of the Ashes* (Los Angeles: World Impact Press, 1996), 97.

14. Brannon Claxton et al., "A Heart for the Future," unpublished church study report, East Grand Avenue Baptist Church, Dallas, Tex., Oct. 1994.

15. American Intercultural Press, P.O. Box 700, Yarmouth, Me 04096. books@interculturalpress.com.

16. Susan Hogan-Albach, "Scholars: Plan Relies on Faith Not Facts," *Dallas Morning News*, 4 Feb. 2001.

17. Barna, *The Power of Vision*, 79.

18. Ibid., 28.

19. Malphurs, *Developing a Vision for Ministry*, 32.

20. Frank Tillapaugh, *Unleashing the Church: Getting People out of the Fortress and into Ministry* (Ventura, Calif.: Regal, 1982), 110.

21. See Tom Brokaw, *The Greatest Generation* (New York: Random House, 1998).

22. Tom Sine, *Mustard Seed vs. McWorld: Reinventing Life and Faith for the Future* (Grand Rapids: Baker, 1999).

23. Bill Hybels, "Vision Night '96," cited in Malphurs, *Developing a Vision for Ministry*, 207–24.

24. Malphurs, *Developing a Vision for Ministry*, 69–75.

25. Introductory brochure, Asian-American Baptist Church, Richardson, Tex.

26. Tillapaugh, *Unleashing the Church*, 132.

27. Tillie Burgin of Mission Arlington, a ministry of the First Baptist Church, Arlington, Tex., speaking at the regional meeting of the Evangelical Missiological Society at Dallas Theological Seminary, March 1996.

28. Telephone interview, 17 Feb. 2001.

29. Student report on intercultural contacts assignment, Introduction to World Missions, Dallas Theological Seminary, fall 2000.

30. Poul Prip, internship report on ministry at Asian-American Baptist Church, Richardson, Tex., 20 Feb. 2001.

31. Staishy Bostic Siem, "Religious Freedom: Ethiopian Baptist Church Marks Its Independence," *Dallas Morning News*, 19 Feb. 2001, 1A.

Resources

Secular and Christian Perspectives on Cultural Diversity

Adeney, Bernard. *Strange Virtues: Ethics in a Multicultural World*. Downers Grove, Ill.: InterVarsity Press, 1995.

Appleby, Jerry L. *Missions Have Come Home to America: The Church's Cross-Cultural Ministry to Ethnics*. Kansas City: Beacon Hill Press, 1986.

Bibby, Reginald. *Mosaic Madness: The Poverty and Potential of Life in Canada*. Toronto: Stoddart, 1990.

Breckenridge, James F. *What Color Is Your God?* Wheaton, Ill.: Bridgepoint Books, 1995.

Brown, Mary E. *The Shapers of the Great Debate on Immigration*. Westwood, Conn.: Greenwood Press, 1999.

Chandler, Paul Gordon. *Divine Mosaic: Windows on God from Around the World*. London: SPCK, 1997.

Chandler, Russell. *Racing toward 2001: The Forces Shaping America's Future*. Grand Rapids: Zondervan, 1992.

Cohen, Robin. *The Cambridge Survey of World Migration*. Cambridge, U.K.: Cambridge University Press, 1995.

Cose, Ellis. *A Nation of Strangers: Prejudice, Politics and the Populating of America*. New York: William Morrow, 1992. Backgrounds of immigration movements that make America what it is today are explored. Shows how legal and social reactions have varied in bringing us to our present situation.

Fitzpatrick, Joseph P. *One Church, Many Cultures: The Challenge of Diversity*. Kansas City: Sheed and Ward, 1987. The multicultural challenge for the Roman Catholic Church in America.

Foster, Charles, and Theodore Brelsford. *We Are the Church Together: Cultural Diversity in Congregational Life*. Valley Forge, Pa.: Trinity Press, 1996.

Guthrie, Shirley. *Many Voices, One God: Being Faithful in a Pluralistic World*. Louisville, Ky.: Westminster John Knox Press, 1998.

Harley, David. *Preparing to Serve: Training for Cross-Cultural Mission*. Pasadena: William Carey Library, 1995.

Henriques, Joseph. *Designing an Intercultural Ministry: A Guide for Serving Your Culturally and Religiously Different Neighbors*. Centreville, Va.: People of the World, 1999. People of the World, P.O. Box 1784, Centreville, VA 20122.

Herrera, Marina. *"A Strategic Plan to Prepare Ministers for the Multicultural Church: A Response to the Demographic Changes Facing Our Society and the Catholic Church in the 1990s and Beyond."* Washington, D.C.: Washington Theological Union, 1992.

Hopler, Thom and Marcia. *Reaching the World Next Door: How to Spread the Gospel in the Midst of Many Cultures.* Downers Grove, Ill.: InterVarsity Press, 1993.

International Students Inc. *A Movement of God's People: Changed Hearts, Changing Lives, Changing Nations.* Colorado Springs: ISI, 1993. The case for involvement with international students—eloquently stated.

Jupp, James, ed. *The Challenge of Diversity: Policy Options for a Multicultural Society.* New York: Australian Government Publishing Service, 1990.

Kennedy, John F. *A Nation of Immigrants.* New York: Harper and Row, 1964. This is an interesting perspective of a former U.S. president, himself a descendant of Irish immigrants. It underscores the positive contribution of immigrants to America. Originally published by The Anti-Defamation League of B'nai B'rith, 1958.

King, Joyce, ed. *Preparing Teachers for Cultural Diversity.* New York Teachers College Press, 1997.

Kohls, L. Robert, and Herbert Brussow. *Training Know-How for Cross-Cultural and Diversity Trainers.* Duncanville, Tex.: Adult Learning Systems, 1995.

Kohls, L. Robert, and John M. Knight. *Developing Intercultural Awareness: A Cross-Cultural Training Handbook.* 2d ed. Yarmouth, Me.: Intercultural Press, 1994.

Miller, John J., ed. *Strangers at Our Gates: Immigration in the 90s.* New York: Manhattan Institute, 1994.

Motz, Arnell, ed. *Reclaiming a Nation: The Challenge of Re-Evangelizing Canada by the Year 2000.* Richmond, B.C.: Church Leadership Library, 1990. This work faces the fact that the Canadian evangelical movement is losing ground to secularism and to the many religions espoused by new waves of immigrants. It proposes a plan of action to "reclaim the nation" for Christ.

Novak, Michael. *The Rise of the Unmeltable Ethnics.* New York: Macmillan, 1972.

Ortiz, Manuel. *One New People: Models for Developing a Multiethnic Church.* Downers Grove, Ill.: InterVarsity Press, 1996.

Pederson, Paul. *A Handbook for Developing Multicultural Awareness.* Alexandria, Va.: American Association for Counseling and Development, 1988. Guidance in counseling minorities.

Perkins, Spencer, and Chris Rice. *More than Equals.* Downers Grove, Ill.: InterVarsity Press, 1993.

Retta, Edward. *Hispanic Community Concerns and a Hispanic Evangelical Agenda.* Dallas, Tex.: Cross Culture Communications, 1996.

Rhodes, Stephen A. *Where Nations Meet: The Church in a Multicultural World.* Downers Grove, Ill.: InterVarsity Press, 1998.

Sanders, Cheryl J. *Ministry at the Margins.* Downers Grove, Ill.: InterVarsity Press, 1997. Sanders emphasizes participation of marginalized people in ministry rather than their being simply recipients of ministry.

Schaller, Lyle E., ed. *Center City Churches: The New Urban Frontier.* Nashville: Abingdon Press, 1993. Case studies of effective urban ministry, several of which are distinctly multicultural.

Schlesinger, Arthur. *The Disuniting of America: Reflections on a Multicultural Society.* Knoxville: Whittle Communications, 1991. Author voices concern that the promotion of multiculturalism will tend to break down national unity.

Spencer, William David, and Aida Spencer. *The Global God: Multicultural Evangelical Views of God.* Grand Rapids: Baker, 1998.

Summerfield, Ellen, and Sandra Lee. *Seeing the Big Picture: Exploring American Cultures on Film.* Yarmouth, Me.: Intercultural Press, 2001.

Thornstorm, Stephen. *Harvard Encyclopedia of American Ethnic Groups.* Cambridge: Harvard University, Balknap Press, 1980.

Volf, Miroslav. *Exclusion and Embrace: A Theological Understanding of Identity, Otherness, and Reconciliation.* Nashville: Abingdon Press, 1996.

Zeigler, Lee. *Film and Video Resources for International Educational Exchange.* 2d ed. Yarmouth, Me.: Intercultural Press, 2000.

Electronically Accessible Resource Centers

American Bible Society, 1865 Broadway, New York, NY 10023. 800-32-Bible. abs@webzone.net or www.americanbible.org. *For foreign-language Bibles, portions, and tracts.*

American Field Services (AFS). *A secular facilitator of exchanges between U.S. students and those from other countries. AFS is regionally administered, and links to one area can be given by any regional office. For example, going to the Puget Sound web site would provide links to those of other localities.* www.afsgreaterpugetsound.org.

American Tract Society, P.O. Box 462008, Garland, TX 75046. 800-548-7228. www.goshen.net/AmericanTractSociety. *ATS publishes effective, attractive tracts in several languages spoken by ethnic groups in North America.*

Cross Culture Communications, Edward and Marilyn Retta, P.O. Box 141263, Dallas, TX 75214. 214-827-8632. Fax 214-824-9861. eretta@acrossculture.com; www.acrossculture.com. *Evangelical organization that specializes in helping North American and South American businesspeople get together and enhance their intercultural working skills.*

Gospel Films, P.O. Box 455, Muskegon, MI 49443. 800-253-0413 or 616-773-3361. Fax 616-777-1847.

The Intercultural Press Inc., P.O. Box 700, Yarmouth, ME 04096. 800-370-2665 or 207-846-5168. Fax 207-846-5181. books@interculturalpress.com or www.interculturalpress.com. *Valuable helps for those who work or teach or live with other cultural groups in North America and around the world. I.P. is a secular organization. Write for a catalog.*

International Bible Society, 1820 Jet Stream Drive, Colorado Springs, CO 80921. 719-488-9200. Fax 719-488-3840. www.gospelcom.net/ibs. *Contact IBS for foreign-language Bibles, portions, and tracts.*

International Christian Youth Exchange (ICYE) International Office: GroBe Hamburger Str. 30, D-10115 Berlin, Germany, or e-mail at icye@icye.org. Web site: www.icye.org. *Facilitates exchange of Christian students or places children of non-Christian background with Christian families.*

International Students Incorporated, P.O. Box C, Colorado Springs, CO 80901. 719-576-2700. Fax 719-576-5363. In the Dallas–Fort Worth area, the contact is Derrah Jackson at 214-321-4933.

Multi-Language Media, P.O. Box 301, Ephrata, PA 17522. 717-738-0582. *Evangelical organization with catalogs that offer hundreds of films, videos, books, Bibles, tracts, etc. in thirteen languages (Bibles in fifty-three languages), for ministry to five major religious groupings.*

People of the World, P.O. Box 1784, Centreville, VA 20122. *Helps American churches respond to newcomers from abroad and helps individual Christians share their faith through genuine friendships.*

SIETAR International, 808 17th Street NW, Suite 200, Washington, DC 20006. 202-466-7883. Fax 202-223-9569. *SIETAR* (Society for Intercultural Education, Training and Research) *specializes in examining and interpreting cultural behaviors among and between diverse groups. SIETAR encourages interaction between differing cultures and concerns itself with developing skills for learning, acting, and communicating in a culturally diverse milieu.*

SIM International, Ethnic Focus Ministry. Contact Dr. David L. Ripley, Director, Ethnic Focus Ministry, P.O. Box 1251, Wheaton, IL 60189. 708-653-4221.

Urban Evangelical Mission, Willie O. Peterson, Urban Research Consultant, 17311 Dallas Parkway, Suite 238, Dallas, TX 75248. 214-931-9265. Fax 214-991-3624. *This organization specializes in concerns and ministry in the African American community.*

Selected Culture-Specific Resources

Alexander, George. *The New Americans: The Progress of Asia Indians in America.* Cypress, Calif.: P and P Enterprises, 1997.

Dolan, Jay P., and Jaime R. Vidal *Hispanic Catholic Culture in the U.S.: Issues and Concerns.* Notre Dame, Ind.: Notre Dame University Press, 1994.

Evans, Anthony T. *Let's Get to Know Each Other: What White Christians Need to Know About Blacks.* Nashville: Thomas Nelson, 1995.

Goizueta, Roberto S., ed. *We Are a People: Initiatives in Hispanic American Theology.* Minneapolis: Fortress Press, 1992.

Hispanic Task Force of the Baptist General Convention of Texas. "Vision 2000: Winning Hispanics for Christ. Goals and Recommendations 1992–2000." Baptist General Convention of Texas, 1992.

Jo, Euntae. *Korean-Americans and Church Growth.* Seoul, Korea: Cross-Cultural Ministries Institute, 1994.

Kim, Hyung-chan. *A Legal History of Asian-Americans, 1790–1990.* Westport, Conn.: Greenwood Press, 1994.

Lane, Eddie. *Parenting in Context of a Spiritual Deficit.* Dallas: Black Family Press, 1997.

———. *Reclaiming the Village: The African-American Christian Man.* Dallas: Black Family Press, 1997.

Maynard-Reid, Pedrito. *Diverse Worship: African-American, Caribbean, and Hispanic Perspectives.* Downers Grove, Ill.: InterVarsity Press, 2000.

Mirande, Alfredo. *The Chicano Experience: An Alternative Perspective.* Notre Dame, Ind.: University of Notre Dame Press, 1985.

Montoya, Alex D. *Hispanic Ministry in North America.* Grand Rapids: Zondervan, 1987.

Nydell, Margaret K. *Understanding Arabs: A Guide to Westerners.* Yarmouth, Me.: Intercultural Press, 1987.

Ortiz, Manuel. *The Hispanic Challenge: Opportunities Confronting the Church.* Downers Grove, Ill.: InterVarsity Press, 1993.

Pannell, William. *The Coming Race Wars?: A Cry for Reconciliation.* Grand Rapids: Zondervan, 1993.

Peterson, Willie O. *Understanding Current Black Concerns: The Community at Large and the Black Evangelical Agenda.* Dallas, Tex.: Urban Evangelical Mission, 1996.

Purvis, Gene. *Hispanic Church Planting Guide: A Guide to Ministering in the Hispanic Community.* Dallas: CAM International (8625 La Prada Dr., Dallas, TX 75228, www.cam international.org).

Ratliff, Joe S., and Michael J. Cox. *Church Planting in the African-American Community.* Nashville: Broadman, 1993.

Sanchez, Daniel, and Ebbie Smith. *Growing Hispanic Churches: What Is the Holy Spirit Using to Grow Hispanic Churches in Texas?* Fort Worth: Scarborough Institute for Church Growth, Southwestern Baptist Theological Seminary, 1996.

Sandoval, Moises. *On the Move: A History of the Hispanic Church in the United States.* Maryknoll, N.Y.: Orbis Books, 1990.

Yang, Fenggang. *Chinese Christians in America: Conversion, Assimilation, and Adhesive Identities.* University Park, Pa.: Penn State University Press, 1999.

Yau, Cecilia, ed. *A Winning Combination: ABC-OBC: Understanding the Cultural Tensions in Chinese Churches.* Petaluma, Calif.: Chinese Christian Mission, 1986.

Selected Resources: Major Religions and Christian Response

General

Da Costa, Gavin. *Theology and Religious Pluralism: The Challenge of Other Religions.* Oxford, U.K.: Basil Blackwell, 1986. Da Costa is an Indian Catholic born in East Africa, currently teaching in England. He studies pluralism from the viewpoint of the pluralist John Hick, the exclusivist Hendrik Kraemer, and the inclusivist Karl Rahner. Da Costa considers himself a follower of Rahner.

Halverson, Dean C. *The Compact Guide to World Religions.* Minneapolis, Minn.: Bethany House, 1996.

Matthews, Warren. *World Religions.* 3d ed. Boston: Wadsworth Publishing, 1999.

Romo, Oscar I. *American Mosaic: Church Planting in Ethnic America.* Nashville: Broadman Press, 1993. This is an excellent Southern Baptist work on how America became so multicultural and how we can minister to our cultural mosaic.

Salley, Columbus, and Ron Behm. *What Color Is Your God?* New York: Citadel Press, 1995.

Buddhism

Harvey, Peter. *An Introduction to Buddhism: Teachings, History, and Practices.* New York: Cambridge University Press, 1990.

Niles, Daniel T. *Buddhism and the Claims of Christ.* Richmond: John Knox Press, 1967.

Hinduism

Flood, Gavin. *An Introduction to Hinduism.* New York: Cambridge University Press, 1996.

McCune, Kelvin M. *Effective Hindu Evangelism: Contrasting the Concept of Salvation between Hinduism and Christianity*. Columbus, Ga.: Brentwood Christian Press, 1996.

Islam

Mcdowell, Bruce A., and Anne Zaka. *Muslims and Christians at the Table*. Phillipsburg, N.J.: Presbyterian and Reformed Publishing Co., 1999.

Robinson, Neal. *Islam: A Concise Introduction*. Washington, D.C.: Georgetown University Press, 1999.

Turner, Richard B. *Islam in the African-American Experience*. Bloomington: Indiana University Press, 1997.

Specific Issues in Multicultural Ministry and Church Planning

Axelson, John A. *Counseling and Development in a Multicultural Society*. 2d ed. Pacific Grove, Calif.: Brooks Cole Publishing Co., 1993.

Barna, George. *The Power of Vision: How You Can Capture and Apply God's Vision for Your Church*. Ventura, Calif.: Regal, 1992.

———. *Turnaround Churches*. Ventura, Calif.: Regal, 1993.

Bennett. Milton J., ed. *Basic Concepts of Intercultural Communication: Selected Readings*. Yarmouth, Me.: Intercultural Press, 1998.

Berry, John W. *Cross-Cultural Work Groups*. Grand Rapids: Sage Publications, 1997.

Loden, Marilyn, and Judy B. Rosner. *Workforce America*. Yarmouth, Me.: Intercultural Press, 1991. How to foster teamwork in a diverse workforce.

Malphurs, Aubrey. *Developing a Vision for Ministry in the 21st Century*. Grand Rapids: Baker, 1999.

Ponderotto, Joseph G. et al. *Handbook of Multicultural Counseling*. Thousand Oaks, Calif.: Sage Publications, 1995.

Romano, Dugan. *Intercultural Marriage: Promises and Pitfalls*. Yarmouth, Me.: Intercultural Press, 1988.

Salins, Peter D. *Assimilation, American Style: An Impassioned Defense of Immigration and Assimilation as the Foundation of American Greatness and the American Dream*. New York: Basic Books, 1997.

Schaller, Lyle E. *Strategies for Change*. Nashville: Abingdon Press, 1993.

Stanley, Andy. *Visioneering: God's Blueprint for Developing and Maintaining Personal Vision*. Portland, Ore.: Multnomah, 1999.

Warren, Rick. *The Purpose Driven Church: Growth without Compromising Your Method and Mission*. Grand Rapids: Zondervan, 1995.

Washington, Raliegh, and Glen Kehrein. *Breaking Down Walls: A Model for Reconciliation in an Age of Racial Strife*. Chicago: Moody, 1993.

Wilkerson, Barbara, ed. *Multicultural Religious Education*. Birmingham, Ala.: Religious Education Press, 1997.

About the Authors

Michael Pocock is chairman of the department and professor of World Missions and Intercultural Studies at Dallas Theological Seminary in Dallas, Texas. He received his masters of theology and his doctor of missiology degrees from Trinity Evangelical Divinity School. He has served as president and south-central vice-president of the Evangelical Missiological Society.

Having immigrated to this country from England when he was thirteen, Dr. Pocock understands the concerns of our immigrant population. He has also served as a missionary and church planter in Venezuela and pastor of a multicultural church in Chicago.

Michael travels extensively in ministry abroad. His hobbies include fishing and boat building. He and his wife, Penny, have three children and one grandchild.

Joseph Henriques is vice president and dean of Moody Graduate School in Chicago, Illinois. He received his doctor of ministry degree from Dallas Theological Seminary.

Concerned with the needs of America's immigrant population, Dr. Henriques founded People of the World to teach individual Christians how to develop genuine, intercultural friendships, and to equip churches for outreach to an ethnically diverse community. With a bicultural and bilingual background, Dr. Henriques is uniquely qualified to lead workshops on various issues dealing with multicultural outreach and sharing faith with people of other ethnic groups.

Joe and his wife, Bonnie, have five children and two grandchildren.

Michael Pocock can be contacted at Dallas Theological Seminary, 3909 Swiss Ave., Dallas, TX 75204. 214-841-3689. mpocock@dts.edu.

Joseph Henriques can be contacted at Moody Graduate School, 820 N. La Salle Boulevard, Chicago, IL 60610. 312-329-4129. Joseph.Henriques@moody.edu.